Fashionable Asheville

To order additional copies, please contact us.
BookSurge, LLC
www.booksurge.com
1-866-308-6235
orders@booksurge.com

Fashionable Asheville

David Coleman Bailey

2004

Fashionable Asheville
1880-1930

CONTENTS
VOLUME ONE
PART ONE
CROSSING THE CLOUDS

PART TWO
BUILDING FOR TOMORROW

PART THREE
SPECTRUM OF STYLE

CREDIT

Illustrations for this publication furnished courtesy and cooperation of the North Carolina Desk at Pack Library.

This book is dedicated to my loyal and patient wife, talented and creative, whose tireless & imaginative efforts at home & business management have not only proved highly successful but made possible the time required for me to perform the research, write the text and complete the manuscript. In the process, she long ago became expert in residential design and knowledgeable on the subject of Biltmore Forest, the beautiful town in which we live.

mired in the churning mud of unpaved streets, had been evolving into something distinctly different. Miniature but metropolitan.

In the process, strong, lanky characters, squinting and squirting strong streams of tobacco juice out from the sidewalk, would be gradually replaced with a more cultured character from a more eclectic background. Something fashionable had arrived. Some would scoff or remain non plussed while others hastened to embrace the subtle blandishments of what was en vogue or high fashion.

And when famous ladies like Grace Coolidge came to shop, attracted by word of something different in conversation circulating at the higher echelons of social interest, there could be little doubt that this evolution had gone beyond local perception and participation.

The Altamont and Biltburn and Old Catawba of Thomas Wolfe's powerful manuscripts provided grist for the prolific word master's mill. Other writers addressed the subject as well. And many books and articles have been published, each dealing with some phase of the larger subject, but the distinctive social history of this ambitious little city, the tall tale that made it famous, has been left largely to oral accounts.

In the midst of it all, of course, sat the Old Kentucky Home, the boarding house on Spruce Street where Wolfe and his parents and family lived, a vigorous place known to readers around the world as *Dixieland*. A strong source of inspiration for many years.

We seek here to address the ambiance that made it "wear so well" in the eyes and minds of those who thought it did…and those who had a dreamer's vision of something far beyond limitations of reality.

INTRODUCTION

In a sense, every place is unique…Boston, Cincinnati, St. Louis or Denver. But these famous places are real cities. On the other hand, thousands of towns have certain distinguishing characteristics yet many are just that…small towns, hardly distinguishable to the traveler one from another.

There are social watering holes for the old guard, the dynastic rich, the nouveau riche. Enclaves for the educational elite, avant garde, radical chic. Compounds for bohemian cults, free thinkers, and the socially embittered. Resorts of every kind and description. Conference centers. Each with a story of its own.

It may be easier to tell what Asheville wasn't than what it was. It certainly wasn't Savannah or Richmond. Palm Beach or Sarasota. It wasn't southern or northern. Continental or chic. Rural or country. Ethnic or xenophobic. It definitely was not western or mid-western. And it was neither fast track nor slow. Even Hot Springs or White Sulphur it was not.

A philosophical observer might see it as some kind of natural amalgam. A mingling of entities. A coming together of bloodlines. A commonality of divergent interests beneath a scenic ceiling of environmental influences.

The gargantuan Wolfe, whose ongoing surge of descriptive passages was probably unsurpassed, addressed the subject from time to time. We received the results courtesy of Scribner's and his editors who harnessed the hot fires of creative but unbridled energy enough to get this open ended lifetime manuscript into manageable pieces or sections, referred to for want of a better name as novels.

Whatever they are or some may think them to be, no one puts the matter at hand quite so well. His first major work, *Look Homeward Angel*, was published in 1929 as this period was coming to a close. Early on, he remembered a scene from early childhood. Here is one house that remained etched on the arc of his memory…

> Craftily, he wormed his body through the wide wires of the fence, into the cindered alley that wound back to the Swains, and up to the ornate wooden palace of the Hilliards.
>
> They were among the highest aristocracy of the town: they had come from South Carolina, "near Charleston," which in itself gave them at that time a commanding prestige. The house, a huge gabled structure of walnut-brown, which gave the effect of many angles and no plan, was built upon the top of the hill which sloped down to Gant's, the level ground on top before the house was tenanted by lordly towering oaks. Below, along the cindered alley, flanking Gant's orchard, there were high singing pines.
>
> Mr. Hilliard's house was considered one of the finest residences in the town. The neighborhood was middle-class, but the situation was magnificent, and the Hilliards carried on in the grand manner, lords of the castle who descended into the village, but did not mix with its people. All of their friends arrived by carriage from afar; every day punctually

at two o'clock, an old liveried negro drove briskly up the winding alley behind two sleek brown mares, waiting under the carriage entrance at the side until his master and mistress should come out. Five minutes later they drove out, and were gone for two hours.

This ritual, followed closely from his father's sitting room window, fascinated Eugene for years after: the people and the life next door were crudely and symbolically above him.

He felt a great satisfaction that morning in being at length in Hilliard's alley; it was his first escape, and it had been made into a forbidden and enhaloed region.

In young Tom's adventure, he found his head beneath the moving foot of a horse, an event from which he almost miraculously recovered, in short order, but which set off a wild exchange of words and actions among the various immediate participants.

Combining with such events were passing sights and sounds from certain points in time, sometimes noticed and remembered by their eventual disappearance. The image of a tree shaded house. Late afternoon light on a particular mountainside. Personality perceived through an individual person's voice on the sidewalk. Muffled din of conversation in a tavern or tea room. Appearance of an exotic automobile. A busy, hard grinding noise from passing street cars. Children playing idly under falling leaves in a quiet old school yard. Or excited stirring of anticipation about going uptown.

Here the subject is examined with a mixture of affection and curiosity, tinged with an occasional touch of dismay at the course of people and events. It is hoped that in so doing, the curiously fashionable feeling of the times may be recreated with some measure of success for anyone who found it of either passing or permanent interest. And for those who wish to learn more.

One who expects Pittsburgh millionaires, mountain grilles, the urban 400, pedants of intelligentsia, anti-social critics, or sycophants of high society will be disappointed. These were colorful characters but they brought their own molds.

FOREWORD

As time goes by, changes in the urban structure make old patterns extinct and some scenes unrecognizable. This city was no exception and no effort is made here to bring it up to date with a confusing series of alterations and metamorphoses, simple or complex.

Updating is a relative term anyway. A publication date does not cause environmental elements to be frozen in a time warp. Forces of preservation have slowed destruction of our architectural heritage but it has not ceased altogether and some things actually need to be demolished.

If he is unfamiliar with the city's geographics, the reader need not be concerned. Like many towns, Asheville had a central square and a main street, and a few principal thoroughfares. Two of them, Charlotte and Merrimon, were named in the year our narrative begins. Most towns have a Broadway and a Depot Street too and Southside ran down to the depot.

Patton is pure Asheville while Haywood is derived from a neighboring county known to ever more visitors. Montford is an integral part of Asheville history, street and town. So is Coxe. And Biltmore is known far and wide. With the town becoming a city, name changes turned streets into instant avenues. Penland became Rankin, Bailey to Asheland, Water to Lexington, Academy to Montford. Depot to Clingman, Beaverdam to Merrimon, Bridge to Central.

In 1916, Main became Broadway and Biltmore Avenue. Generally speaking, the pavement got better, or appeared for the first time, but for the most part, old routes remained what they were. Narrow, winding mountain streets.

As fashion replaced farmer, Best became Biltmore. Biltmore was described as Vanderbilt Park. Forest Hill turned into Kenilworth. Public square became Court Square and then Pack Square. The post office became Pritchard Park. Doubleday turned into Five Points, Ramoth into Woolsey, Vernon Hill into Victoria...and then were absorbed into Asheville.

We will not assume that one knows names, however, and our story is not dependent on them other than as incidental factors of identification in the passing scene.

PART ONE

CROSSING THE CLOUDS

ONE

THE NAME ASHEVILLE

"Time is like a fashionable host that
slightly shakes his parting guest by the hand."
—Shaks.

The name Asheville evokes poignant images of a mountain mosaic in which sophisticated social fabric of an urban little enclave rested lightly upon bedrock of native conviction and personality. Character of the place comes into focus through an elusive elixir as pervasive as mists passing over Beaucatcher in the early morning hours.

Physical dimension has something to do with creation of a sense of place. Although they are opposites in many respects, Charleston and Manhattan share a similar peninsular foundation. New Orleans is dominated by water, San Francisco by the bay. Asheville's setting was in the clouds and as a municipality, it was both the smallest cosmopolitan city in the East and the highest in elevation.

Thus situated between heavily wooded hillsides and silhouettes of low hanging clouds or drifting fog banks, it worked a certain spell on the inhabitants. At times the mood was almost ethereal as the spirit of a higher plane began to permeate this Scottish atmosphere. And then suddenly one might be drawn by the immediate lure of deep azure skies on those surprisingly clear, cool days that inspired Wolfe to write of "October's bright blue weather."

Townspeople developed a cohesive sense of closeness, a sharing of common experience, like members of a colony brought together in a pre-designated place for some vague but instinctively perceived purpose. So it was that thoughts of Asheville brought smiles to the faces of persons in distant places. Few could define the synergism but many would refer to some element of it, or perhaps describe an experience or event that seemed amusing or significant.

As in the old village days of Chapel Hill, the vibrant and congenial atmosphere of heterogeneous boarding houses provided a mystic glue which brought about hearty social intercourse in a manner difficult to visualize in the world of combustion engines that would follow. Thus these institutions and their siblings became a sort of center stage to which others were related.

Around the peripheries flowed a diverse collection of mondes aparte...separate spheres of Groves & Vanderbilts, Wolfes & Fitzgeralds, Coxes & Cheeseboroughs, Pattons & Weavers, Davidsons & Morrisons. A long parade of physicians & attorneys, artists & writers, architects & engineers, eminent in professional disciplines. Not to mention retired industrialists from the Eastern business world.

To be a part of the Asheville scene was to become a player with a role in a kind of stage play...a whimsical bit of Shakespearean conspiracy to make light of the workaday world. To see the plot unfold in that classical vein or relish with Wolfe the intense drama of turmoil & struggle on the seamy underside. Whether with the smiling countenance of comedy or weeping face of tragedy, the playwright is the linchpin and real characters were in tune with the manuscript.

During his early writing days, Wolfe became so fascinated by facets of this crosstown pattern that he wrote a celebrated scenario in which disparate characters awoke from ordinary night-time slumber, somewhat simultaneously, to face questions of a new day, each in his own little niche of town. Presbyterian minister, successful businessman, flamboyant workingman, calculating lawyer, imposing whore. All members of the city's cast and caste.

In retrospect, the town often seemed to be a mecca for interesting characters. Strong minds found solace from the conventional market place, along with creative challenge in an inspirational environment. A mode enhanced by healing balm of restful nights and imaginative ideas. This was an incubator for second careers.

***

The ambiance did not spring from out of nowhere, of course. Before it was anything other than a commercial crossroads, the Asheville area was a center of natural beauty, which attracted nature lovers and prominent naturalists from distant points.

The object of their interest lay equidistant between Canada & Florida, where two geographic and climatic zones met, a region containing the greatest variety of flora & fauna on the continent, and the widest variety of gems & minerals as well. Here amid the oldest mountains in the world could be found the rarest of plants, spectacular high waterfalls, and a green wilderness which included nearly a hundred peaks reaching almost 5,000 feet or more...including 43 above 6,000 feet.

In 1737, John Brickell of Philadelphia wrote of this diversity, indicating that he was almost overwhelmed by it. To catalogue the plants, he observed, "would be the Work of many years, and more than the Age of one Man to perfect, or bring into regular classes..." In an ocean of deep foliage, singularity of growth was remarked by all.

In the years following, John Bartram of Philadelphia asked his son William to spend several years studying and sketching in the state. In 1753, the great Swedish botanist Linnaeus described certain of the plants in his *Species Plantarum.* So did Thomas Walter of South Carolina in his classic *Flora Caroliniana.* One of the most famous of these botanical explorers was André Michaux who sent rare plants back to France for the palace grounds at Versailles. And Professor Asa Gray of Harvard became widely known for his investigations into mountain plant life in a number of these counties. He is remembered by the rare and delicate lily that bears his name.

John Lyon of Scotland was a leader in botanical research and became so interested in the area that he took up lodgings at the Eagle Hotel in Asheville and remained until ill health led to his demise in the city. Geologist Elisha Mitchell, for whom the tallest peak and that county are named, became a legend in mountain folklore. And Charles Short, Charles Sargent, and Arnold Henry Guyot are all remembered among pioneers in this field of study.

***

In the center of this region was a geological feature known as the Asheville peneplain, a relatively long, flat stretch of land spreading out along the French Broad Valley. With its two million acres of land, this configuration was the focus for those with development in mind. And this Asheville Plateau had attracted the attention of the first explorers.

As a result of an agreement with chiefs of the Cherokee nation, the State opened (1783) the land between Blue Ridge & Pigeon River for settlement. In the following year, Samuel Davidson and his family left protection of an established fort, their base at the foot of the mountain barrier, and ventured along an old Indian trail. Their intention was to become the first settlers of the inviting valley on the other side, an ambition fraught with unknown difficulties.

Mr. Davidson reached the ruins of a Cherokee village and is believed to have been reassured by this that the Indians had been cleared out. He built a cabin on Christian Creek and every evening his horse was set free to forage. Seeing smoke coming from a white man's chimney, a band of Cherokee hunters kept the place under surveillance and formulated a scheme.

They quietly took the horse, removed the bell from around its neck and cleverly used it to lure Davidson up Jonas Mountain in search of his animal. After hearing what proved to be the fatal shot, his family waited until dark before fleeing back to their base at the fort. The extended Davidson clan held conferences of their own and then promptly went to recover the body. This completed, they took out after the assailants, succeeding before long in shooting, killing and scattering that branch of this famous tribe.

Once assured that the job had been done, they began a steady settlement of the Swannanoa Valley that leads west into the site of Asheville. Along the way, they were joined by Vances, Alexanders, Pattons, Bairds, Killians, Moores, Forsters, Davises, Gudgers, Weavers, Samses, Rices and others, primarily of Scotch-Irish extraction from Ulster. Composed of previously transplanted Scots, this hardy line had emigrated from Belfast or Londonderry to Philadelphia and two lesser American ports nearby.

From there, they had followed the highway westward through Pennsylvania to a point just west of Greensburg and then turning south through Maryland on the Great Wagon Road, continued on down through the majestic Shenandoah Valley of Virginia. Alongside some Germans from the Palatinate, they settled heavily around Lexington & Staunton, the rest coming on down to Salisbury and the surrounding region.

Some of the fearless, like the Davidsons, elected to push up into the mountains. While living in the Swannanoa Valley, one of the men married one of the Patton women and went on to become a symbol of America's frontier. His name was Davy Crockett. Others also went on to become scouts and guides, opening up The Great West. The Pattons and many fellow arrivals remained to develop basic institutions of Buncombe County, then a vast area.

The task required exceptionally strong men, and women. By the turn of the century, transport routes were still rudimentary, consisting largely of trails and pathways, augmented by crude ferries over the principal streams and rivers. In 1800, Bishop Francis Asbury, the famous circuit riding Methodist, made his first trip to Asheville and the surrounding area. In his historic diary, he gave a clear description of the situation.

"...my roan horse...reeled and fell over, taking the chaise with him; I was called back, when I beheld the poor beast and the carriage 'bottom up' lodged and wedged against a sapling...Not far off we saw clothing spread out, part of the loading of household furniture of a wagon which had over set and was thrown into the stream."

As to the French Broad, he wrote: "We crossed the ferry, curiously contrived with rope and poles for half a mile along the bank of the river, to guide the boat by, and O the rocks, the rocks!"

Endnotes

1. The term "Scotch-Irish" is frequently misused, as is Scotch. Scots call themselves just that, Scots, and things, such as whiskey or food, Scotch. The so-called Scotch-Irish migrated from Scotland to Ulster to America.
2. The Scotch-Irish were not half one and half the other. This is an American slang term used to refer informally to former Ulstermen who were Orangemen, followers of William of Orange, after they came to America. In other words, some Americans used it to describe other Americans. The term "Scots-Irish" is also incorrect, having been manufactured by confused journalists.
3. Most Americans also seem befuddled by the situation in Ulster, counties in the north of Ireland loyal to the Crown.
4. In the extended migration, a few continued all the way to the Carolinas border, where Andrew Jackson was born.
5. The post was later re-named Ft. Davidson. A small community that grew up around it became the town of Old Fort.
6. Through many sub-divisions, the original Buncombe would be included in most of the latter western counties. (See appendix.)
7. *Travels of Wm. Bartram*, Philadelphia, 1791. More than 200 native plants were described. The Bartrams have been cited & used extensively for reference by many leading writers in British & American literature.

***

1. A pioneer Scot, Lyon had made exploratory trips to the area since the turn of the century. He came to Asheville (1814) because the hotel's original frame structure had been erected earlier that same year. His health failed rapidly, however, and he died there.
2. Cause of death was tuberculosis, another forerunner of things to come. After he was buried in the cemetery at the Presbyterian church, friends in Edinburgh sent his tombstone to America, oldest such stone bearing an inscription west of the Blue Ridge.
3. In 1887, remains were removed to Riverside, along with the grave marker, shortly after that repository of famous persons was opened as a private burial ground.

TWO

ORIGINS OF THE CITY AS A RESORT

Origins of the city as a resort may be traced back to Sulphur Springs just west of town...and that development came with completion of the first turnpike, which opened Asheville to the world.

As the 19th century got under way, conditions of transportation led political leaders to begin agitating for general improvements. Finally, the Buncombe Turnpike Company was chartered and incorporated (1824) with a thousand shares of capital stock at fifty dollars each.

Construction records are fragmentary but at various times during the following year, contractors began work on different sections. The first started at Saluda Gap where the road from Charleston ended. At Paint Rock near the state line, the turnpike joined a Tennessee road that branched in several directions.

The route generally followed existing trails and paths. Work in Buncombe, as the county was then defined, was completed in 1827 and the last sections down the river toward Warm Springs and beyond were finished during the next year. In the following October, the first toll gate was opened. And John C. Calhoun would become a visitor to Asheville.

Much of the institutional development that followed was related to church congregations. While they predominated among pioneer settlers, Presbyterians tended to stick to themselves. The result was that Methodists, and later notably independent Baptists with their autonomous church structure, grew in membership at a far faster pace. Eventually Baptists would outnumber all others combined.

Still, the Presbyterian influence was fundamental because of their conviction that education was essential. They wanted to be able to read and understand the Bible without having to rely on church authorities. And they were determined to provide an education for their children. They founded most of the schools in the area, the basis for education until the turn of the century when the Aycock era brought a general level of basic learning across the state.

Among them was one Robert Henry, who instructed students at Union Hill Academy, the first school. He was known as a fine physician among early residents and like his counterparts, when trying to heal the sick, was as much botanist as anything else. The wide variety of plant & animal life provided cures both imaginary & real.

With completion of the turnpike at hand, Henry went on one of his exploratory hikes and there at a place four miles west of the river, he and his slave, Sam, named for the first settler, discovered the main spring of what proved to be a group of such springs. One tested white sulphur; the other principal spring was said to be of blue sulphur. A slight particle of iron and "perhaps a little magnesia" was reported. Not far off was a chalybeate spring.

The waters were very cold and pleasant to the taste. In cases of dyspepsia, it was said to have no superior and those using it claimed that "it certainly gives one a most excellent appetite." The breeze was soft and cool at this spot and the view outstanding. In the west, Mt. Pisgah & the Haywood mountains, including Cold Mountain. Close at hand a little vantage point, named Mt. Yeadon after the editor of the *Charleston Courier.* The top was about two and a half miles from the springs. From it, the appealing view expanded in several directions.

Some years later, with traffic flowing through over the fine new turnpike...some said it was the best in the impoverished state...Henry's son-in-law, Col. Reuben Deaver, started building a hotel there. The place had come to be known as Sulphur Springs and from that the hotel acquired its name. By 1848, it was a rambling resort with accommodations for 200 guests, as well as their servants and carriages.

After it was compared favorably with Saratoga by Charles Lanman, a professional traveler whose books gave the area its first publicity, the hotel became popular with visitors from Columbia & Augusta & Charleston, at its peak accommodating as many as 500 guests, far greater than anything in the city itself. Climate and clear waters had already established a widespread reputation for health related benefits of the Asheville Plateau. A cool respite from swampy & malarial climes of the tidewater South.

Although people had been coming here for their health since the turn of the century, the turnpike set new standards. Nature was still in control but out of isolation, an artery of commerce was now emerging...a link with Greenville in South Carolina and Greeneville in Tennessee.

In addition to passengers, there was an even more basic element. The Midwest produced a large quantity of animals and the Southeast a strong market. Skilled drovers with flocks & herds slowly grew to a veritable flood...the largest concentration in the country...as hundreds of thousands of hogs, cattle, & turkeys poured through this narrow funnel on their way to towns & plantations from Columbia southeast.

Results of this torrent were mixed but generally on the favorable side. A road has two directions, of course, and as early as 1829, a newspaper correspondent reported that from eight wagons a day to double that number were passing through Asheville. Loaded with persons headed west to seek more favorable economic conditions. On the other hand, animals require feed and farmers who supplied it readily understood the monetary benefits. And those who catered to visitors in any way stood to benefit increasingly as well.

In the Swannanoa Valley, a day's ride from the city, George C. Alexander had bought property (1818) along the river. He established an inn which his descendants enlarged and renovated many times. And north of the city, a brother, James Mitchell Alexander, contracted to build a section of the turnpike along the river there. After it was completed, he bought a large tract of land and erected a handsome and comfortable hotel, one later substantially enlarged. The turnpike passed between hotel and riverbank and a small community grew up around that point.

While presence of mineral waters was an early attraction, there was more to it than that. In a time of spas, travelers seeking curative & restorative powers for medicinal purposes often were drawn to places with social amenities. Resorts like Saratoga in the North and Hot Springs & White Sulphur Springs in the South were widely known. With the size of its clientele, Sulphur Springs was obviously considered to have the right amenities. And in time, Warm Springs, later known as Hot Springs, became an even greater attraction.

In 1858, the Asheville *Spectator* observed that "none deny the infallible efficacy of Warm Springs in cases of rheumatism and like diseases...It has been our good fortune to have been at many watering places, but never at one where the comfort of the visitor was more looked to." A drawing (1874) from *Scribner's Monthly Magazine* shows a bridge across the French Broad near Patton's hotel, a stagecoach stop on the way there. The spa had started in 1831 as a small inn.

The innkeeper was Mr. John E. Patton, a pioneer hotelman's name in these parts as well as the family name from which the appellation for Asheville's main street was derived. And many a stagecoach passenger stopped in town en route to these popular resorts.

***

As the Fifties drew to a close, a volume entitled *Mountain Scenery* called attention to the comparatively unknown condition of this "heavenly region" and chided residents of the state for allowing others to discover it. The author was Henry E. Colton.

"There is perhaps no section embracing so small a compass," he wrote, "for which nature has done so much as that composing" this area. "All roads seem naturally to converge at Asheville," he went on, and here "the rising ground from the valley, upon which the town is built, enables one to obtain from almost any point...a fine view." Indeed, "the eye tires as it sweeps over the seemingly interminable ranges which rise above and beyond each other."

In his *Alleghany Mountains*, Lanman describes the view from a hill nearby. "It was near the sunset hour, and the sky was flooded with a golden glow, which gave a living beauty to at least a hundred mountain peaks...from the centre of which loomed high towards the zenith, Mount Pisgah, and the Cold Mountain, richly clothed in purple...In the middle distance...columns of blue smoke were gracefully floating into the upper air...and whence came the occasional tinkle of a bell, as cattle wended their way homeward, after running among unfenced hills.

"Directly at my feet lay the little town of Asheville," he continued, "like an oddly shaped figure on a green carpet; and over the whole scene dwelt a spirit of repose, which seemed to quiet even the common throbbings of the heart."

Colton commented on private residences of the citizenry and handsome houses of the South Carolinians. "One of the most luxuriantly adorned meets a traveler's eye just as he leaves the Swannanoa River to go into town," he wrote. (Once home to Dr. J.F.E. Hardy.) "The people...are everywhere noted for their hospitality. The court house...is situated on what might...be called the culminating point of the town, as the hill there reaches its greatest height, and then slopes gradually on every side. From the cupola of this building, 96 feet from the base, a fine view...is to be had. It is a pleasant place to sit, of an evening, witness the sunset, and enjoy a cool breeze.

"The Female College, in a building of some size, is flourishing. During the past year, it numbered about 240 pupils. There are three churches, Methodist, Presbyterian, and Episcopalian, all (with) regular preaching, and three good hotels, of which the Eagle is chief. It is kept by Messrs. Patton & Blair, formerly by Dr. J.D. Boyd...The Buck is kept by J.H. Gudger, who has been its proprietor for many years. The Buncombe House is sufficiently near for all purposes, yet away from (the) dust and bustle. In connection with the Eagle, an excellent livery stable (is maintained) by Messrs. Sullivan & Patton."

Another writer describes the trip from Salisbury and is complementary of the accommodations. "By noon the next day, we reached the headspring of the Catawba, which is about 50 yards from the top of the Blue Ridge. There we stopped to take a lunch. 'Tis a wild looking place. The spring is thickly overshadowed with pretty trees, and surrounded, except on the side next to the road, with a rich carpet of green moss. Waked by a noisy little storm cloud from the nice nap, to which the coolness and pleasantness of the place invited us, we bestirred ourselves and were, in a few moments, over the summit of the ridge, and descending into a delightful country.

"Nor were we at any loss for company. On both sides of us were clusters of the sweetest flowers of the Ridge; and, ever and anon, a merry brooklet coming from the Black and spurs of the Ridge, would dash across our path in frolicsome glee. After a few hours' travel, we discovered ourselves rolling alongside that nymph of beauty, the Swannanoa. Its waters are unusually clear and pure, and its grassy banks look as if they had been washed; and the walnuts, sycamores, water-birch, hollies, and sugar maples, which hang over it, throw down a deep shade upon its green-colored waters.

"When you come within five or six miles of Asheville, on one side of you is this river, and, on the other, splendid residences and rich farms. No one can fail to admire that part of the Great State of Buncombe."

In describing his trip over this same gap, Lanman gives us a glimpse in the opposite direction. "It was a wilderness of mountains, whose foundations could not be fathomed by the eye; while in the distance, towering above all the peaks, rose the singular and fantastic form of the Table Mountain. Not a sign of the breathing human world could be seen in any direction, and the only living creature which appeared to my view was a solitary eagle, wheeling to and fro, far up towards the zenith of the sky."

As the years passed, the number of routes reached eight...Counter clockwise from the meridian, north via Sams Gap to the towns in Upper East Tennessee and the Lost State of Franklin, northwest along the French Broad to Marshall and on to Greeneville, west from Sulphur Springs to Waynesville and beyond for junctions to Atlanta & Chattanooga, south via Flat Rock to Greenville via Caesar's Head, southwest to Rutherfordton & Charlotte via Hickory Nut Gap & Gorge, east across the Blue Ridge to Marion & Morganton, and northeast across the lofty Blacks to Burnsville & the Toe (Estatoe) River Valley to Blowing Rock and other isolated communities of the northern mountains.

At one time, terrain, transport, & travel made Asheville a center for the most extensive system of stage routes in the East. One that required an army of men & horses. There were perhaps 25 inns with varying degrees of quality in meals & accommodations to supply needs & wishes of the traveler. The heyday of stagecoach routes was reached after improvements & refinements had been made to roadbeds. Each was important in days of slow travel & formidable distances. It was 272 miles to Raleigh, nearly 500 to Washington & almost 300 to Charleston.

Antebellum writers were few & far between but still they managed to turn out hundreds of pages for flatlanders to read about joys & perils of journeys over these various routes. The phrase "wild grandeur" was perhaps one most commonly used to explain their lure for pleasure seeking travelers. The one through Hickory Nut Gap, as described by Colton, begins like this...

"...leaves the North Carolina Railroad at Charlotte and proceeds west through Shelby into the mountains...This region was home (to) Alexanders, Brevards, & Grahams...The road passes near several iron works, some of which have been operated for many years. A ride of about 35 miles brings the traveler to Lincolnton, where, if he be in the stage, he will probably take supper. A night ride brings him the next morning to breakfast at…Rutherfordton, where he will most surely get that which will tempt & satisfy his appetite…

"Leaving that place, he begins to enter the mountains in reality." There follows a graphic & detailed description of the route winding along river banks, "the river foaming & boiling all along the course. Glimpses of distant mountains, edges of frightful precipices, grand panoramas, clouds of spray, a series of high bluffs, narrow gorges, stone holes, granite outcroppings, shooting waterfalls, retinues of clouds. Isolated rock formations against the sky, a small stream leaping over a cliff nearly a thousand feet high, appearing & disappearing aspects of elements in deep natural pools.

Beyond Chimney Rock & Bat Cave, Sherrill's at Fairview was one of the best known inns. West out of Asheville, the first tollgate was established at Turnpike just east of the Haywood County line. Much later, John Smathers built a rustic inn & tavern there and later on, Smathers Inn had accommodations for 70 persons. Patton's seven miles north of Hendersonville & Roberts's, the Halfway House just ten & a fraction miles from both Asheville & Hendersonville, provided a popular choice of necessities & luxuries.

Probably most famous of the stage operators was Valentine Ripley. Among his schedules was Mt. Sterling, Kentucky, through Cumberland Gap, 245 miles. Greenville to Greeneville, each 60 miles for a total of 120 miles. Warm Springs 37, Salisbury 140. Baxter & Adams were well recommended. In 1871, E.T. Clemmons began running various & sundry lines. Wolf Creek, Tennessee, via Warm Springs. Old Fort, Greenville and others. He was succeeded by Weldin & Bailey in 1876 but they phased the business out as the railroad approached.

As the years of our epoch neared, daytime trips and overnight sojourns into the realm of forest primeval had become commonplace. Visitors seldom left unimpressed and post cards from Asheville & environs would remain a major factor for standard inventory of national card collectors & dealers. As the decade of the Eighties began, Mayor Edward J. Aston launched a campaign to clean up the city…from trash to tramps…but new arrivals were often willing to overlook the object of his efforts.

"Oh Asheville," one Raleigh matron exclaimed. "Behold the scene! Drink deep in the beauty and grandeur of its surrounding country. Your very senses will be steeped with an intoxication. As far as the eye can reach, you behold these everlasting mountains…and the city lies like a dream at your feet."

Endnotes

1. Construction of the Asheville section of the turnpike commenced on February 26, 1827.
2. Union Hill Academy was opened around 1790. In 1793, a log structure was erected on eight acres of land acquired that same year.
3. A Kentucky drover boasted of having run 2,785 hogs through on a single run. In the early period, some were vicious, half-wild animals, a condition attesting to strength & character of these men.
4. George Alexander's inn was a stopping place for many famous persons, reportedly including Henry Clay. In the 1920s, Floridians built summer homes nearby, without kitchens, and used the inn's dining room. Cooper's Station became Swannanoa Station on the railroad.
5. James Mitchell Alexander's inn was augmented by a store, tanyard, shoe shop, harness shop, blacksmith shop, wagon factory & grist mill. A ferry & bridge were located there.
6. The railroad later encountered much difficulty along the riverbank north of the city. One side of the French Broad canyon

was formed of solid rock that required almost continuous blasting to overcome. From Marshall to Warm Springs, the right-of-way occupied the turnpike bed and this saved the railway company considerable expense.

7.   Principal routes developed regular schedules; others were intermittent or sporadic. Some could be chartered.

8.   The little mountain above the town was called Beaumont and for a time Beaux-Catcher Knob.

THREE

THE INFLUENCE OF CHARLESTON

The influence of Charleston on the social philosophy and fashionable fabric of Asheville was a topic of conversation...but it is one of those subjects that does not readily lend itself to specific analysis. It was felt rather than understood.

The spirit of that venerable place, home of so many new enterprises, is in itself elusive. Along with the cavalier society of Tidewater, its leadership represented the highest level of American aristocracy as it emanated from the Mother Country. Not generally recognized is the fact that the original settlement was, in effect, a royal colony. A site planned by the court of monarchy as a form of extension of the capital of London itself. It was unique.

From the standpoint of Asheville, it was foreign, yet there was a connection, one evolving out of circumstance and geography. Landlocked communities need access to the sea and this was the most accessible port. The Turnpike pointed in that direction. The first families of Virginia were Southern and tended to live on their great estates, but they did not have to cope with the malarial swamps of the Low Country. Hampton Roads was oriented to Baltimore, Charleston to Barbados.

Waters of the Wateree & Congaree and the great banks of the Santee provided a lifestream for planters but also an impetus to leave their empire of rice, indigo & cotton for sophistication of the royal city. And by means of the country's first railway passenger service, from there to the Upstate. Some said inhabitants worshipped their tightly knit yet cosmopolitan world, but they also nurtured a dream. The exciting vision of a rail line running up the peninsula from Meeting Street and not stopping until it found a terminus in the wilds of the west.

Urbane Charleston had urban facets of a true city, paved streets, office buildings, public utilities, townhouses & theaters, long before Asheville had progressed very far beyond yoked oxen lying in the mud. And so we may conclude that it would have been of interest to Ashevillians under any circumstances. But there was something else. There was another Charleston. And it too was different. And while the mother city was 275 miles away by winding ways of the times, this other Charleston was nearby. Just down the road at the second stop of the stage line. One night at Fletcher, the next at Flat Rock. And not only that, settlers of the satellite were drawn from upper echelons of the mother metropolis.

Near Asheville, Robert Henry had just discovered Sulphur Springs while here in the wilderness. And the first self sufficient southern social settlement was about to begin. From the land of palm and live oak to the land of pine and white oak, a colony of style and elegance would emerge. Over the following decade, the brilliant side of life in Old Charles Towne transplanted to the hills, with materials transported in hundreds of wagons & carriages, all part of a yearly pilgrimage.

***

In the 1820s, Webster of New England spoke for the North, Clay of Kentucky for the border West, and Calhoun of South Carolina for the South. In 1824, Calhoun became Vice President and the following year, the Erie Canal was opened, bringing in a new era. Slowly the burning issue became trade, tariff and transportation.

In Baltimore, they were talking about a railroad to the Ohio. The Charleston leadership had been first in everything else and now it wanted to do the same. The initial stage would be to Columbia, then Spartanburg, Flat Rock, and on into Asheville where the Turnpike crossed the French Broad just south of the city. There it would follow the river to Knoxville or run north through the mineral district of the Toe River Valley to Johnson City. There was even talk of eventually extending it via Cumberland Gap to Cincinnati, where it could be linked with others to form a transcontinental route.

Following completion of the Turnpike, two representatives of Charleston's foremost families, Frederick Rutledge & Edward King, were dispatched to Asheville in the spring of 1828, to determine feasibility of an engineering survey, based on the city. After crossing Saluda Gap, they moved along Howard Gap Road until they reached a place that had been a hunting grounds for the Cherokee nation. Its predominant feature was a large, fairly level rock. They were accompanied by William McAlpin who put up a temporary structure that could be demolished if needed.

The party was taken with the pleasing aspect of the situation in general. A thriving little community of perhaps a dozen pioneer families had established grist mills with brick masons and several inns. As soon as their primary task had been completed, Mr. Rutledge took it upon himself to have a substantial log structure built. He named it *Brookland.* And so here at Flat Rock, the Charlestonian vision of commercial supremacy led to an unexpected development.

The sight of this residence and its owner, a member of the state's leading political family, led others to envision this place as a refuge from heat, insects & disease, such as malaria & yellow fever. King was the first to act. Visiting his companion the following year, he decided to build something really worthwhile. He transformed an 1815 mill house into something worthy to house and entertain a large family, which included 23 relations. Completed in 1830, it was named *Argyle* for their ancestral home in Crail, Scotland, where he was born.

A successful export merchant doing business with Baring Bros. of London, this distinguished attorney and his family became the linchpin of the community. However, the social narrative of this elegant enclave became a legend in large measure through flair of an early arrival who burst upon the scene to become a flamboyant organizer. As wife of Charles Baring, Susannah Tudor Heyward was sparkling and witty and while several of her characteristics were questioned, she was a skilled writer of dramatic works, with some ability as an actress.

Decked in royal purple, headgear often of graceful plumes, she and her dress were not to be ignored. Nor was she…by Charlestonians or anyone else. She wore magnificent diamonds for every occasion and never lost her love of flowing ribbons and sashes, usually of royal blue or other shade of that color.

A native of Exeter, England, Charles had come to the confluence of Ashley & Cooper for his firm and also on a mission from Lord Ashburton, who "sent him to arrange a match between himself (Ashburton) and the wealthy and charming widow Heyward" of that distinguished family name. It seems that on this fiduciary visit as knight errant for his kinsman, he found the widow so fascinating that the mission, which brought him here, was somehow forgotten. Whatever the circumstances, he became "Susan" Heyward's suitor.

Kings & Barings became better acquainted. Because of asthma, Mrs. King had come to Asheville but obtained no relief. En route home, they stopped at Flat Rock Inn & Tavern, where for the first time in many months, she found her distress alleviated. Judge King enlarged the grounds of *Argyle* to 900 acres. By 1833, Baring had acquired nearly 3,000 acres, the larger tracts by grant from the state. His friend was also moving rapidly in this direction and eventually his holdings came to about 7,000 acres, mostly through a number of private purchases.

While Barings proved to be the chief social catalyst and Kings the principal civic pillar, family names were filling the social register as visitors, guests, or even permanent residents. Laurens, Taylor, Moultrie, Rhett, Smyth, Vincent, Maybanks, Lowndes. Pringle, Huger, Elliott, & Barnwell were direct descendants of the first lands proprietors of the Carolinas. Eventually more than fifty houses…cottages, manors & mansions…were completed and occupied. And names included rulers of the province.

Leading families of Charleston, Rutledge, Middleton, Pinckney, were educated in England. Between the three were a number of signers of the Constitution or the Declaration, ministers to England, France & Spain, royal governors, state governors, chief justices, and generals. Several were candidates for President or Vice President. And others were numbered among those who officiated at every constitutional convention.

Social intercourse of the mountain colony was also enhanced by presence of members of the *corps diplomatique*…most notably French & British ministers to Charleston & Savannah. Count de Choiseul and Edmund Molyneaux acquired fine homes and participated in most activities, the count having fled his native land during authority of the *Directoire* before being readmitted and appointed to his diplomatic position.

Estates had taken form there in the highlands. Winding, tree-lined drives over which fine horses & carriages arrived in expansive park settings. Hunting & horse racing in the English & Low Country manner. Spacious parlors & drawing rooms, making lavish entertainment possible. Cotillions & teas. Formal balls and presentation of popular private theatricals. This was the *Little-Charleston-in-the-Mountains* and as with the mother city, in later years it would be closely associated with the Confederacy.

The more important homes had porter's gate & lodge, rambling stables, servants quarters. Full kennels. There were solid silver doorknobs, golden candlesticks, & rosewood furniture. Architectural aspects of Charleston itself. Red-coated hunters. Liveried footmen. Some of the grounds were immense but as in the home country, an abundance of slaves kept things moving properly. On a relative scale, they enjoyed the good life too.

While antebellum Charleston became a subject of factual & fictional accounts across the land, antebellum Flat Rock was something of a mystery. Even in Asheville, the mystique remained a point of reference in rather vague terms. It was difficult for mountaineers unfamiliar with the scene to visualize exactly the quadrilles danced under candled chandeliers, provocative conversations over three o'clock dinners in silver laden banquet rooms, morning gatherings on spacious latticed porches protected by formal landscaping, or comfortable carriage drives along Little River Road…bordered with banks of violets…where friends exchanged pleasantries in a lighthearted atmosphere…gay feminine voices wafting across a rural landscape…or headed across the way to enjoy elaborate picnics on the mountain ridges.

***

Meanwhile, plans for the railway project progressed and work started. On September 24, 1839, company directors met at the Eagle Hotel in Asheville with Chairman John Young Hayne, a prominent Charleston businessman, presiding. It was an important session. Several decisions had to be reached and the question of route beyond Asheville was on the agenda. Several states were represented since a separate company would be formed in each.

This was potentially the most significant project of its kind in the land and the atmosphere was serious and sometimes tense. Cigar smoke hung in the air with an image of those port cities along the Ohio ever present. Participants went for long stretches without a break. There was some controversy & stress but eventual compromise & accommodation seemed likely, at least to optimists.

After a late afternoon session, Mr. Hayne came out into the lobby and sank into an armchair to relax & rest a bit. Before long, he was gripped with a seizure and then suddenly slumped over. A physician was called but it was too late. Dead of a heart attack or stroke. Judge King was elected to succeed him but it was a serious setback to the project and its patient planners.

***

While the highly visible role of national leadership played by the Old Dominion was unparalleled, the cosmopolitan, concentrated city of Charleston represented a unique source of quiet power as well. Behind artistry of handcrafted doorways and inner courtyards, there was control & influence. A velvet glove.

Among hundreds of city leaders, perhaps none possessed quite the scope of the Rutledge-Middleton-Pinckney connection. It epitomized philosophical influence. And helps explain why the aura of Flat Rock went beyond pleasure of social functions made more enjoyable by flow of cool mountain breezes. A few vignettes suggest the scene…

Charles Cotesworth Pinckney was a joint commissioner with John Marshall to the *Directoire* of France. Talleyrand assured them that a gift of money was necessary, preliminary to negotiations, and that refusal might bring on war. Pinckney's response is classed in early history as one of a dozen most quoted challenges by an American patriot. "War be it, then. Millions for defense, sir, but not one cent for tribute!"

Under pseudonym of *Andrew Marvel*, Arthur Middeleton wrote brilliant political essays. He served so ably that he was chosen president & commander-in-chief for his state, but declined. One of the boldest opponents of royal authority, he was captured & imprisoned at St. Augustine and later in the prison ship, *Jersey*. His son, Henry, was President of the first continental congress. Their home was superb Middleton Place.

Edward Rutledge signed the Declaration, his brother the Constitution of the United States, only brothers to do so. Affectionately called *Dictator John* by constituents, John Rutledge was the only American public official ever granted dictatorial powers of his office. George Washington appointed him first Chief Justice of the United States. With Madison and several others, he was an actual framer of the Constitution.

Endnotes

1. Mosquitoes or heat of summer doldrums caused Charleston families to seek refuge on nearby Atlantic shores. Earliest of these beachfront colonies was Pawley's Island, off the coast at Georgetown, reached by rail & boat, perhaps around 1780. About 1880, natives began making hammocks for sale to visitors.
2. Charlestonian personality evolved out of basic English character seasoned with Scottish salt and French Hugenot spice. A solid Germanic strain and a trace of Scandinavian bloodlines were later blended with a touch of Barbadoes & Caribbean.
3. A single drove of ten thousand hogs passing through Flat Rock held up the stage for six hours.
4. To escape "fever of the country," a trip to England was sometimes considered simpler than rigors of a journey to the mountains.
5. A trip was likely to require two weeks. Two servants came along in accompanying wagons for each task so none would have more than he or she could do in half a day.
6. King took an interest in architecture and was an early member of the faculty at the College of Charleston. He also established a school that became the Medical College of South Carolina.
7. Educated in Germany, he was classmate & friend of the unpopular Bismarck, who was later chancellor & emperor, and maintained correspondence with him in later years.
8. A distinctive rock formation was believed to be an old Indian landmark, used for smoke signals & other tribal purposes.
9. First of these pioneers was Wm. Mills, who had a land grant. He settled in 1807 and was followed by Abraham Kuykendall.
10. Gatepost crests at *Brookland* contained the initials "F.R."...one for name of the owner, the other for name of the colony.
11. The original Celtic family name of Kingo had been Anglicized.
12. By outbreak of war, only one route connected the seaboard with the Mississippi Valley. The Charleston & Memphis was an expansion of the line to Hamburg (later Bamberg) after it was extended to Terminus (site of Atlanta) and Birmingham, then on to the river via Corinth, Mississippi.
13. The Haynes were also among early visitors at Flat Rock.

***

1. Born in Wales, Susan Tudor had lived in England and north of the Mason-Dixon Line. Always socially active, she was reported to have had half a dozen husbands during her flamboyant life.
2. Unlike settlers who pushed on, Charles Baring was largely ignorant of basic agriculture. His mind somehow connected soil fertility with an unhealthy climate, this having been his experience along the coast.
3. First of the Baring tracts were recorded in 1831.
4. At *Mountain Lodge*, bricks stamped MANCHESTER were found during later remodeling, confirming statements that they were made in England, shipped to Charleston, and hauled to Flat Rock in ox-carts.
5. In the basement, other artifacts were later located, including a ceiling beam in which were fastened iron snap-cuffs suspended from chains; in the floor were fastened leg-irons. Punishment for wrongdoing was administered here, in the absence of public courthouse and jail facilities.
6. At the Old Mill was a furniture factory, established to obviate need for long hauls from the coast. Mr. Farmer was builder in charge. Among products were the widely known Flat Rock Sofa and walnut-crafted Flat Rock Chair.
7. Each manor house was architecturally distinctive, interiors furnished by a master craftsman named Freeman, a Scottish shipbuilder who, after coming to Charleston, made woodworking his occupation.

***

1. Under circumstances of impoverishment, Memminger was left (1807) in the Charleston Asylum for Orphans, described by observers as probably the best place of its kind in Europe or America.
2. Recognized as exceptionally capable and dedicated, he was adopted by the governor, Thomas Bennett, entered college at age 12, small in stature but mature in character, a serious personality type later described as a prodigy.
3. After the war, the Union army of occupation seized the Memminger house in Charleston and, in an ironic act, used it as a home for "colored orphan children."
4. His detractors believed some of his policies were misguided and many historians agree. Some suggested that he and Judah P. Benjamin should have changed cabinet seats.
5. When Trenholm was imprisoned, some went so far as to suggest that they had incarcerated the wrong man. A victim of bloodthirsty radicals, he was rescued by the more humane President Johnson.

***

1. Some said facetiously that unless one wished to become a professional genealogist, the easiest course was to assume that they were all related in some way.
2. Some family members were buried in the family crypt at Washington & Lee University or the family plot at Magnolia Cemetery in Charleston.
3. St. John's was consecrated by the bishop in 1836.
4. Most early estates had private lakes.
5. Saluda Cottages became known as *Sans Souci.*
6. The Lowndes family acquired property of Henry McAlpin, son of William, and reconstructed it into a fine home known as *Dolce Far Niente.* (Loosely meaning pleasant idleness.) Completed in 1836.
7. King later gave part of these lands for a seat of government by Henderson County. It was named Hendersonville.
8. Among the triumvirate, Rutledge was of Scotch-Irish extraction, Middleton & Pinckney of English derivation.
9. Inherited by the family of Alexander Campbell King, *Argyle* may have the longest continuous possession by the same family of any house in the Asheville area.

Other Milestones

Beaumont. Andrew Johnstone, Georgetown, rice planter. *Pleasant Hill.* William Johnstone, son of Andrew. Next door. (Both 1839-41.) *Greenlawn.* Arthur M. Huger. (1840) *Brooklands.* Edmund Molyneaux. Acquired in 1841, original place rebuilt. *Many Pines.* Jas. Pringle. (1847) *Dunroy.* David Williams, Camden. (1852) *Teneriffe.* Dr. J.G. Schoolbred, early settler. (about 1855) *Elliott Place.* Col. Wm. Elliott. (1877) *Tranquillity.* Edw. G. Memminger. (1890)

A Salute

Charleston appears to have been the epicenter of the Great Earthquake of August 31, 1886.

In 1893, it was struck by a massive & devastating windstorm of the highest magnitude, with more than a thousand lives lost.

Fire, flood, cyclone, tornado, hurricane, explosion, bombardment, demolition, earthquake, plague, pestilence have been visited upon it.

It has yet to suffer earthquake & hurricane simultaneously but the Federal bombardment was by far the longest anywhere in American history.

No other city has endured such physical catastrophe.

Throughout it all, the great church bells kept pealing.

As refuge for its citizens, Asheville and its sister county to the south have been blessed.

Flat Rock was birthplace to the lemon julep.

So here's a toast to this ancient city and the mountain colony to which it gave birth.

FOUR

FROM FLAT ROCK TO THE SWANNANOA

At the Little Charleston of the Mountains, E.C. Jones, prominent Charleston architect, provided special designs for summer pleasure as well as urban elegance. In 1852, he produced plans for an Anglican church. St. John in the Wilderness, a distinctive structure built by Ephraim Clayton, Asheville's leading contractor.

In 1859, Henry T. Farmer built the Flat Rock Hotel. Sometimes called Farmer's Hotel, it was later named Woodfield Inn.

Near Fletcher, *The Meadows* and *Rugby Grange*, both big, bracketed stone houses, resembled certain lines of Flat Rock work. Near Asheville, *Newington* was a stone house with peaked roof, bargeboards, and substantial porch.

In 1879, the Asheville & Spartanburg Railroad was completed across Saluda Grade, making the stagecoach connection to Flat Rock relatively easy. According to a church history, "families remained from May through September, while men (still actively employed) went to and fro as their work dictated."

Many overlooking extensive grounds, residents indulged a shared taste for the Picturesque style developed by A.J. Downing. They built their "cottages" in the steep gabled Gothic style and in various Italianate modes, with deep porches and long windows, often French doors at the first story.

Rock Hill

On land purchased from Charles Baring, Christopher Gustavus Memminger built (1839) his Greek Revival summer house, a symmetrical dwelling set high on a raised basement, part of a farmstead he called *Rock Hill*. At the turn of the century, Ellison A. Smyth, a South Carolina textile manufacturer, purchased it and changed the name to *Connemara* after his ancestral homeland in Ireland. To formalize it as his mountain country estate, he added farm buildings, stone walls and a lake.

Argyle

About 1830, Judge Mitchell King remodeled an 1815 dwelling into a summer residence. The 2½ story frame house was enlarged by a deep, double-tier porch. As with other such Flat Rock houses, it gained lattice and bracketed trim in the mid-19th century and then in the early 20th century, was reworked in neo-Classical fashion.

Tall Trees

Margaret King Huger received this land as a wedding gift from her father, Judge Mitchell King of *Argyle*. This hip-roofed house with bracketed eaves was built about 1840 for her and her husband, Arthur. A full height portico with Doric columns was added early in the 20th century.

DAVID COLEMAN BAILEY

***

1. Dedicated August 21, 1859, this church was named after one in New York City. A North Carolinian named Hawkes had been rector there and Mrs. Daniel Blake, who was married there, had been a member.
2. Early rectors came largely from pulpits in Charleston, rotating certain weeks of the month. Among them was the Rev. A. Toomer Porter, founder of the military academy in Charleston. Several were headmasters at Ravenscroft, an Episcopal training school around the corner from Trinity Church in Asheville.
3. When work on the building was finished, Miss Frances Helen Blake immediately gave an additional 13 acres and built a one-room school of hand hewn timbers with a roof of hand rived shakes or shingles. During early days, the church was closed during winter months but she carried on year round, week-days as well as Sabbath, and was responsible for many of the converts.
4. One of the finest houses in the Blake Settlement was the William Heyward place. Uncompleted when the Rev. George M. Everhart purchased it in the summer of 1866, he lived in some of the "outside rooms" and conducted services at the church for a season, 1867-8. The estate was later acquired by Mr. G.A.G. Westfeldt.
5. Robert B. Blake donated four acres on the west side of the road for construction of a rectory and Mrs. Overton M. Price organized women to raise money. Having none to contribute, two members gave stone from the "Great Stable" at their estate on Blake Mountain.
6. Calvary churchyard became the leading burial ground in the Asheville region for Episcopalians and various relatives.

***

1. Beale came to Shufordsville a few years after close of the war. He built Arden House in 1870. Name derived from an idyllic forest in Warwickshire, used as scene for some of Robin Hood's travels as well as episodes in Shakespeare's *As You like It*.
2. In 1883, Fletcher & Shufordsville were incorporated, the latter under the name Arden, and the post office was moved to Fletcher.
3. Frederick Rutledge of Montford also grew up at Fairfields with sojourns in Charleston. His gentle reminisences of fine English hunting guns and other similar subjects were contained in a modest little volume entitled *Fair Fields of Memory*.
4. Fire broke out on Sunday before Christmas, December 22, 1935. Firemen were unable to extinguish the blaze.

***

1. Members of all families that established principal gardens of Charleston were represented at Flat Rock. John Galsworthy found them the most beautiful to be seen anywhere, as have many professional gardeners.
2. The Rutledge plantation on the Santee, *Hampton*, later became hereditary home of Archibald Rutledge, poet laureate of South Carolina. His poems, short stories, & numerous books were widely published and became nationally popular. One of the best known titles was *Home by the River*, a title also used for a collection of his works.
3. Other than the time that *Newington* was under construction & finishing, the property remained in the Blake family for nearly a century, finally being liquidated in 1923 during the Boom.
4. After a major fire near outbreak of war, *The Meadows* was rebuilt by Daniel Blake's son, Robert.
5. The property at *Straun* was acquired for the campus of Christ School; the house was allowed to deteriorate into abandoned ruins.
6. Not to be confused with the community at Azalea Station, about five miles further upstream.

FIVE

WAR & RECONSTRUCTION

The War Between the States left isolated communities of the Southern Highlands in abject poverty although they had certain advantages, some said, in that they were close to the soil *and* they were poor to begin with. And it raised a question that continued to confuse strangers: Is Asheville Southern?

To the Coleman brothers, a leading social and military family of the town, it was. But in very truth, as one conceded, it really wasn't. It was part of Appalachia. And Appalachia was a kingdom of its own, one that knew no state boundaries or other artificial lines of civil demarcation.

In the civil conflict that rent the nation asunder through a fratricidal bloodbath, mountaineers sometimes found themselves in one lost cove estranged from neighbors in another and some wounds never healed. Confederates would remain Democrats, Unionists Republican.

The state as a whole, vale of poverty and humility as it may have seemed to many, gave more men and *materiele* to the cause than any other. Its proudest boast, stamped in gold on the heavy grey volumes of official history, was...First at Bethel. Farthest to the Front at Gettysburg and Chickamauga. Last at Appomattox.

And Asheville provided some of the most determined officers of all, led by David and Thaddeus Coleman who served from the first day of the Confederacy to the last, without interruption. It furnished the first volunteer riflemen's units, the last home guards, and reinforcements for every army and theater of battle from Maryland & Pennsylvania to Mobile & New Orleans...from the Army of Northern Virginia to the Armies of the Trans-Mississippi and the West. And David Coleman led his men to victory at Chickamauga, highwater mark of the Confederacy.

As for those who never knew what the simple granite shaft centered in the town square was about, it provided the state's great wartime governor, Zebulon Baird Vance, who furnished emergency supplies to Jefferson Davis and his administration when warehouses were running low because of the federal blockade. During later days of conflict, Davis acknowledged that without him, his task might have been beyond reach.

Vance was considered a literal prototype of the Anglo-Saxon. When Commodore Maury of Lexington, Virginia, the famous "pathfinder of the seas," carried out his project to prepare an encyclopedia of ethnic types races of the world, Vance was selected unanimously by judges because "physiognomy embodied the best and strongest in the Anglo-Saxon, dominant among Caucasians." One of two men chosen to represent the state at Statuary Hall in Washington.

Pillage & destruction, epitomized by Sherman's notorious March to the Sea, left the Asheville area relatively unscathed. In December of 1862, the main structure at Sulphur Springs burned down but not as a result of warfare. There was looting & shooting by bushwhackers but demolition was rare. The four-year horror of war was followed by the vindictive ten-year ordeal of so-called

Reconstruction, an ironic euphemism for no construction or reconstruction or economic assistance at all…but when it finally came to an end, the winds of change were blowing for what Atlanta's Henry Grady would later call the New South.

And the people of Asheville were looking forward to a direct connection with the rest of it. In those quiet days, the scene was still much a part of the broader panorama…with stagecoach lines following winding routes around sharp spines of the mountain cordillera. In 1875, *Appleton's Journal*, a popular magazine, published a serialized, fictionalized account of late summer travel over "mountain by-ways" around Asheville. Written by Mrs. Frances Christine Tiernan under the pen name, Christian Reid.

Reliable pairs of men "drove the mountain" and she recounted her adventurous trip from Henry, east of Old Fort. Henry Station was the terminus for service from Salisbury while Thaddeus Coleman prepared engineering plans for extension of the line to Asheville. She was transported "in a coach drawn by six fine white horses." Their destination was the Eagle and passengers could ride with considerable confidence. Over all the years, never an accident.

The stage coaches, traveling in *stages* from one stopping place to another, would in time disappear but the title of her little work lingered on. *The Land of the Sky.* Hundreds would use it as a line for their own work without ever knowing its source or *nom de plume.* It proved particularly popular during times of economic prosperity & optimism, notably with arrival of new forms of transportation & development. Whenever engines of promotion were cranked up & moving in high gear, it became a central theme & slogan.

After seeing a copy of Christian Reid's charming narrative the following year, Newton Pearce Chedester left his mercantile business across the mountain in Johnson City to assess prospects. While staying at the Eagle, he purchased four town lots at the end of the first block west of the square. There on the northeast corner of Water Street, he erected the first brick store building in Patton Avenue and on the upper floors, established a 65-room hotel, the first high class, modern hotel in the business district. It was called the Grand Central and it advertised accommodations to please any traveler. Operated as S.H. Chedester & Son, the business flourished, both mercantile and hotel, and it became a fixture of the district.

With arrival of telegraph service the next year, Asheville was ready to become a nerve center for the region and Western Union opened an office in the lobby of the Eagle, thereby providing a convenient central point for stagecoach schedules and other communication.

In the year after that, substantial frontage was acquired by unknown parties across the street from the Eagle, and the year following, the library association was organized on that same corner. It became site of the city's first major hotel. The Swannanoa was regarded as one of the most beautiful streams in the South…many an ode to beauty was penned in its name by poets impressed with the pristine serenity…and the long stretching newcomer was named in its honor. In Union, South Carolina, Charles Rawls had followed progress of the railroad from Charleston for many years and now he purchased the hotel and sent his two sons up to manage it.

Later, an affluent businessman named Pack arrived as a permanent guest but insisted on modern plumbing. The enterprising new management obliged, getting our epoch started in style by installing it in prompt fashion. Progressive young Charles later became mayor of the town, which by then had become a city.

One day a young Presbyterian scholar stopped there with his bride. On his way from Staunton, Virginia, to his father's new home in Columbia, where the elder Wilson was pastor of the church. The young man's name was Woodrow and the honeymoon was the beginning of a happy married life what would take him to the White House. The best educated and most conscientious of all Americans to preside there.

This was not the easiest place in the world to reach but a glance at the map would show that east of the Mississippi-Ohio river valleys and south of the Mason-Dixon line, it was just about dead center. And one after another, additional inns & hotels were opened around the Square, providing a somewhat citified ambiance yet enabling guests to feel that pleasure trips into the countryside were well within reach.

Endnotes

1. Prof. R.R. Hunter explained the selection process. He said 250 photographs from Europe & America were submitted and one by one eliminated from consideration. As committee members gradually discarded them, "they finally had six photographs remaining. All were photographs of Vance." Dr. Hunter was agent for Maury, naval hydrographer & meteorologist, and author of *Physical Geography of the Sea*.

2. *Zeb Vance: Champion of Personal Freedom.* Glenn Tucker. Bobbs-Merrill, a subsidiary of Howard W. Sams & Co., publishers, Indianapolis, New York, 1965. 564 p. Mr. Tucker also quotes an elementary geography published by Commodore Maury.

3. A Hoosier by birth, Mr. Tucker was a distinguished American historian, author of *High Tide at Gettysburg, Dawn Like Thunder,* & the definitive *Chickamauga: Bloody Battle of the West.* He came to Asheville at the height of his career and made his home at Sugar Hollow Farms, founded by a group of Chicago Presbyterians.

4. Hundreds of babies in North Carolina were named for Zebulon Baird Vance, particularly in the west. (Sometimes the initials Z.B. were used as well.)

5. Vance was compared to Lincoln in personal oratorical style, plain & lucid, replete with incident & analogy.

6. Tucker narrates the following: "In a later generation, one of the highly rated Congressional story tellers was Tom Heflin of Alabama, who served in both houses. Locke Craig asked Robert Watson Winston which told the better story, Vance or Heflin. "Locke," he answered, "which is greater, lion or mouse?" He added that the latter told funny stories to amuse the crowd, while Vance's tales 'drove home the point and carried the day!' "

7. Watson also spoke of the relationship between the state's two most famous governors. "Of the young man Aycock, Vance was very fond. He seemed to feel that the mantle would some day fall on the shoulders of this youthful Elisha."

8. In 1903, it was published in book form by D. Appleton & Co.

9. Established in 1814 by one of the Pattons, James by name, the Eagle had shown the way and there were many guests of national reputation. Early in its career, it had been converted from the original frame building to an enlarged, three-story brick structure. Frame hotels came to be regarded as firetraps and it was a credit to city firemen that apparently no serious damage or injury resulted from hotel blazes in the central district. In time, most of the others burned down.

10. Just north of the Square stood the Buck with livery stables, competing for the "carriage trade" on later site of the Langren.

11. Actually, the first hotel may have been J.M. Alexander's small inn near the Eagle.

12. Directly on the Square itself, old photographs (circa 1850) show the Bank Hotel just around the corner from the Buck. Believed to have been named for a nearby bank.

SIX

AN ADMIRABLE VANTAGE POINT

While the Charlestonians stopped along the Swannanoa, the taproot from which the city's social oak tree grew was planted just above it on a majestic knoll with a circumferential view that included the town itself.

Where Main Street terminated at the river, migration of South Carolinians from the south and Scotch-Irish from the east reached a common ground. The choice part was a tract of 640 acres, a grant under date of August 7, 1797, from the state to William Stewart. Among these veterans of the war and the 436-mile Great Wagon Road to the Yadkin, Daniel Smith had married Mary Davidson of the original settler's family.

Their first child was a healthy boy who arrived on June 14, 1787, the first white child born west of the Blue Ridge. This infant was named James and he grew up in a sturdy manner. He married Polly Patton, whose family was starting to play a leading role in development of the town, now beginning to emerge by stretching north to the top of the hill and beyond. And they were the parents of nine children who lived to maturity and married, except for one who died a bachelor.

Thus began the career of James McConnell Smith, a natural entrepreneur. At this time, there was need of competent merchants who could bring in a broader supply of well made goods from producers in other states. Properly managed, a general store should prove successful. Smith filled that need with a shrewd eye of prices and values. He also understood the value of land. On July 24, 1817, now passed his 30th birthday, he purchased 8½ acres on Main Street near the three-year-old Eagle and added an acre the following year by purchase from the proprietor.

On February 16, 1821, he acquired nearly 30,000 acres in the county at favorable prices and now he began seeing the Eagle as a possible competitor. Over the next couple of years, he was making plans for another hotel on the other side of the square. Work began in late 1824, ten years after the Eagle had opened its doors, and the following year, the Buck was in business as well. Together, they became a center of conversation and information about the turnpike project. The next year, word came there from Raleigh that a charter had been granted for that purpose.

On November 13, Smith acquired 123 acres of the noble knoll from his father, a tract to which 465 acres were added on March 31, 1830. As soon as the turnpike was seen approaching on its route to this site, the point at which it would connect with Main, he invested heavily in the turnpike company. Traffic began increasing but it soon became apparent that there was a serious drawback. At river crossings, travelers found themselves coping with perils of ferries only moderately changed from those described by Bishop Asbury.

Bridge building was an art not yet acquired in the mountains and years passed with fervent complaints and no results. Finally, Smith decided to act himself. Where Sams Ferry had been in operation, he had the first mountain bridge constructed late in 1833. Like the turnpike, it was chartered as a monopoly, with the county fixing toll rates, and like the ferry operation it replaced, they were exactly the same as those authorized and charged in 1801. It continued in operation until damaged by flood in 1852 when it had to be repaired.

By then, James M. Smith had become a wealthy man…and a man of many parts. In time, he would be referred to as "the merchant prince of Buncombe."

The time of the new bridge marked the beginning of social aspirations. James Silk Buckingham, an English visitor of the 1840s, described the town as "encircled by ranges of mountains of varied heights and distances, with swelling slopes and delicious valleys, such as one might travel a thousand miles without finding surpassed in beauty." On August 16, 1852, shortly before the flood, Zeb Vance wrote to his fiancee: "Our village is very gay at this time. The South Carolinians are crowding both our hotels to overflowing. The streets sound with the noise of carriage wheels from morning until night." Mollie Carrie Gudger was writing to her niece that she had observed "a good many people riding out" from the town "some in buggies and some on horseback in riding costumes looking quite like *city folks* and *city life*."

Around 1848, Mr. Smith decided to build a substantial town house on the knoll. Smith & McDowell, his big store, was prospering in partnership with his son-in-law, William Wallace McDowell. Among other things, they were catering to the female interests with somewhat fashionable clothing and accessories, along with fancy foods and delicacies and other specialty items for the growing carriage trade.

In town, the Smith residence was a comfortable place. Rooms were spacious and well appointed. It had a nice garden, both flower and vegetable with attractive accoutrements, an orchard, and several outbuildings. Now he wanted a place more "in the country" where he would have plenty of elbow room. Here he built a rectangular structure of solid brick with interior woodwork in Greek Revival style. Its double-pile, five-bay plan featured a double-tier porch semi-engaged beneath an extension of its main gable roof. Walls were laid in Flemish bond.

Times were good. The Revolutionary War and its naval subsidiary, the War of 1812, were over and great civil strife was still on the horizon. When Smith died on May 18, 1856, he had already completed his various commercial enterprises. He was the owner of a large and thriving barn along with herds of horses and other livestock. He had a prosperous tannery and a profitable slaughterhouse whose business was expanding. He also owned a number of large lots in various parts of town.

And there was another measure of his wealth. At the century's halfway mark, his property accounting listed 44 slaves, a remarkable number for the mountain economy, and this figure may have grown somewhat prior to his demise.

***

When Smith died, his country place passed into the hands of his son, Joseph P. Smith, who lived there, but the father had never given up his place in town. Two years later, McDowell purchased it and lived there until the war, when he organized the Buncombe Riflemen, one of several small units that were among the first to ride out in response to events in the harbor at Charleston.

What followed tested the mettle of every Southerner and tales of bravery and heroism are legion. One of them concerns us here…

A native of Richmond, John Kerr Connally was descended from Thomas Graves who arrived at Jamestown aboard the *Mary & Margaret* a dozen years before the *Mayflower* landed in 1620. The family line originated with the Dukes-de-Greve who left Normandy with William the Conqueror for England where they changed the name to Graves. Of Anglo-Norman stock, the Kerrs (pronounced Carr) came to Williamsburg around 1730 from Ulster

Orphaned at an early age, Connally spent his childhood years at the home of an uncle, Col. Joseph Williams near the end of the Great Wagon Road at Panther Creek on the Yadkin. He studied law and had begun his practice in Richmond when hostilities broke out. The spirit of his ancestors was still strong in him and he joined the 55th North Carolina Regiment, of which he was elected colonel. He dreamed of victory and took defeat with personal pain.

The high water mark of the Confederacy was reached at Chickamauga and at Gettysburg. At the latter place, a severe crisis developed. After Pickett's ill-fated charge resulted in carnage, the men in Longstreet's final assault began to falter. Young Connally could not bear the sight. Impetuously, he snatched the colors from the standard bearer and in the last wave of attack, rushed forward at the head of the line. In the process, he became a visible target.

A volley of fire caught him. The colors were shot from his hand and then his left arm was shattered. He also received a wound in the hip. He collapsed to the ground where he was left for dead. The symbolism of this gallant act rallied his men to make a successful if eventually futile charge. Left on the field of battle, he regained consciousness but fell into enemy hands. Bewildered, he somehow managed to survive his wounds but his arm had to be amputated and he was imprisoned.

After a long incarceration, Connally was subject of a prisoner exchange. He made his way back to Richmond and the two arms of his sweetheart, a member of a prominent family there. Despite his partial disability, he earnestly proposed marriage to her and she accepted. Rumors of impending disaster were circulating at the time and, in truth, evacuation of the city was imminent although no one knew for sure what was going to happen.

The object of John Connally's affections was Alice Coleman Thomas, one of six eligible daughters of James and Mary Thomas. Their father was a prosperous tobacco merchant dealing on a substantial basis with foreign firms, notably a British enterprise with merchant banking connections. He directed his correspondent there to maintain his cash holdings in gold. As a consequence of his foresight, he was insulated from a currency collapse. When many fortunes in the city were ruined...this was then capital of state and nation...he found himself in a comfortable position.

In their hospitable home at 112 East Grace Street, Mrs. Mary Woolfolk Wortham Thomas was a matron of calm authority. Dignified even in time of great crisis, she was a source of strength and wisdom to all the family. Her daughters...Mary, Elizabeth, Katherine, Laura, Alice, and Gabrielle...were popular in social circles of the city and they learned well the skills of diplomatic negotiation. In time, Mrs. Thomas found herself with six sons-in-law whose varied and successful careers enhanced their fortunes...a situation further enhanced by James Thomas who provided an extremely generous dowry for each of his children.

Alice and her husband settled down to a relatively comfortable life in the impoverished city where he became a prominent attorney, having resumed his practice there. His ancestor Graves had sat in the first governing body in the land, the opening session of the House of Burgesses in Virginia, and he inherited a similar interest. He ran for office and was elected a senator in the state legislature functioning not far from his home.

In 1870, he was walking inside the State House one day on business, when suddenly the floor collapsed. He was pinned in the rubble, the body of a man resting on him on one side, a combination of beams so placed as to leave his head free. He had space to breathe but he was trapped. In this terrifying situation, flashes of his final battlefield experience crossed his mind.

He had been spared, only to be confronted with a mysterious blow. He was again bewildered. Only God Almighty could save him from a horrible death. He prayed fervently. If only the Lord of all Creation would work a miraculous resolution to his plight, he would give up his comfortable career and devote himself to His work through a spiritual conversion. Rescue workers eventually managed to free him without serious bodily harm, and he kept his earnest promise, winding down his practice and taking leave of the bar to follow other pursuits. He entered the ministry and did good works although he did not have a regular church assignment. He honored the Sabbath day to the letter, seeking to confine Sunday activities to walking in the open air and sojourns in the hills.

Later he and his wife visited Panther Creek. On one of these trips, they decided to make a journey up into the mountains. They boarded the cars for Icard Station and changed for the stagecoach waiting there at the end of the line. As it started up Main from the river, headed for the Eagle, they noticed the wooded hillside on the left. He came back to visit the site, met Major McDowell, and walked around the property. He observed that one of the crests there had a particularly good view, looking over to the town at one side of the panorama. He could not get it out of his mind. He returned and purchased this tract above the house James Smith built.

Here in the center of his approximately 350 acres, Connally began building his house and as Reconstruction came to an end in 1875, it was completed. It would become home to four daughters, first of which was Mary Wortham. It was a fine Italianate structure of brick, hand made from clay taken from the property. There were 14 rooms, lavishly detailed with parquet flooring, rich molding, curly poplar paneling in the dining room, arched doorways, and a stairway with delicate balustrade and caged newel. A pedimented central pavilion projected slightly on the three-bay facade while a trabeated entrance composition contained a fanlight and sidelights with Palladian motif.

He named it *Fernihurst* after the Kerr family castle in Scotland. Although conversion had resulted in his becoming a teetotaler who disapproved of drinking, it was obviously a mansion perfectly suited for social entertainment on a scale unknown to this part of the country except for the Charlestonians. A large porch, wings, and frame additions were added from time to time until there was a total of fifty rooms, 29 of which were bedrooms, surrounded by terraces, lawns, orchards, flower gardens and greenhouses. The colonel planted many excellent trees, yew, elm, magnolia, including varieties imported from England and other places.

While she did not want to cut ties with complex family relationships centered at the big house on Grace Street, Alice Connally was a woman experienced in the subject of entertaining from her days there and before long, things began happening.

***

A contemporary, James Evans Brown arrived in Asheville with his father, John, in 1841 from Lewisburg, Pennsylvania, to pursue land grants. John Brown had come in 1795 to purchase tracts for eastern investors, both in the Asheville area and in Mitchell, Avery & Yancey counties, a region sometimes called Mayland. North Carolina was the leading gold producing state.

John Evans Brown became one of the "49ers" who struck out for California in the excitement that followed discovery of gold at Sutter's Mill. He kept diaries of his six-month quest in which others perished from disease such as cholera or lost resolve while he persevered. Nevertheless, in the end, he came up empty handed like so many others and returned home. The lure of the Pacific was in his blood, however, and a couple of years later he was back in Northern California by stagecoach, for passage Down Under.

There in New Zealand he married the adopted daughter of a wealthy merchant and established a large sheep ranch that brought him wealth & fame. Returning to Asheville, he built a landmark in 1889, the year *Richmond Hill* was erected. Located on the mountain overlooking the city. He called it *Zealandia*. Patterned after *Haddon Hall* in Scotland. Shortly before *Biltmore* was opened, he passed away but his family stayed on in the mining business and his mansion remained a prominent fixture of the city's profile.

***

Meanwhile, the youngest of the Thomas girls, known as Gay, had accompanied her sister on trips to Yadkin County, west of the towns of Winston and Salem. From their connections with the diplomatic service, they had all traveled abroad and were beginning to enjoy many exciting and romantic experiences in certain foreign lands. As part of this life, they became involved in activities of the diplomatic corps in Washington as well and Gabrielle had met a highly cultivated young gentleman there, handsome, agreeable, and humorous.

Now it turned out that he was a resident of Yadkin and she found herself invited to his ancestral home, *Richmond Hill*. His name was Richmond Pearson and among other accomplishments, he was proficient in languages. He knew Colonel Williams. He knew her family and mutual acquaintances in the foreign service. He shared with the others the same respect for Southern traditions. He enjoyed making trips up into the mountains. And he was coming to find her a beguiling subject for further study as well.

The Thomases always had numerous servants, some of the domestic help being of English, French, or other European origin. Each daughter had a personal maid. There were French chefs and cooks to prepare meals that included specialties favored from experience in foreign capitals. Social life grew naturally and with advent of full railway connections, the pace increased, with travel back and forth between Richmond, Washington, Asheville, and down along the Yadkin, as well as foreign capitals. Eventually there were receptions and parties for as many as five hundred persons, including local residents and out-of-town visitors and guests.

Among these was Theodore Roosevelt, who enjoyed playing chess with his friend, Richmond Pearson. In 1882, there was an elaborate wedding ceremony there, as Gabrielle and Richmond were united in the bonds of holy matrimony. He was entering the diplomatic service, would go to various capitals around the Mediterranean, and a number of members of the diplomatic corps were present for the occasion. Some guests stayed on for a week or so, a custom that prevailed in those days and for many years to come.

In 1884, Pearson changed course and embarked on a new career. The couple set up temporary residence at *Fernihurst* where he had an office or study. He ran for office and was elected that same year to serve in the General Assembly. They loved their new residence but both wanted a home of their own and began thinking and planning for it almost immediately. The question was where to find another place, another splendid hilltop like this. In due course, a second site was located down river on the other side, across from the place where a community of substantial homes to be known as *Montford* was under consideration. He was able to consummate purchase.

In Washington, he discussed his ideas with James G. Hill, supervising architect for the U.S. Treasury. Mr. Hill came down and looked the place over. Favorably impressed, he went back to the capital and began laying out the design. The result was a large, comfortable, rambling house whose interior contained a profusion of high quality woods, wall coverings of fine fabrics, and mantels in Neoclassical Revival style. Work was started in 1888 and completed late the following spring. Its owner named it *Richmond Hill* after the Yadkin house. It was a fortuitous circumstance for the Thomas family as there were now two houses for social activity.

The Pearson children, Marjorie, Thomas, grew up there and Richmond Junior began following in his father's footsteps, becoming proficient in every major European language and one or two Middle Eastern ones as well. After entering the service, he was assigned to the same part of the world as his father.

As with others, Mrs. Thomas was a frequent visitor at both houses. In 1897, she spent the summer at *Fernihurst*. On the morning of October 7, she came in from a walk on the grounds, something she particularly enjoyed, and started to enter the house. There were two doors, side by side...one leading into the house, the other providing access to the furnace room in the cellar. She mistakenly entered the cellar doorway and fell down the steep stairway, a distance of about nine feet. The impact broke her wrist and fractured her skull near the top of her head. She died about four hours later.

Colonel Connally believed that the social order so many had been willing to die for would survive only if coming generations were also able to make sacrifices to ensure that it would. He maintained his position with respect to responsible conduct and behavior and to abstinence. He reportedly withdrew to his study or a room in one of the outbuildings when strong drink was in evidence at parties. He purchased a large tract of land east of the city near Black Mountain for use as a retreat, particularly for the purpose of encouraging family & friends to join in the practice of long family walks.

Resolute to the last, the old soldier died on January 31, 1904, here at his home. His widow remained there until her own death in 1917. Mary Wortham lived on there until 1929 when sudden contraction in the investment structure led to the house being vacated. As the great social era neared its conclusion, days of glory along the river came to an end along with it.

Endnotes

1. A handsome hand painted sign out front was remembered by a number of persons. Swaying slightly in a breeze, it depicted a great buck with large antlers.

2. On March 11, 1828, he bought ten shares. On the following January 9th, he added two more plus one from David L. Swain. On February 2nd, he added a final share.

3. At one time, Smith also operated a ferry of his own.

4. The bridge outlived early popularity. In the year following flood damage, the county decided to take it over and did so the next year. It gradually fell into disrepair again and became a dangerous hazard, wrecked in the flood of 1916. Foundations remained visible for many years.

5. Beginning in the late 40s, Smith served as a director of Greenville & Columbia Railroad Company.

6. On June 29, 1852, Vance reported that he had received an invitation to attend a social function at the Smith house. In his inimitable humorous manner, he described the amateurish efforts of at least one young man to be comical & entertaining.

7. Each three-bay end wall had a pair of interior chimneys while a two-story porch had six fluted columns at each level.

8. As noted, the Old North State was reliable. It might be said that the Charlestonians ignited it, the First Families of Virginia took charge of it, and the Tar Heels bore the brunt of it, an oversimplification with an element of truth.

9. The Constitutional Convention was in session. The Virginia Plan was presented the day before he was born, the New Jersey Plan the day after he was born.

***

1. After moving to Asheville, Pearson promptly established law offices in the old Legal Building at 28 Patton Avenue, along with Foster Sondley and other luminaries.

2. In addition to life as ambassador in Madrid, Dr. Curry had a distinguished career as an educator and was founder of several colleges.

3. Among others who lived in the big house on Grace Street was "Dr. Quesenberry," a Santa Claus like character who married Ellen, another member of the family, and like Mr. Alison, had been left a widower.

4. Upon return from the war, McDowell resumed residence and lived in the house until 1881.

5. In the Square, United Daughters of the Confederacy placed a bronze plaque at the base of the monument. Embedded in a boulder, it was dedicated to his record. They dedicated another on Monument Avenue in Richmond.

6. Just before evacuation of the city, Mrs. Thomas went hunting for some material at Hutzler's with the intention of making a veil. When Mrs. Hutzler heard about it, she brought out some *illusion* that she was saving for her own daughter and pressed it upon her customer as a present.

7. At one time, three clergymen were staying there as delegates to a church convention while three of the daughters were on the top floor in maternity care, all waiting to give birth at the same time.

8. Pearson was born on January 26, 1852. Under certain pressure of temporary annoyance, he had a fast temper that vanished just as quickly.

9. Other Italianate features included round arch windows, a Tuscan porch, a blind second story lunette on Tuscan pilasters, and a fully developed & bracketed cornice.

10. Walls of the main building at *Fernihurst* were 15 inches thick. The structure was unique in this part of the country, acclaimed by the architectural society for "purity of lines seldom equaled."

11. Under certain conditions, Alice & Gabrielle could each see the other's house.

12. The Yadkin originates in the Blue Ridge east of Blowing Rock and its waters find their way to the sea in the Grand Pedee and Catawba of South Carolina, finally emptying into Winyah Bay at Georgetown.

***

1. On June 15, 1892, Mary Wortham Thomas Connally was married to Otis Mills Coxe, brother of Franklin Coxe, and their son, Tench Francis Coxe, born in Richmond, also grew up at *Fernihurst.*

2. On February 13, 1919, Tench Francis Coxe married an Englishwoman, Anita Emily Mynott Remington, in London. They had fraternal twin daughters, Mary & Frances, born in Philadelphia, the original Coxe family seat. On January 12, 1923, he died of pneumonia at *Fernihurst* at the age of 29.

3. Alice grew up a beauty with wistful violet eyes, leaving a trail of earnest male admirers across the Atlantic, including the Duke of Alba in Spain. She was only 17 when he was smitten by her but he was more than twice her age.

4. Alice usually spent the winters with members of the family in Washington & Richmond. The route of cosmopolitan beaux & suitors ended with a love match back in Asheville when she married Dr. Thos. Patton Cheesborough of *Azalea.* They had two sons.

5. Mary Curry married Walter Andrews of New York and had three sons. She later lived in Washington.

***

DAVID COLEMAN BAILEY

1. The Rutherfoords' grandson, Ellsworth Lyman, lived in Asheville. He was a descendant of the Ellsworths of Connecticut, a family that included Oliver Ellsworth, a member of the Constitutional Convention and a friend of John Rutledge.
2. Ellsworth & Rutledge served with Edmund Randolph of Virginia on the Committee of Detail which gave the United States its name, a suggestion attributed to Ellsworth. In March of 1796, he was appointed Chief Justice, the position to which Rutledge had originally been named.
3. Gladstone said that the Constitution was "the most wonderful work ever struck off at a given time by the brain and purpose of man" so it is small wonder that special attention is given to anyone who had anything to do with it.
4. Ellsworth is not listed among the Signers but definitely had "something to do with it," having been largely responsible for adoption of the Connecticut Compromise by which two senators are authorized from each state.

***

1. Nicknamed Lady Mary, Mary Wortham was an accomplished horsewoman. She rode sidesaddle, won numerous awards.
2. When Southern Railway built a roundhouse for the Asheville division, it was considered an eyesore marring the view. Mary Wortham Connally sued for a large sum and won her case in U.S. District Court but the jury awarded one cent in compensatory judgment. She moved to Canada and contributed the same amount to a religious movement. Years later, she returned home practically penniless.
3. After his retirement following The Crash, John P. Curran, a wealthy New York cosmetics manufacturer, went all over Europe searching for just the right spot to establish a retirement home. "Always we found ourselves comparing other places with Asheville," his wife said later. In 1933, he purchased *Fernihurst.*
4. Curran spent a substantial sum restoring the property. The 38-room addition was removed and Colonial Revival porches and other elements added. It was renamed *Viewmont.*
5. The new owner correctly analyzed conditions in Asheville and concluded that they would eventually recover. On that premise, he invested in downtown business property, and went bankrupt in the process. The First National Bank & Trust Company took possession shortly after the Currans left the city.
6. As war in Europe was getting under way, the eldest son of the founder of Champion Paper & Fibre Company was in Asheville visiting. He inspected the property, now vacant again, and purchased it.
7. Company headquarters were located in Hamilton, a suburb of Cincinnati. He continued to maintain a home there and in Winter Park. One daughter lived at one house, the other at the second. He owned the Asheville property until March 23, 1960, when he suffered a fatal heart attack there.
8. The Connally preference for pure drinking water over alcoholic spirits took a happy turn. The property near Black Mountain later became basis for acquisitions leading to a new city reservoir on the North Fork of the Swannanoa, a source of some of the best city drinking water to be found anywhere in the world.

***

1. The two ran for representative from the ninth congressional district. Despite vigor & intensity of debate, they traveled as friends, maintaining a cordial attitude and often staying at the same hotels.
2. Although cable had been laid from Ireland to New Hampshire in 1875, undersea telegraphic service had not been perfected and was still considered somewhat of a recent innovation.
3. The match lasted a week, seven full days, and was reported on a daily basis. It ended with a draw, each team winning two and a half games. At conclusion, Pearson spoke for the American side and shouted, "Three cheers for Her Majesty the Queen!" The British captain answered with a rousing, "Three cheers for the President of the United States!"
4. His house had its own communication system and a pulley operated elevator for transporting heavy items such as baggage between all floors.
5. Men congregated in the library after dinner. Ladies were inclined to retire to the parlor. Two were provided for that purpose and for entertaining guests. The elegant front parlor was a six-sided room forming an octagonal bay with windows ten feet tall. The second was also a comfortable room.

6.   Downtown hotels were an hour's carriage drive away and guests often remained overnight, departing after breakfast. The electric car line shortened the trip but was not extended to the river for several years.

7.   A grand entrance hall was paneled in rich native oak. The grand staircase turned several times on its way to the second floor, where the ceiling, 12 feet in the hall, rose to a majestic 23 feet above the floor of the hall itself. There were ten master fireplaces with elaborate mantels in neo-classical revival style.

8.   Born in Virginia, the Pearson grandfather was a patriot of the Revolutionary War, planter, merchant, mill owner with 5,890 acres and 110 slaves at the turn of the century. His son became a member of the North Carolina Supreme Court and one of its most famous chief justices. Richmond Pearson grew up in his father's home with a respect for proper order.

SEVEN

RAILROAD ENGINEER

The beginning of our saga was marked by two related events. The first occurred during the spring of 1880 when railway passenger service was inaugurated at Azalea. The second took place that fall on a "bright blue" Saturday...October 2nd.

The first regular train to Asheville came through Royal Gorge that morning, puffing its way along the center of the Swannanoa Valley...Grey Eagle, Alexander's, Glen Ingle...stations that the railroad would rename Black Mountain, Swannanoa, and Azalea...and formally rolled to a steaming stop. The place had just been named Best for an official of the company.

Passengers bound for Asheville had been boarding stagecoaches, lined up on the other side of the platform at Azalea, for the last short leg of their trip. Since 1855, when the Western North Carolina Railroad had been chartered, a quarter century of peace, war, reconstruction, and finally peace again, the drivers had been losing their route from Salisbury piecemeal as tracks were extended forward in fits and spurts from connection with the North Carolina Railroad there. Now all that had been left were those 3.75 miles to Swannanoa Bridge at the foot of Main.

The location was known as Asheville Junction, the point at which the turnpike crossed, and a hotel had been built, along with railway passenger station and freight depot. On April 27, the railway company had been purchased by William J. Best with a promise to extend it in two directions from the city. West to Waynesville and on to Ducktown via Nantahala Gorge...147 miles...and north along the French Broad to Warm Springs & Paint Rock...53 miles...for connections with Chattanooga, Morristown, Knoxville & Cincinnati.

The path across the crest of the Blue Ridge had been a terrible ordeal...many lives lost over a decade of drilling, blasting and hauling from Henry Station west of Old Fort. By hand. A series of difficult tunnels culminated in the seventh...the great Swannanoa Tunnel. Highest in the East and longest in the South, it ran 1,832 feet from McDowell County into Buncombe at an elevation of 2,516 feet.

The railroad lines of Asheville were designed by Thaddeus Coleman, former officer, Corps of Engineers, C.S.A. The line from the south would join with the line from the east at a junction a few yards east of Best...and the two lines on the other side of town would form at a second junction, just beyond a trestle (later concrete viaduct) leading out across the river from the Asheville yards.

Along with the saga of the Clinchfield, these five routes represented the foremost achievement of mountain railroad building in Eastern America. To some, the task appeared virtually impossible, particularly since funds and equipment were usually limited, at one point stolen. Completion of the entire route structure required efforts of thousands of men over a period lasting more than half a century. Hundreds lost their health or their lives along the way, a little known story.

Now at last, the railroad had come to this isolated but promising town. It would employ hundreds, directly and indirectly. The immediate vicinity would become a small village of its own, where the world could discover what a few already knew. One day Mr. Vanderbilt would alight there and see far beyond the station platform. Eventually the village and the town would become one but that lay half a century ahead and the closing months of our narrative.

For now, crowds that gathered were excited about something more tangible. The shining locomotive engine that stood panting before them, passenger cars trailing behind, represented promise of the Industrial Revolution in a natural world of arts and crafts.

***

A significant but overlooked part of the economic picture in those days was the great tobacco boom. The variety was Virginia bright leaf, introduced into Chunn's Cove by a resident of that state who moved there in 1868. Two years later, more than 30,000 pounds were grown in the county. In 1880, a decade later, the figure was over 475,000. The first warehouse was opened in 1879 and by the 1882-3 market year, there were four down along or near South Main below the Swannanoa Hotel. One and a half million pounds were sold that year. Four years later, the annual total had surpassed *seven million pounds.*

At its peak, tobacco was king. Three factories were turning out plug, twist, and pipe tobacco. As down in the Piedmont, the smell of tobacco and the auctioneer's chant filled the air during season. Streets were crowded with wagons carrying hogsheads of leaf and buyers from many other places were registered in hotels and boarding houses. Money filled a lot of pockets. By 1890, however, the figure was back below one and a half million again and in 1897, the last tobacco warehouse in the city was closed. At the turn of the century, the total was 568,260 and a decade later it was nearing extinction below thirty thousand.

Thus over a period of four decades, statistics went from 30,689 in 1870 to seven million in 1886-7 and back to 29,788 in 1910. Various reasons, social, agricultural, commercial, industrial, have been advanced by way of explanation for this phenomenon but apparently no one knows for sure. Perhaps it was a combination of many factors. In the late 1920s, burley became a crop in demand; its development pattern was more stable and lasting, leading some to speculate that it was better suited to mountain cultivation.

The situation in agriculture and industry was one thing, travel and hospitality another. In the year the Battery Park opened, there were 30,000 summer visitors. By 1890, when a comparable structure opened in Kenilworth, the figure had grown to 50,000. By outbreak of war in Europe, it would reach a quarter million.

EIGHT

ORIGINS OF FASHIONABLE ASHEVILLE

Origins of fashionable Asheville may be traced to the Coxe family of Philadelphia, inheritors of a mammoth land grant through the lords proprietors in colonial days. Its members were possessed of considerable energy, vigor, and drive.

These lands were centered in the region around Rutherfordton on a trail that became the turnpike from the mountains down to Charlotte. They would become the site of early Southern textile manufacturing enterprise, an industry founded in New England from roots in Old England. And this in turn led Col. Franklin Coxe to some familiarity with the isolated community that is our subject.

Colonel Coxe was a descendant of Tench Coxe, 1755-1824, prominent American economist who was a member of fledgling early congresses and served the federal government in several capacities, including that of assistant secretary of the treasury at the time of the Continental Congress. A contemporary of Alexander Hamilton, he was an early commissioner of revenue before Jefferson made him purveyor of public supplies.

Coxe was a ready champion of the principle that our weak domestic manufacturing industry should be encouraged and that competition from foreign commerce should be curtailed, including access to coastal trade. He urged the South to cultivate cotton and was sometimes called the father of that industry. Thus his *View of the United States,* a compilation of his papers published in 1794, led to broader understanding of life below the Mason-Dixon Line.

His great-grandson grew up at Green River Plantation and his background & experience gave him a familiarity with social & business considerations and the role of hospitality in the advancement of commerce & communication.

As the expansive decade of the Eighties began to unfold, the structure of Asheville started to take form. It was the first of two such decades, the other following forty years later, that would make it into a cosmopolitan city.

Utilities were the key. Gas & electric service, followed by the telephone. City water & central sewer lines. A fire alarm signal system. Modern street lighting. Expanded police & fire departments organized with updated maps. And most significant from a standpoint of social chronicle, Colonel Coxe, an active director of the incoming railway company, started studying the prominent geographic feature within the town, with a view toward making it fashionable.

Once known as Old Stoney Hill, this feature was now known as Battery Porter after a Confederate artillery unit stationed there for protection under command of Capt. J.A. Porter. Its commanding rise would soon become known as Battery Park Hill and it was destined to play a leading role in city history. Architects studied possibilities. A winding road was cut through great trees covering much of its surface. And Colonel Coxe set his sights above them.

In 1882, the rail line west to the tip of the state had reached Waynesville and now it had been completed to Murphy. Service from South Carolina was still long awaited. In fact, its origin was the little *Best Friend of Charleston*, known simply as *Best Friend*, the nation's first operating line locomotive. And Best had been called Asheville Junction in anticipation of the road's arrival there.

On July 12, 1886, the Battery Park Hotel officially opened its doors to the public. A large, rambling Queen Anne style hostelry, it stood atop its impressive vantage point overlooking the heart of town, within easy walking distance of principal thoroughfares. One of the first in the South to boast a fine electric elevator & electric lighting throughout. And the view was not limited to the town. This dignified structure commanded a position overlooking surrounding mountains far beyond.

And Colonel Coxe played a dual role. The following day, the first train from the south arrived with passengers who included guests with reservations for the hotel, and other hotels. They were met at the Depot with a line of carriages to bring them straight uptown. Little had been left to chance, including means to tell their story far & wide.

Before long, the Southern Railway System and other lines began advertising Asheville as an easily available destination, not only for nature lovers of old but for eminent persons whose affluence would permit travel to the best spas and other resorts in the land. With arrival of sleeping car accommodations crafted & operated by the ubiquitous Pullman Company and its subsidiaries, all this became conveniently possible.

Visitors to northern places such as Saratoga & Cape Cod, and southern places such as Hot Springs & White Sulphur Springs, found attractions worth inclusion in one's seasonal itinerary. It was also noted that those whose interests lay in the more common forms of cheap entertainment might find little here to attract their curiosity.

Writing in the *Atlanta Constitution* early the following year, C.T. Logan commented: "Today no city of her size is doing more to perpetuate the glory of this generation in the New South than Asheville, and I have scarcely passed a square (block) without finding some sort of building improvements going on."

This was the era of Queen Anne style in hostelries. Arrival of the rails brought construction of a handsome hotel in this fashion, directly across the street from the main entrance to the Depot. Its considerably smaller but graceful frame silhouette provided a welcome & immediate convenience to the many travelers there, including those awaiting connections to all points at all hours of the day & night. The Glen Rock also found favor with those who lacked leisure time for pleasant pursuits of longer stays, ranging from a few days to many months.

While the Battery Park was under construction, E.G. Carrier of Summerville, Pennsylvania, southeast of Erie, came to take a look, having heard that it was going to be something special. Like Mr. Pack, Edwin George Carrier was a prosperous lumberman and he knew what the Coxe family was.

Mr. Carrier had invested in timberlands & orange groves in the Tampa Bay area, where St. Petersburg had close ties with Asheville. He decided to make a side trip to Asheville on the way there, in order to find out for himself what was going on. He met with Colonel Coxe and then, to see more of the countryside, rode the train west through the beautiful Hominy Valley. This caused him to believe it would be a good place for a resort, catering to the class of clientele that interested Coxe, but in a rural setting rather than urban.

The following year, he returned as a guest at the Swannanoa and acquired several hundred acres near the future site of The Asheville School, the first of some 1,600 acres he would acquire there. This included the abandoned Sulphur Springs resort, which became known locally as Carrier Springs, and where that hotel had stood, he built a luxurious new, three-story brick Sulphur Springs Hotel nearby. The next year, his hotel and the Coxe hotel both opened that summer. After arrival of some eminently fashionable names, the name was changed to the Belmont, that socially prominent family name providing a desired connotation of fashion, being associated as it was with a popular Eastern spa & race track in the splendid age of the moguls.

In 1889, a wing was added containing a beautiful, modern high speed passenger elevator, said to be the last word in "lifts" to be found anywhere in the South, including Coxe's castle across the river. And he stole a march on his competitor, if this more rural operation could be called competition, by organizing the West Asheville & Sulphur Springs Electric Railway Company to build a car line from the Belmont to the Depot. Running along Hominy Creek and across a 250-foot high bridge also built by him, it became an attraction for visitors & residents alike and Carrier Bridge was considered a modern marvel of construction.

Having successfully entered into competition for traffic at the bustling Depot, Carrier then obtained a franchise to extend service from that point up the hill to Patton Avenue where Uncle Sam was getting ready to build an imposing post office in Victorian style at the Haywood Street intersection. This burgeoning business, including mail & freight, was expected to be profitable. The location put him in the center of town, as well as right at the doorstep of the Coxe Estate and its 25-acre grounds, which ran down from the high flagpole to Government Street, as the stub end of College would soon be known to townspeople.

Meanwhile, he was bringing his abilities as a pioneer dairyman, cattleman, & orchardist to bear on his properties. Before Mr. Vanderbilt introduced Jerseys nearby, he introduced purebred Herefords from Blue Grass country around Lexington, Kentucky. He also acquired some Jerseys and established a racetrack along the river bottoms, primarily for entertainment of hotel guests. On July 13, 1892, a crowd of 3,000 well dressed persons came by electric railway & horse drawn carriage, assembling in the stands to watch the first program. Spectators of perhaps half that number were attracted by trotting & bicycle races, baseball games or other popular sporting events. Training & racing horses became a hobby & pastime. And there were elaborate tournaments in competition on what was called the Cross of Gold. The lands also served as fairgrounds for various activities, becoming known locally as Carrier's Field.

As a result of continued success, the French Broad Racing Association was organized with three-day events and generous purses that attracted leading Southern stables. After visiting the spa at Warm Springs, now Hot Springs, fashionable visitors journeyed up the river to take part in these activities.

Mr. Carrier had already built a small dam & hydroelectric generating plant, the first in the mountainous region of the state, first of its kind to furnish power for a commercial street car, and a means of providing the first reliable street lighting system in the city. All this was created after needs of the hotel had been met. Things were going well. The hotel was leased to Dr. Karl von Ruck for ten years. On May 26, 1892, the new post office opened, thereby securing a substantial downtown terminus for his car line. But on the night of August 24, a raging fire destroyed the Belmont, just as it had its popular predecessor in 1862, three decades before. A glow from the flames could be seen from vantage points all across town.

Undaunted, this imaginative developer began building guest cottages and laying out a residential community, with streets named for states of the union. It extended westward from the river bluffs. A number of houses of moderate cost were included for interested employees of the resort business in the area. The development was called West Asheville. Then another disaster struck. In the winter of 1905-6, the citrus crop failed and he was left in difficult financial straits. In 1907, he left the city and returned to his successful lumber business.

Some measure of his attachment to the Asheville dream may be seen, however, in the fact that when he died in March of 1927, his body was returned for burial at Riverside, across the stream from the scene of those memorable activities.

Endnotes

1. On October 21, 1886, the Rev. B.E. Atkins, president of Asheville Female College, made this entry in his diary: Tonight for the first time, Asheville was lighted by electricity. These lights consist mainly of four iron towers 125 feet high with four globes on each…In addition, there are drop lights at various intersections…The light is brilliant and gives general satisfaction." The towers were located around the Square.
2. The field later became the city's first landing strip for aircraft.
3. An engineer, his son, Heath, became R.S. Smith's partner.
4. Haywood Road was extended south to connect with the West Asheville Bridge, opened to traffic in 1914.
5. Asheville & West Asheville merged in 1917 and after the war, Haywood Road began to be developed as a business thoroughfare, culminating with financial collapse of the city.
6. After leaving the city, he organized a lumber business of cypress timberlands near Wilmington, an enterprise he gave to his sons upon his retirement.
7. The city system had the Farinholt franchise. The company did not want Carrier as a competitor and sought an injunction to prevent his crossing their line near the Depot. Resourceful Carrier dispatched a crew of men under cover of darkness. They ran the crossing without the threatened interference, then pushed a hand car across the new track, thereby establishing their position outside of court.
8. His street railway company was reorganized and added a route to Biltmore. The railroad crossing there prevented it from making a crossing to the passenger station but it connected with carriages at the end of the line. Many passengers simply walked across. Eventually a series of complex reorganizations brought all operating companies into one, under aegis of Asheville Electric Company.
9. The small powerhouse & wooden dam harnessed Hominy Creek. The bridge was located a few yards from confluence of the rivers, adjacent to railway yards and what had become part of entrance grounds to Biltmore Estate.
10. The hotel was not to be confused with a large, heavy brick boarding house of that name erected later at No. 57 Spruce Street, near the *Old Kentucky Home* at No. 52.
11. The Carrier properties were situated in Orange County in the heart of Indian River country.
12. The right-of-way extended about 3.5 miles from the Depot and approximately five miles from the intersection of Patton & Haywood.

NINE

ROLE OF THE COXE FAMILY

The pioneering role of the Coxe family relates not only to establishment of a great hotel but to the imagination and dedication displayed by the owner as host to his many appreciative guests, local and otherwise, as well as to the railroad that made it possible.

In Philadelphia, the family could trace its lineage to the court of King Charles II. Tench Coxe had been a contemporary of William Cathcart in acquisition of original tracts of land in the New World. The North Carolina plantation had been established by his son, Francis Sydney. Family members had both the means and the experience to entertain in a proper manner.

Named for the Quaker City's foremost citizen, Franklin Coxe was born in Rutherford County. At age of 19, he was an outstanding athlete, six feet, four inches tall, weighing 220 pounds. He inherited a large interest in anthracite coal lands in southeastern Pennsylvania from his grandfather who was head of Coxe, Furman & Coxe, a major commercial house, where he had established a reputation for financial acumen. Frank became one of the founders of Coxe Bros. & Co., later merged with the largest private coal operators in the country, Cross Creek Coal Company, in which he retained a substantial interest.

As our saga began, the Richmond & Danville Railroad Company became assignee to the interests of W.J. Best & Associates syndicate in the financially weak Western North Carolina Railroad and Coxe became owner of a large majority of the one fourth of shares belonging to private stockholders. By that time, the road was fast approaching Asheville. Two years after its arrival, financial & economic conditions during the winter of 1882-3 put still another strain on the company's equity position and he supplied capital needed to stabilize the situation.

Coxe continued to play a responsible role in viability of the regional rail system. In 1886, as the Battery Park was gearing for operations, he was elected president of the Charleston, Cincinnati & Chicago Railroad Company. By 1890, it would complete 175 miles of track from Camden, South Carolina, to Marion, North Carolina. Eventually it became part of "the Clinchfield" to Spartanburg where it connected with the line from Charleston through Asheville.

The great era of railroading and related hotel systems was about to begin and insofar as the Land of the Sky was concerned, he was in a central position. At the Battery Park, each room had its own fireplace, modern steam radiators, and the new Edison electric light bulbs. Bar and billiard rooms catered to gentlemanly pleasures. With the arrival of E.P. McKissick as general manager, French chefs & cooks came on and European dishes were combined with local specialties to provide a distinctive cuisine. Entrees of note included pineapple pigeon, Oriental Simla chicken, and roast breast of guinea hen a la Parisienne. Opossum dinners on Thursday and mountain trout on Sunday became standard features, not to mention Rococco cream from Europe as a dessert.

The first anniversary dinner party set the tone for future events. Flowers were in profusion.

Fern & palm graced the main ballroom while "rich colors of bunting from flags of each of the 19 southern states" decorated the main dining room. Thousands of Chinese lanterns cast streams of red, green, & blue light upon carriages stopping at the *porte cochere*. More than 1,200 guests were recorded in attendance, crowding the grand piazzas and gathering in the spacious ballroom where the formal hotel orchestra opened proceedings with a grand march. The evening began with champagne punch served at handsome striped tents, especially erected, and went from there to daybreak, when festivities ended with *Tipsy Pudding.* . .a concoction based primarily on milk, eggs & cornstarch.

Many ladies costumes & *accoutrements* "excelled in richness of material and elegance of design," according to newspaper accounts of the day. One of the most perfect, it was reported through social correspondents, was that of Mrs. A.J. Lyman who attracted admiring glances with "a court train of heavy (layers) of heliotrope satin over a petticoat of pansy velvet, ornaments, diamonds, pearls, and a garniture of *duchesse* lace." From that time on, prominent families began to conduct socials and the number of balls & receptions increased. The anniversary dinner dance was continued and to it was added a rhododendron ball in August, a German party to greet the fall, and a festive Christmas hop.

Among notable persons on the list of distinguished guests was one George Washington Vanderbilt, esthetically preeminent in that prolific family whose members built many of the nation's most magnificent homes. He would walk corridors of the Battery Park, converse with dinner companions, and sit in comfortable big chairs on the wide verandahs there. . .observing through a characteristic skyline haze the late afternoon & early evening panorama. Layered distances far out and across to Mount Pisgah & The Rat, central feature of this noble scene at dusk or other suitable times.

At some point in that leisurely time, his mind started formulating something that gripped his considerable imagination. Some say he told companions that he wanted to acquire everything from here to there, pointing directly to the mount with its famous biblical name. By some reckoning, that could amount to a quarter of a million acres in two counties and more, substantial even by flat ranch standards of the Lone Star State. Whatever the exact sequence of events, he knew what he wanted and the result was one of the great masterpieces of all time.

Soon after his return to Fifth Avenue and the landmark family residence there on Vanderbilt Row, his secret agents began the formidable task of acquiring what he had envisioned. As time passed, large tracts were assembled, piece by piece, along with some of the best architectural & engineering minds to be found. An army of workers was painstakingly brought together, including skilled artisans & craftsmen from many parts of Europe, along with reliable & dedicated native workers.

On Christmas Day in 1895, six years after work had commenced, the doors of *Biltmore* were opened to guests with a splendid party. Even a rustic oaf could have seen that it was as close to perfection as the genius of master builders & brilliant decorators could make it. Some of the best that Europe had available, personally selected by the owner, was included in furnishings & décor. Indeed it was the finest private home in the western hemisphere.

Endnotes

1.   John Motley Morehead built the 223-mile North Carolina Railroad from Goldsboro to Charlotte by way of Salisbury. The right-of-way formed a crescent that led to economic development of the Piedmont, often called the Piedmont Crescent.

2.   In 1885, George F. Baker purchased control of the Richmond & Danville, later the basis of the Southern, including the line from Salisbury to Asheville.

3.   A native of Lincolnton, Robert F. Hoke became president of the Seaboard Air Line system that connected with lines of this region. As a Confederate officer, he served with distinction throughout the war and had been designated by Lee, among his generals, as successor in the event of his death. Hoke made the final surrender at Durham Station on April 26, 1865.

4.   Daniel Coxe of Somersetshire was a member of the court of Charles II in the middle of the 17th century, during time of invasion by Cromwell. His son was Dr. Daniel Coxe of London and *his* son, Col. Daniel Coxe came to America (1702) and settled in New Jersey near Philadelphia. His son, William, married into the prominent Tench family of that city and a child was named Tench.

5.   Tench was one of the lords proprietors, specif., that of the governing body of West New Jersey and also the province of *Carolana*, consisting of what lay between 31st & 36th parallels of north latitude. Thus he was responsible for governing a sizable portion of what would become the continental United States, everything south of North Carolina (then including Tennessee) and the Missouri territory, excepting, of course, colonial territories of France & Spain, which became the states of Florida, Louisiana, & South Texas.

6.   A smaller formation next to Pisgah, like a double mound, resembled, at a distance, a mouse or rat. Hence the phrase. Everyone in the Asheville area was familiar with the expression. Pisgah & The Rat.

***

1.   Some 125 feet above the Square in a 25-acre park, it was "a massive ramble of frame construction," as described by Katherine Bishir, "nearly 500 feet long with broad porches running around its length, bow windows breaking the front and numerous gables adorning the whole." In summer, porches adorned with great boxes of flowers. In winter, enclosed with glass.

2.   A description, published seven years after the opening, stated that within its walls, "all was comfort and elegance. Every evening, the spacious entrance hall displayed a brilliant gathering of guests in little groups. Ladies with fancy work and gentlemen with cigars passed the hours in informal sociability."

3.   Special entertainments were given in the ballroom, with a stage of its own.

PART TWO

BUILDING FOR TOMORROW

ONE

THE STREET RAILWAY SYSTEM

While *Biltmore* was beginning to take tangible shape on planning sheets and diagrams of designers offices, the city was beginning to take a small but significant first step toward physical mobility which would unify disparate elements.

Late on the morning of February 1, 1889, with one Frank Sprague standing by, the first cars of a brand new trolley line moved smartly off to inaugurate regular transit service between Square and Depot. As cheers sounded from a small crowd, they disappeared around the first curve, site of a trolley barn that would later be rebuilt into a structure still standing.

At the foot of the hill on South Main, motormen successfully circumvented danger by navigating a sharp curve into Southside and proceeded proudly on to their destination. There a luncheon ceremony greeted municipal dignitaries. Men had filled the first car to ensure that well dressed ladies to follow would make the trip safely and without unpleasant incident.

Thus began the world's first all-electric street railway system to enjoy continuous, uninterrupted usage from opening day. Others had started as horse-drawn conveyances but these were not "hay burners," they had current and sometimes showed sparks. And no one was more pleased and gratified with results than Mr. Sprague himself, father of the electric trolley car and the modern electrical motors that made their operation possible. Henceforth skeptics would have to pay attention.

An imaginative graduate of Annapolis, Sprague had pioneered the first such system in Richmond before coming to Asheville. It broke down for a time on hilly street sections there before his crew was able to get it perfected and they were hoping to get it right this time. By the time they got to the *real* hills of Asheville in 1888 and improvised a few things along the way to connecting bustling depot with busy square, the kinks & bugs got worked out and once started, things kept going and never quit. Some day, almost every civilized city in the world would have street car lines but few ever knew where they originated.

The new service solved the problem of a crippling bottleneck. Old buses, horse drawn, from the busy Broadway line in New York City had been acquired and pressed into service for several years but by general consensus had failed to provide a satisfactory answer. Now there was a growing feeling of potential civic success. Soon there was an extension out Charlotte Street and addition of other lines continued in all directions until the first world war.

"This town had the best little old trolley system you ever did see," an old timer remarked with a broad, jovial smile. Then with changing expression, he added, "I never could understand why they closed it down." The object of his admiration, and that of many others, performed several functions, not least of which was that of a connecting vehicle for social activity, a direct link between stations & hotels, lodging & dining places, clubs & locations of amusement.

Special varnished vestibule cars took businessmen from street corners in the most fashionable quarter of town, directly to the depot for the best connections, or dropped them off in the center of town. A special junction enabled passengers to go directly from an important mountainside inn to the depot and return. There was a private spur line from the main street up through the hotel grounds to the Battery Park, and the Battery Park Special ran it at frequent & appropriate intervals. A heavy suburban line connected to Lake Louise in Weaverville.

With Pullmans and other cars arriving at all hours from all parts of the East, the depot line was a busy one. So was service between Grace and Biltmore. The connection between the Grove Park Inn and West Asheville became the busiest of all and employed the largest cars. There was a line to the amusement park on Lookout Mountain north of the city, to the park at Overlook on Sunset Mountain, and to the many attractions of Riverside, the popular favorite beyond Montford. All connected at the central square.

Most people wanted to live near one of the lines and so demographic patterns were influenced by their presence. The first town houses, so to speak, had already been established. They were situated on Haywood Street along the stretch that would later become an avenue of fashion. From there, they advanced to all points, down Main in both directions, along College & Charlotte to Chestnut, and out Beaver Dam Street, later named Merrimon. Plans for a crosstown connector route along Chestnut were developed too late for implementation.

Among the earliest of residential streets was Woodfin, the Woodson of Wolfe's childhood descriptions, and here houses ran in continuous sequence past the home of Nicholas Woodfin, noted attorney & horticulturist. Shortly thereafter, structures began appearing down Patton to the end of the street where it converged with Haywood and on to the end where it merged with Park at the end of the car line. Homes had been established there since before memory of any survivors although most records vanished along with original property owners.

Here on the bluffs overlooking the river, a residential neighborhood for the socially inclined held its place until a new concept came along, a planned development beyond Haywood Street in the northwest quadrant. Known as *Montford*, it was a town until incorporation into the city in 1915. The broad & stately main thoroughfare, unusual for these hills, was double tracked by the street railway company. Vividly described by Wolfe as Montgomery Avenue, it was remembered for a pleasing aspect of broadly branched trees arching out over the street.

Foliage provided shade for bold young swains holding & hanging on to open platforms of excursion cars, laughing girls chattering on rattan seats inside, along with everyone else in a gala mood of anticipation at the prospect of reaching the entrance to Riverside Park with its rides & amusements. A large motion picture screen in position within its frame, on a small island in an inlet from the river behind. Anyone who knew Asheville probably knew Montford with its variety of Victorian styles in architecture & comfortable life style…and at least a few members of the "Montford Gang" whose leaders were among foremost social, business & civic personalities of the city for more than half a century.

The street railway system gave Asheville an integrated social system as well. During the year prior to its inauguration, there were more than 40,000 visitors and 184 buildings built. And once cars got rolling, there was talk of a cultural meeting place. It would take another decade for the city auditorium to materialize but there was something that could be done more readily. The life span of professional theatre in Asheville mirrors our social epoch almost exactly, having commenced the year before it began and terminated the year after it ended. By 1879, there was a pioneer music hall on the third floor of the court house. After arrival of railway passengers, interest in an opera house was expressed, an ambitious concept for a town this size.

On the evening of October 22, 1883, the Metropolitan Opera House was opened in New York and the initial performance of *Faust* drew national attention. Outside of Atlanta and a few major port cities, opera as a community enterprise was virtually unknown in the South but certain businessmen responded to the challenge by building a small opera house directly opposite the Swannanoa Hotel. Patronage was inadequate, however, and with rise of the tobacco market, it was turned into a warehouse and when that era ended, it became a popular livery stable catering to the hotel trade in particular.

As work started on the street railway, buildings were leased at 41-43 Patton with E.W. Burkholder as architect, under commission from the Asheville Grand Opera House Company. On the evening of September 27, 1889, a brand new curtain went up behind the footlights for the opening performance of *La Belle Marie* or *A Woman's Vengeance* with Agnes Herndon in the title role. House seating capacity was 850 on the main floor with an additional 350 seats in galleries & private boxes.

A report by one present, published in the *Citizen* next morning, declared "the interior of the house was beautiful last evening and impressive in size, particularly as seen from the gallery. Coloring of white was harmoniously toned with bright coloring of the stage curtain and red curtains of the boxes and (illuminated) with nearly 400 electric lights." The ceiling was decorated with fresco paintings of classical composers, the work of French-born Eugene Cramer, who maintained a studio in Columbia. With collaboration of one Joe Physiox of New York City, he spent eight months on the job. Work on site was executed, cream on light blue, by Mr. F.A. Grace of Detroit.

Writing for the *North Carolina Historical Review*, Donald J. Rulfs describes the theater in Asheville, 1879-1931, as a vibrant & vigorous proposition. The regular 1890-1 season saw the house in full operation with a total of 59 performances, including plays, opera and other musical productions, along with an occasional lecture. During 1896-7, there were 65 events.

Hoisting of heavy sets & equipment from College Street into the second story stage entrance and back proved fascinating to young boys. They formed a small audience of their own on the sidewalk. Arrivals of formally dressed men and their ladies, alighting from carriages at the front, provided an attraction for general street audiences.

Endnotes

1. Much later, Sprague Electric was absorbed into General Electric, which at one time controlled the street railway system during its early years.
2. The name Grace applied to a community whose area extended about a quarter mile or more from Grace Chapel.
3. How Montford was so named became a lost figment of time but many residents believed that it was derived from nobility of English literature, specif., possibly as the Duke of *Montfort*. And there was a Montford Street in Charleston.

TWO

A PROLIFERATION OF HOTELS

During the decade following arrival of the railroad but prior to arrival of the street car, the flight of the Eagle as a social bird began to wane with competition from more modern entities. There was still a feeling of escape from more mundane matters in the world at large. To the visitor, at times everything seemed extravagant and romantic.

One remarked that "they are laughing, talking, dancing, flirting, as they do at summer resorts everywhere." Other accounts described Asheville in terms that were idyllic and occasionally poetic. The lingering influence of Sidney Lanier and others who extolled virtues of beauty was being felt. The scene was in tune with literary qualities.

According to Richard Thornton: "With the coming of brick structures in the 1880s, there was a strong Scottish-Northern European feeling. Building during the Victorian period was not (primarily) decorative. The style was very practical, simple, typical of the small cities in Northern Europe. The buildings (tended to lack) decorative details. They were pragmatic in appearance, almost Germanic in style."

On the western side of the Square, the Western Hotel had been established in the southernmost building early in the decade. The Presbyterian seminary at Church & Patton was now the centrally located Stevenson House and at No. 91 Patton, Slagle's was open for business, with the special car line track entering grounds of the Battery Park at that point. By 1890, there were eight major hotels and more than thirty prominent boarding houses.

More visitors were riding electric cars up from the Depot and into the Square. From upper floors of the Grand Central, the Chedesters could watch construction at the Battery Park and they wanted to utilize this increasingly valuable property. They started construction of their own, erecting a new building with fifty additional hotel rooms across the street, connected with a pedestrian flying bridge.

With *Biltmore* under construction, commerce flourishing, a transportation system operating, and Asheville's reputation as a resort spreading, the city would enter the Gay Nineties with a developing character of its own. In 1892, the business district was anchored by construction of two large, heavy buildings, the stone faced city hall at the east end of the Square and the brick masonry federal building filling the small triangle formed by Patton, Haywood, and College.

Down South Main, it was hard to keep track. The Swannanoa was attracting many smaller competitors. Things were busy around the Depot as well. The Glen Rock captured a substantial portion of passenger traffic but also attracted a collection of rivals. East of the Square, there was more of a boarding house atmosphere in the four blocks along College leading to the road over Beaumont. Midway there, an elegant 1893 mansion would become known appropriately as the Van Gilder House. Guests could enjoy themselves in a comfortable setting of old fashioned manners and service without hustle or bustle. This stretch ran from the Buck to grounds of the institution from which the street derived its name.

Here several hundred young women from all over the country made Oak, a short connector street, a landmark of activity. On the left was the stately Oaks Hotel, a five-story ante-bellum structure from 1856, now advertising that it was conveniently positioned for walkers from the Square and "on the car line" for others, with frequent service and a stop at the front door. Adjoining at the right was Asheville Female College with heavily tree-shaded grounds of its seven-acre campus. In early days, the hotel served as a dormitory and dining hall, with private parlors, dining rooms, and reception areas used by faculty, students, and friends. Both structures were imposing in a large, ornate, old fashioned manner with high ceilings, roofs, and cupolas.

But the *piece de resistence* was Kenilworth. Opened to the public in 1890, it was built as a fitting counterpart to the Belmont and Battery Park. The undertaking was financed by a consortium of Philadelphia capitalists who were impressed by those two hotels and by plans for Biltmore House. Comfortably placed on the hill above the little station at Best, this great edifice with the appearance of a Scottish baronial castle offered some 260 well appointed rooms. Again it was in Queen Anne style of the day, on a site situated to attract visitors yet convenient to residents.

Along with formal neo-Gothic, this flexible mode had emerged in the late 1870s with door cases & dormers, mullioned or segmentally pedimented windows, handsome brickwork or shingle patterns, and imposingly grouped chimneys. Contemporary with Romanesque, it was a cozy, individualized variation of neo-classical tradition, one that fitted the prevailing mood of romantic attitudes.

Meanwhile, these forms were also being employed for residential purposes. Richmond Pearson was a prominent exemplar in this respect and John Evans Brown retired as a rancher in New Zealand and built his stone castle, *Zealandia*, overlooking the city on the crest of Beaucatcher, as Beaumont was coming to be known. Two years later, William E. Breese of Charleston built his own captivating Queen Anne creation, later known as *Cedar Crest*, on South Main at the entrance to Kenilworth.

With all these goings on, social activities, arrivals and departures, trends in fashion, professional means of communication was desired and so the enterprising *Asheville News & Hotel Reporter* was established. This lively journal kept everyone informed as to what was happening of general social interest. The community chronicle concept was rather distinctive and as much as anything else, epitomized ambiance of the era. Other publications began carrying social news, along with articles by prominent physicians such as Battle and Ambler, explaining climate from a professional viewpoint and why it was so pure and beneficial.

Wilder & *Cloudland*

If this were a land of dreams, one of the lofty visions came from an unlikely source, an Ohio iron master. John Thomas Wilder had commanded the Union Army's famous "lightning brigade" so successfully that he was selected to lead the advance on Chattanooga and participated in the Battle of Chickamauga, greatest of all battles. In all, he took part in 219 other battles and skirmishes.

The experience had not left him embittered. On the contrary, he liked Confederate soldiers and the Battle Above the Clouds had implanted a highland mystique upon his soul. After the war, he settled in Chattanooga, in the most romantic setting of the South. He visited Asheville and other resorts and went to see Sulphur Springs.

He established a prosperous business, naming it Roane Iron Company. He acquired other companies manufacturing rail for rebuilding war-ravaged roads and extensive lumber interests in Upper East Tennessee. From there he climbed The Roan, a profound experience. Active in civic affairs, he was appointed postmaster and in 1872 was elected mayor, of the city he had helped conquer only a decade before. The railroad from Cincinnati arrived at Chattanooga the same year the road arrived at Best and he returned to Asheville to explore possibilities, staying at the new Swannanoa.

And then later he was aboard the first train from Spartanburg for opening ceremonies at the Battery Park. There to greet him was Colonel Coxe. They had some significant common interests, notably hospitality and transportation. Indeed Wilder had completed a spectacular resort hotel on Roan the year before. It was named *Cloudland.* Sitting on the hotel's wide verandahs, they talked with Mayor Edward J. Aston and some leading businessmen about the general's plans for a hotel-rail-mining network. The Toe River Valley in one direction, Copperhill mining district in another. A chain of resorts through Waynesville and the Sapphire Valley all the way to Bristol and the gateway to the Shenandoah Valley. Like a stagecoach on ribbons of steel. Rail vs. trail.

Ironically, his first priority, a rail line between Asheville and Chattanooga, never materialized, even though the gap was only a few hundred yards. The so-called Murphy Branch was completed into that far western town and just down the street, a branch of the Louisville & Nashville (L&N) ran to Chattanooga yet the two stations were never connected for line traffic. No one has ever come up with viable explanation although some believed that a selfish desire to retain revenues rather than share them was the primary consideration. If so, it was a narrow point of view since through traffic would have generated far greater total results. (An electric car line to Charlotte failed because of cost.)

Wilder had bought part interest in a Chattanooga hotel and purchased land on the crest of the Roan, which straddles the North Carolina-Tennessee line. According to scientists & naturalists, the 25,000-acre Highlands of Roan is the most significant natural treasure in the Appalachian cordillera. He had developed an interest in the iron mines at nearby Cranberry. Under his original plan announced in 1882, a line had been constructed within two years by the East Tennessee & Western North Carolina from Allison's Mills on the Watauga in Tennessee to the state line, a distance of about 30 miles.

Before the year 1886 was out, the erstwhile commander of "the lightning brigade" had the Charleston, Cincinnati & Chicago Railroad Company (3C) incorporated and under construction, from both ends and in both directions from the middle. The goal was the river at Ashland, Kentucky, a distance of 621 miles. The line to Murphy would extend to Chattanooga, a logical destination. At the outbreak of war, it, along with Atlanta, had become the rail hub of the South. And Asheville was a sister city. The mayor and his colleagues could easily grasp the scheme. Spokes of a wheel. Traffic from Chattanooga moving through the city on its way to Tidewater. Washington & New York. From Atlanta to Bristol & Roanoke. From Augusta & Columbia to Charleston. West Virginia. Durham & Raleigh to Nashville & Memphis.

The dream that faded when Mr. Hayne collapsed in the lobby of the Eagle had never totally expired and now it was like the phoenix emerging in the form of a lion. At the heart of it all was black gold. Around Clinch River, there was enough coal in the ground to fire the nation's furnaces and stoke the country's trains. It was too expensive to transport anthracite by land from Philadelphia to San Francisco but once the dream of a canal across Central America could be realized, trains from mineshaft heads of the Clinch fields to Cincinnati and Charleston could reach low cost water navigation. By barge down the Ohio and Mississippi, by ship out of Charleston harbor. A cargo conveyor to the Pacific, and the world.

Meanwhile, guests at *Cloudland* were enchanted. Going there was like being suspended from a balloon, free from insects, reptiles, and disease, even heat waves and lightning bolts. Writing under date of August 6, 1881, Dr. Daniel C. Holliday was quoted in the *New Orleans Democrat*. "Here we are enjoying a morning temperature of 48 degrees. Noon is 65, night 48 to 52...and this only 48 hours from New Orleans! It really appears like fairy land." Amid wild glens and great soaring cliffs of naked granite was the highest human habitation east of the Rockies. Rhododendron, azalea, laurel, and mountain heather in clumps from a yard wide to ten acres. The grasses of Roan, acres undulating like waves in the wind, were known as the *balds.* A challenge to science. Thousands of botanists would seek to unravel this mystery without success. The Roan would not reveal its innermost secrets.

Old time guests long remembered the main dining room of the hotel and beautiful cherry wood dance floor of the spacious ballroom. No ice was needed in the water since it came from a pure spring with a natural temperature 13 degrees above freezing. The state line was drawn down the middle of the floor and the main banquet table. One might pass the biscuits to a fellow diner in another state, but not alcoholic beverages, which were illegal in North Carolina although not in Tennessee.

The hotel had a pool, a billiard room, and an infirmary, a resident physician, postmaster, librarian, engineer, tailor, barber, baker, butcher, bandmaster and bartender. The latter was in clear view. A couple could take the floor and after a few turns, go for a drink...hard or soft...by waltzing into Tennessee.

Endnotes

1. Hotels there included the Oxford and something called Strauss European, along with the Asheville, not to be confused with Hotel Asheville on Haywood. In 1909, the Eagle was sold & refurbished to survive as Burnett House.
2. On North Main, Carolina House became Magnolia House, across from the Masonic Temple.
3. Hotels in the depot district included Meisenheimer, French Broad, Florence, Gladstone, & Highland.
4. The Van Gilder became the Knickerbocker. In 1924, it was sold to the county and used as an annex to the courthouse next door until being town down to make way for the new courthouse.

***

1. Dr. John Samuel Dickson, a Presbyterian minister, organized a group for Bible study (1833) in the basement of the Methodist church. Two years later, it became a seminary for young women, operated at the corner of Church & Patton.
2. A music teacher there, Miss Elizabeth Blackwell was also interested in medicine. When Dr. Dickson's health failed, the school was closed and she went to Charleston with his widow to live with his brother, a physician. She became the first woman to receive a medical degree and later went to New York to establish clinics for women patients there.
3. In 1850, the Holston Conference (Methodist) organized Asheville Female Academy. After the war, it was moved to Oak and became Asheville Female College, housed in a large, ornate edifice.
4. When appearing in public, they wore white Jaconet dresses in summer, blue Mazarine worsted in winter. A plain straw

bonnet or hat trimmed in blue lute string ribbon accompanied either costume. Wearing of jewelry forbidden, elocution, literature, manners and social history required subjects, attendance at Sunday school & services mandatory.

5. In Wolfe, Oak is Ivy. The two buildings dominated the entire block and he describes the scene with familiarity, the hotel corner being at Woodfin where he lived and the car stop on the corner a scene of his father's arrival, which he described so vividly.

6. Beaumont Street ran from the site of the Swannanoa Hotel across Valley to the old road that crossed the mountain. The female college was less than half a mile from the foot while Col. Stephen Lee's military school was at Chunn's Cove about the same distance on the other side. Sometimes boys & girls met on the summit, ostensibly to enjoy the view. In a whimsical fashion, the girls began calling Beaumont Beaucatcher and eventually the old name was forgotten. Colonel Lee died in 1879 and as the span of our story began, the school was closed.

7. After the female school was closed, the building remained vacant until around 1910 when Asheville High School was established there from classes at Montford and nearby Orange Street, near Central. In 1916, the structure was demolished and replaced by a modern brick building.

8. In 1908, the hotel became Cherokee Inn. There was lingering concern over hotel conflagrations and later it too became vacant. From 1920 to 1925, it was home to the Y.W.C.A. before being acquired by the Baptists as a building site.

***

1. As an officer or director of some 25 corporations, Joseph Murphy Gazzam of Philadelphia was one of that city's foremost citizens. A prominent financier, he organized Quaker City Bank and was an organizer of a railroad that came under the Vanderbilt network.

2. Following Mr. Vanderbilt to Asheville for the groundbreaking at Biltmore, he immediately saw possibilities for a great hotel across the way from the proposed entrance to the estate. He formed an investors syndicate for the purpose. Designed after a Scottish castle, the structure was named Kenilworth Inn. When the building was destroyed by fire, architectural & construction records were lost.

3. Distinguished in the field of arts & letters, Senator Gazzam was appointed commissioner from Pennsylvania to the Inter-State & West Indian Exposition in Charleston (1902) and the Louisiana Purchase Exposition at St. Louis (1904). He met Mr. Grove at the hotel and in St. Louis and they discussed common business interests.

4. A native of Pittsburgh, he moved to the Quaker City in 1879 and became senior partner of Gazzam, Wallace & Lukens, attorneys-at-law. His grandfather was a prominent English journalist.

***

1. The inn was located on the crest in a private park of 160 acres, overlooking the Biltmore Estate. It included open lawn of 20 acres, bridle paths and walking trails, tennis courts and a golf course, the latter described as "equal to any in the South."

2. For a time, Branch & Young were the proprietors. Later, it was managed by Edgar B. Moore, who also managed Mountain Park Hotel at Hot Springs.

3. As with others, it eventually had its own spur track to connect with the street railway system.

4. An electric car line to Charlotte was proposed but the project failed because of cost.

5. It combined Renaissance with native associations and like the *palazzo* mode, permitted either symmetry or asymmetry.

6. At this time, Battery Park Place, the front of buildings for the Coxe Estate, became known as Government Street, the name derived from the post office & federal building, a central hub of activity. Later it was added to West College as the western stub and then finally "West" was dropped and it became College all the way.

7. In those days, physicians offices were clustered around the intersection of Haywood & Patton, especially in or near the Medical Building (still standing) in the middle of Battery Park Place. This created an incongruous combination in the heart of town…prominent practitioners of the art of medicine alongside practical practitioners of the questionable art of splicing a string of film frames in series & sequel.

Wilder & Cloudland

1. When the war broke out, he enlisted as a private in the Indiana artillery at Lawrenceburg where he had established a business. He rose rapidly through the ranks, eventually becoming brigadier general.

2. Wilder is credited with having originated the mounted infantry. He later joined Sherman's Atlanta campaign but in September of 1864, ill health forced him to relinquish his command and soon afterwards, he resigned his commission.

3. Because of friction with city council, he resigned as mayor a few months later.

4. He held many other civic positions, including that as a member of the Chickamauga National Park Commission, in charge of by far the largest & most elaborate battleground memorial in the nation, with statuary, monuments & maintenance provided by all the states, north & south.

5. A member of the Royal Geographic Society and the Iron & Steel Institute in London, he was also a founder and life member

of the National Geographic Society. A member of the American Institute of Mining Engineers, he engaged in mining business at Copperhill near Murphy and in the Spruce Pine Mineral District.

6. He assisted in construction of the Cincinnati Southern Railway and became vice president. He was an officer or director of several other large businesses.
7. It was extended to the Cranberry Iron Range.
8. The foremost view provided a prospect of 50,000 square miles in seven states from an elevation of 6,394 feet. Mailing address was either Mitchell County, N.C., or Carter County, Tenn. Hotel grounds were surrounded by a sturdy fence ten miles long, with three gates and security guards.

***

1. His holdings came to approximately 7,000 acres.
2. In 1877, under his direction, L.B. Searle constructed a 20-room spruce log structure at the summit.
3. Hearing about the mystery of the balds, the junior editor of the *North Carolina Standard* paid a visit in 1857. He could not solve it, did not even try, but when he boarded the cars near Valdese for his return trip, his mind was filled with ethereal images and visions. Back in Raleigh, he composed a lengthy, graphic, and detailed account. At one point, he wrote, "After something over an hour's climbing (from a certain place) we stood upon the top...A single glance compensated for all the fatigue of getting there. Of all the mountains I have ever seen, this is the most beautiful. Others are grander, more sublime, and more impressive, but none are so pleasing, so romantic, and so charming."
4. In 1880, J.W. Chickering noticed "enormous chestnut trees, *castanea visca*, up to 24 feet in circumference, and hundreds of others, five and seven feet around, running as much as 80 feet without a limb, straight as a pine." The unforgettable green sward was fringed with huge balsam & spruce, growing from beds of rich lichen & moss.
5. The forest grandeur included other great trees, a wonder to behold. E.G. Britton visited the Battery Park shortly after its opening and went on an expedition into the Toe River Valley. Writing (1886) of his trip up The Roan, he observed that it was "not uncommon" to find logs nearly five feet in diameter. Other botanists found similar surprises.
6. The hotel advertised widely, and even attracted some European royalty, but referrals were most effective, particularly testimonials from those reporting restored health. Respiratory ailments were the most common diseases involved. Access was not easy, however, and one would have to be in fair condition to undertake the trip from originations at low elevation.
7. In early days, travelers took the E.T. & W.N.C. to Johnson City and transferred to the Cranberry narrow gauge road for Roan Mountain Station some 25 miles away. This meant boarding the *Stem Winder* for one of the wildest rides in the world. The route passed through river gorges into a canyon 1,500 feet deep & four miles long, with four tunnels and half a dozen bridges, via rocky clefts about a hundred feet above the pristine stream. A romanticist's unlikely dream.
8. At the station, the hotel company had built a clean, well-furnished hotel for stopovers. There were approximately 300 rooms, of which 267 were guest rooms with bath, meaning a fine copper tub in the bedroom or suite. No bath*rooms.* Other facilities were provided at a general bathhouse behind the main building.
9. The Roan Mountain Station Hotel advertised that it was "950 feet higher than any hotel on Lookout Mountain," the fashionable Chattanooga residential community and resort. It had a Western Union telegraph station with full service.
10. Next door was a livery stable from which a special hack line ran passengers and unlimited baggage 12 miles up a well maintained private road to *Cloudland.* Scenery was breathtaking at every turn. By the time they had reached their destination, awed honeymooners who had made necessary adjustment to the Highlands of Roan were said to regret ever having to leave their exotic circumstances.
11. The Clinchfield station at Toecane was so named because the Toe & Cane rivers merge there. It was established to serve as a transportation point to Bakersville, county seat of Mitchell and eastern gateway to the Roan.

***

1. At Cashiers, High Hampton Inn was built on a 2,200-acre estate established about 1850 by Gen. Wade Hampton, a wealthy planter with family properties in South Carolina & Mississippi. A native of Charleston, he became commander of a Confederate army known as Hampton's Legion. After the war, he was elected governor & then senator. The original inn burned in 1932.
2. Smokemont was established on the site of an abandoned lumber village covering 640 square miles. The Great Smoky Mountains National Park was established by Act of Congress on May 22, 1926. Within its boundaries were 53 peaks more than a mile high.

Panoramic Spectacle

The mystique of The Roan defies challenge. Among its facets was the phenomenon of looking *down* on thunderstorms. "They would fill the deep valleys, while sunshine bathed the mountaintop.

Like islands in the sea, a hundred peaks would rise out of turbulent cloud formations, as lurid lightning bolts cleaved cloud lakes moving through the vale below." Thus there was no lightning at *Cloudland.*

"...a terrific thunder storm visited, not the summit of the mountain, but the valleys below it. It came after dark, and from the porch, we looked out and down upon the world in which it raged. Every flash of lightning was a flash of glory, disclosing a sea of clouds of immaculate whiteness, a boundless archipelago whose islands were the black peaks of the mountains." So wrote Wilbur G. Ziegler & Ben S. Grosscup in *The Heart of the Alleghanies.*

"Not a valley could be seen, nothing but the snowy bosom of this cloud ocean and stately summits which had lifted themselves above its vapors. In the height of the storm, the lightning blazed in one incessant sheet, and the thunder came rolling up the awful black edge of the balsams, perhaps producing somewhat similar sensations to those filling the breast of a superstitious savage at recurrence of an every-day storm above him."

In addition to this fascinating panoramic spectacle, there might appear other displays, including the sight of a circular rainbow. A skeptical naturalist described this experience in the following manner. "Legend has it that the rainbow is God's halo...left by His angels to protect the Roan and its visitors from all that is evil. As I drove up the mountainside with a friend, the fog grew thicker and thicker. Convinced that the weather was not going to give way, I was about to cancel our hike and turn back...when the cloud cover abruptly fell away.

"It (was) as if the whole world had opened up before us. We found ourselves under clear blue skies...with the storms rolling below us in the valleys. Then, looking to the right, I saw the most unbelievable phenomenon I have ever witnessed. A rainbow began to materialize at eye level...and as it developed, it took the form of a complete circle. And then a *second* rainbow formed within the circle of the first! I cannot say how long we stood there. It seemed like a short eternity before the elusive spectrum faded from sight. My faith in legends was reaffirmed on the spot."

Another persistent story, one that could not be confirmed, was that of mysterious music. Herdsmen in the area occasionally heard a strange sound when the wind blew. Some judged it to be normal, a natural amplification of wind noises caused by rock configurations. Others thought the mountain itself was speaking, or that it was a devil's wind which set clouds whirling in a circular pattern.

Those of an opposite mindset ascribed the eerie noise to angels singing in the air and believed that this unique place was blessed with celestial incantations. Whatever the source, it was sometimes described as a sound like buzzing of a thick swarm of bees, heard only when air at the peak was clear beneath a sky of blue, while storms raged down below. General Wilder had heard it and often spoke of it.

When Henry Colton came to investigate, the host and two colleagues accompanied him out to walk around and about. After returning home, he wrote an account of his experience for a Knoxville newspaper. It sounded to him like "a continuous snap of two Leyden jars, positively and negatively charged." He concluded that it was "a result of two currents of air meeting in the suction between the two peaks. Being of two temperatures, (this) generated electricity by their friction and caused a snapping sound."

THREE

BUILDING A MOUNTAIN RETREAT

On his first visit, George Vanderbilt decided to build a mountain lodge. The quality of such a retreat would have been excellent. He had inherited ten million dollars from his father in 1885, however, and with the means available and a magnificent vision rising before him, this knowledgeable young man was soon devoting his energies to something far more challenging.

That something was a true quest for excellence. In an era of great private palace building, this would be the finest, and eventually all of his fortune would be drawn into it. The task was expedited by the fact that that the family's own architect was, by this time, dean of the American architectural profession. The first American to train at *Ecole des Beaux Artes* in Paris. And among private houses designed by him were the New York residence of William K. Vanderbilt and several superb summer houses at Newport, including *Marble House* and *The Breakers.*

The man who designed *Biltmore* was one of the most distinguished architects in American history. Born in 1828 at Brattleboro, Vermont, Richard Morris Hunt began the study of architecture at Geneva when he was 15 years old. After travel in Europe, Egypt, and Asia, he was made inspector of works for the buildings connecting the *Tuileries* with the *Louvre,* under his old master Lefuel, who had succeeded Visconti as architect in charge. Somewhere along the way, he developed an established preference for the Early Renaissance style of Francois I.

Preliminary plans for *Biltmore* were started in 1888 and during the following year, Vanderbilt, Hunt and their aides journeyed through Europe to develop ideas. There in the Loire Valley, they found the ideal they were seeking. Among outstanding *chateaux* there, *Blois* is finely situated in the slopes of a hill on the right bank of the river 35 miles southwest of Orleans. Here the exploratory party encountered something both captivating and satisfying. A bridge across the river connected Blois with the suburb of Vienne, where situated on the highest ground loomed the old castle.

Here Louis XII was born. Under its roof, Charles, Duc d'Alencon, and Margaret of Anjou were married. The courts of Francis I, Henry II, Charles IX, and Henry III were held here occasionally and this is where the latter ordered the murder of the Duke of Guise and his brother, an order he carried out on December 23, 1588. Isabella, queen of Charles VI, here found a retreat. It served as a prison for Maria de' Medici. Catherine de' Medici died within its walls. And Maria Louisa held her Court here in 1814, 75 years before, after Paris had capitulated.

Outer as well as inner facades were richly decorated. The earliest part dated from the 13th century. What fascinated these sophisticated visitors, however, was the Francis I wing built in the 16th century, a masterpiece of the early French Renaissance. Hunt already loved it. Vanderbilt fell in love with it. Their attention was drawn particularly to the admirable staircase, ascending within a projecting pentagonal tower, adorned with exquisite carvings, interior and exterior. It seemed a *motif.* A theme, a centerpiece. A thing of indefinable merit which might lend itself to re-creation.

About 12 miles east, in the midst of a park some 21 miles in circumference, lay *Chambord*, also begun by Francis I, in 1526, and continued by his successors of the houses of Valois and Bourbon. In addition to Francis I, it was the residence of Henry II and Louis XIV and scene of the first presentation of Moliere's *Bourgeoise gentilhomme.* It contained 440 chambers and its most prominent features were six round towers, each 60 feet in diameter. The double spiral staircase was so contrived that persons ascending and descending might pass each other without meeting.

On the Cher, a tributary of the Loire, was *Chenonceaux*, built on piles in the river four miles east of Blere. Francis I was again in evidence; this was a favorite occasional residence of his. Henry II presented it to Diana of Poitiers, who lavished money on its embellishment, as did Catherine de' Medici, after she had dispossessed Diana. Mary Stuart, the immortal Queen of Scots, was there in 1559 on her wedding trip with the dauphin, later Francis II, 24 years after it became Crown property. In the 18th century, it became private property and was long a resort for distinguished men of science and letters, including Montesquieu, Voltaire, Fontenelle, Buffon, Bolingate, and Rousseau. Situated in the Department of Indre-et-Loire, *Chenonceaux* rested nobly on foundations laid in 1515.

The Americans returned with their hearts and minds full of brilliant images, these three in the forefront of their imagination and inspiration.

***

Yet the concept of *Biltmore* was more than a house, it was an estate, a vast preserve. And while much would be left in a natural state, and managed in the best possible way, the immediate grounds and gardens of the house would be landscaped to the same standards. Again, selection posed no great difficulty.

Like Hunt, the man of choice was at the apex of his profession and approaching final stages of a long career. He knew the subject of landscape design in all its subtle complexity. He had studied it from the foundations up and his works made apparent that they were a product of genius that goes beyond technical proficiency.

After special studies at Yale, Frederick Law Olmstead worked on a farm in central New York and subsequently on Staten Island, where the Vanderbilt family had a farm as well. He made a tour afoot in England and on the Continent. He then went on a similar expedition through the ante-bellum South and Southwest. His observations were contained in numerous periodicals, monographs, and books, culminating in *A Journey in the Back Country* (1860) which was reissued with two other books as a two-volume publication, *The Cotton Kingdom,* just as war was breaking out.

Olmstead had a retentive memory that always enabled him to bring together desirable things from many sources. In 1856, he had been made superintendent of the New York Central Park Commission and a plan for this most famous of American urban parks, prepared by him and Calvert Vaux, was adopted the following year. He insisted on philosophical concepts, which earned it the affection and respect of ordinary citizens. He was one of the founders of the Metropolitan Museum of Art and the American Museum of Natural History.

One of the fortuitous aspects of development at *Biltmore* was synergism among those involved with master plans. If they were ever seriously at odds, there seems to be no record of it. Collaborating to produce a fully integrated design, vision transcended means. Olmstead proposed a naturalistic, picturesque park with curving roadways that led the visitor to a sudden vision of the house, a broad and total scene almost detached from the world in a setting of rolling forest planting and stately formal gardens.

A paymaster's office was opened next to the station at Best and a four-mile railroad spur built from that point to the site, for freight and passenger service. The G.W.V.R.R. An office building erected across the street. With hundreds of workmen recruited and employed and experienced supervisors in place, construction began in 1890. By the following year, the entire scheme was underway. In 1892, the understory was completed. The next year, the second story was finished. In 1894, the roof was under construction. And by the end of the fifth full year, the house was furnished and occupied.

As one of the mansions and other monuments built by Vanderbilts and various men of great wealth during the gilded age, *Biltmore* was criticized by some social activists and radical agitators. But their political ideology was a product of urban life in teeming immigrant districts of the North... not a creature of cultural and political mores of the vast region south of the Mason-Dixon line, more specifically the independent kingdom of Appalachia. There thought and mindset reflected not militant revolutionary aspirations of Central Europe but post-medieval psychology and culture of the English speaking peoples and their Dutch Reformed and French Hugenot counterparts. And North Carolina had the highest percentage of native born to be found in any state.

This was a marvel of the modern age that had produced electrical applications, railway sleeping car service, and utility devices previously unknown. Thus it combined beauty of what great artists of the ages had created with functional feasibility of American practical genius that would eventually take over the entire stage. It was one of those rare circumstances wherein the right men and means came together at the right time and place with the right methods and motivation to produce something that would never be equaled or surpassed. Before long, the old social order of Europe would be swept away and new technological superiority of Western invention delayed by economic failure, but for now, all was right in this particular world.

According to authors of *North Carolina Architecture*, Hunt's composition displayed a skillful adaptation of classical architecture to "the needs of a modern palace. The tall roof with steep towers and dormers, confident interplay between balance and asymmetry, open and closed forms of arcades, loggias, conservatory and spiral stair, (taken) in reverse spiral from that at *Blois*, combine to create an intensely romantic house. It is at once picturesque and palatial, vividly French yet perfectly attuned to its site...The flowing plan of oval, polygonal, and rectangular rooms extending from entrance hall and winter garden accommodated purposes of private entertainment and recreation with friends, while presenting to best advantage...art works and architectural elements."

One could visit and never see or imagine a vast downstairs world supporting the orderly, tranquil world upstairs. There a complex operation, well supervised and elaborately equipped, was conducted in an ongoing manner. Kitchens, laundry, storage, and utilities. Somewhere in a section of its own was a spacious, tiled, indoor swimming pool, and a bowling alley, available for residents and guests whenever the mood came on. Upstairs, downstairs. Endless bedrooms upstairs and room after room in the servants quarters. Stables and garages. As guests moved from the pleasant palm court, a glass-roofed conservatory, to the great heraldic banquet hall, or wherever they might wander, décor changed with them.

And if one accompanied his host to disappear into the deep, quiet recess of the library...a walnut paneled masterpiece lined with more than 20,000 books...he would first find himself traversing a 90-foot-long tapestry gallery with adjacent loggia overlooking the mountains to the west. A vista that had set the stage for it all in the first place. This was George Vanderbilt's favorite room. A bibliophile, he had selected a collection from the finest sources and put them in a setting worthy of the most valuable, upper shelves available by means of an extraordinarily handsome circular staircase. Here the steel *Venus* and Vulcan andirons were created by Karl Bitter. Above them an Italian black-marble mantel dominated the room and above it an *overmantel*, also by Bitter, featured large female figures.

This vision of perfection was completed by an Italian allegorical painting...nymphs and clouds swirling across the ceiling.

Endnotes

1. Some reports indicate an early vision of an elegant Southern mansion.
2. Returning to his own country in 1855, he became architect of the Capitol Extension at Washington, Lenox Library and *Tribune* building, both in New York City, United States Naval Observatory at Washington, Divinity College Building at Yale, Administration Building for the World's Fair in Chicago, and Yorktown Monument.
3. With a total length of 620 miles, the Loire is the longest river in France, rising in the Cevannes of Ardeche at an altitude of about 4500 feet and flowing to Orleans and Tours to Nantes, finally emptying into the Atlantic by a wide estuary at St. Nazaire.
4. Its valley or basin contained an unusually large number of *chateaux*, both royal, as *Amboise, Bloise*, and *Chambord*, and private, as *Chenonceaux, Longeais, Chateaudun, Chaumont, Azai-le-Rideau*. Each had its certain appeal.
5. The streets in the upper part of the town were narrow and tortuous, and the houses mean and ill built. The main street traversed a hollow, flanked by elevations, dominated respectively by the cathedral, *St. Louis*, and a castle. Nearby a fine aqueduct of Roman origin, cut in solid rock, supplied the city with water.
6. Following mobilization, he was appointed to a commission of inquiry and advice to monitor sanitary conditions for federal troops and became its general secretary, serving through most of the war in Washington or visiting field armies. A recognized humanitarian, he later became prominent on the Southern Famine Relief Commission, service that would be largely forgotten in the political strife and turmoil that followed.
7. In 1871, he presented to the Territorial Government of the District of Columbia plans for the "parking system" of streets in the capital. The following year, he was made president of the Department of Public Parks in New York. He devised the plan of the street system for the city north of the Harlem River, as well as for Riverside & Morningside parks in Manhattan, Prospect & Washington parks in Brooklyn, Washington & Jackson parks in Chicago, and many others.

FOUR

EXPANSION OF RAILWAY SERVICE

Things had come a long way since the *Best Friend* left Charleston from its tiny station on Meeting Street for the inaugural run. The affluent ante-bellum planter class had its sights set eastward across the Atlantic but under exhortations of Calhoun, leadership had realized that an overland trade route would provide a profitable course westward as well. Double riches for the royal city, and benefits for key stations.

The dream of reaching the Mississippi at Memphis via Asheville remained elusive...but then the unexpected happened. Frustrated by delays, the City of Cincinnati built its own line to Chattanooga via Knoxville and service to the Ohio River was at hand. And the Ohio flows into the Mississippi. It was 1880 and dawn of our new era. The line from Salisbury had arrived. And by following the river past Hot Springs & Paint Rock, the line to Knoxville was completed without undue difficulty.

Despite obstacles, General Wilder was right on the money. And there was enough traffic potential for a second railroad, part of the original scheme. Spartanburg to Forest City & Marion, through the Toe River Valley to Johnson City, an appealing location because that section was near convergence of five state boundaries. Tennessee, North Carolina, Virginia, West Virginia & Kentucky.

Good connections would be available to other roads. And if access from Spruce Pine & Burnsville into Asheville could be provided, via Weaverville, the exotic project would gain additional support.

***

By traversing the Blue Grass State, the alternative being considered would put the route in position to seek the Ohio at Cincinnati. Or Louisville or Ashland. Or all three. A trans-Appalachian course providing a direct link for fast, efficient service between markets of the Southeast & commercial centers of the Midwest.

Development would bring several powerful personalities into play as participants...and lead the city to a frenzy of excitement over prospects for becoming the center in a network of lines. In broader perspective, it was a saga that unfolded over the course of a century. One not fully understood but resulting in a complex series of long forgotten ventures & adventures.

The exact route was confusing because plans kept changing. As the years passed, half a dozen different companies were formed to build one or more segments of the grand scheme. As with other projects involving physical mountain barriers, inadequate capitalization sometimes proved an even greater barrier. And even reliable sources of funds were subject to inevitable rise & fall of world financial markets.

On paper, the scheme looked logical and reasonable. A rich vein of traffic flowing through a potential connecting artery. When projected against topographic maps, however, it was a nightmare of extreme elevations & grim gradients. Particularly intimidating was a tortuous segment extending from Avery at the base of the Blue Ridge to Altamont at the crest. Availability of necessary elements was also questionable. Mountain labor supply, sophisticated engineering acumen, additional capital requirements, transport of materials & supplies, cost of modern equipment, unpredictable weather conditions, cooperative political attitudes.

Some said it could not be done, an impregnable work of nature. Pessimists believed that crossing would never be realized. Enter an optimist.

***

The Appalachians precluded direct rail service to Pittsburgh or Atlanta and, as we have seen, there was no line at all to Charlotte, while lines to Chattanooga were disconnected in a peculiar manner, and later service to Bristol involved transfer at Marion. Wilder's vision of a mountain rail hub was not to be and some thought these failures meant an end to dreams for Asheville as a metropolis.

Nonetheless, service was provided in all directions by means of many tunnels & somewhat circuitous routing. City yards connected with Biltmore yard to form a sausage shaped facility with forks at each end, just east of the latter station for Washington & New York or Atlanta & New Orleans, and just west of the Asheville depot for Knoxville or Murphy over a double tracked bridge.

Boarding the *Asheville Special* at Biltmore around five o'clock in the afternoon, a carriage trade passenger took his leisure…perhaps writing a letter at a desk in the club car. Some time after the train came out of its winding pattern and picked up speed, he would hear the first of three calls to dinner. "Dining car forward." Or he boarded the *Carolina Special* around four for Charleston or around 6:45 and headed down river for Cincinnati. Or a couple hours later, took the *Skyland Special* past Biltmore Forest & Fletcher for Jacksonville, Palm Beach & Miami. There was sleeping car service, through sleepers to all points between New York & New Orleans, Charleston, Cincinnati & Chicago, as well as special Pullman cars to Norfolk, Raleigh, Mobile, Memphis, Nashville, Louisville & St. Louis. Hourly service of various kinds, around the clock.

Arrival of the first train from the East had coincided with full development of the private railway car, a concept emerging for half a century since rudimentary special accommodations were first designed in 1830. In 1880, a complete private car was sent to San Francisco for convenience of President Grant upon his return from a trip around the world. Only a yacht could provide greater prestige for royalty, nobility, and princes of wealth and power, a subject described with great skill in *Mansions On Rails* by Lucius Beebe, the noted epicure, specifically in the final chapter entitled *The Last Resorts*.

Yes, "yachts reigned supreme," wrote Beebe, "but the private railroad car managed to maintain its own *cachet* of ultimate desirability, especially at such advantageous spots as Palm Beach and Asheville, North Carolina, where the Southern Railway thoughtfully established a private car track so that George Vanderbilt's magnificent estate, *Biltmore*, might be available to its owner and his guests."

In *The Vanderbilt Legend*, Wayne Andrews wrote, "On Christmas Eve, 1895, the personal Wagner palace cars of many members of the House of Vanderbilt rolled into sidings at Asheville. Dr. and Mrs. Seward Webb, their children and domestics, Mr. and Mrs. Cornelius Vanderbilt II, their children and domestics, Mr. William Kissam Vanderbilt I, and domestics, then alighted and entered carriages which conveyed them to *Biltmore*, the domain of George Washington Vanderbilt."

Mr. Vanderbilt's own private car, *Swannanoa*, was an element in a traditional line of that famous family, as Beebe points out. "This was, of course, in a time when the New York Central was a patron of Wagner and Vanderbilts were majority stockholders in that company. In a few years, Pullman would enjoy the family custom…but although Vanderbilt patronage was to be a glittering advertisement for Newport, Asheville, and Palm Beach, the resort that basked in reflected glory of the family name first and longest was Saratoga Springs."

And many others had such cars available for use in reaching much smaller destinations, including Pinehurst, Jekyll Island, and also Aiken & Augusta, whose special cars went out of the Pennsylvania Station with the *Asheville Special*. The Southern Railway considered Asheville, with its little suburban satellite station, one of the crown jewels in the railway world of fashionable prestige.

Private car décor ran the gamut from handsome to opulent. Paneling of fine woods, quilted leather banquettes, exquisite lamps, detailed inlays of skilled marquetry, gold portieres, leaded & stained glass, splendid chandeliers. Silk sofas, bevel-edged French mirrors, superb English furniture in royal colors of upholstery, the best Axminster carpets. There were luxurious beds, custom made call bell systems, gold table service from Tiffany. Italian marble baths & lavatories, wine cellars for vintage collections, Turkish baths, ship-to-shore telephones. All served by French chefs & English butlers, with special cars for retinues of personal servants.

Cars available for private rental made a list not generally of the same elegance but were in good company and had a special resonance. Many bore names of celebrated explorers, others words that evoked images of excellence or allure. *Ocean, Traveler, Celtic, Ideal, Superb, Sybaris, Iolanthe, Esperanza, Esmeralda*. Some were named for choice destinations. In the latter category, the roster of 1888 included *Del Monte, Fairmount, Harvard, Raritan, & Rahway*. Five years later, *Casa Monica, Newport & Wildwood* were among additions while later still, the names of Asheville, Boston, Manhattan, Palm Beach & Philadelphia had found company with the others.

Ribbons of steel in the blue ribbon world of recognized society.

Endnotes

1. Murphy was the western end of *From Manteo to Murphy*, the familiar state descriptive phrase.
2. And it gave national recognition to this exotic symbol of ornate luxury, hundreds of which began to be turned out by a variety of carbuilders shops from Philadelphia to Chicago.
3. "From earliest beginnings, the railroad, and close on iron shod heels of steamcars themselves, private cars of the moguls were an integral part of the social scene. Among earliest resorts to achieve national recognition was Hot Springs in the Ozarks…Eventually, private car tracks would become standard fixtures at various springs, such as Hot Springs in Virginia, White Sulphur in West Virginia, Saratoga, French Lick, Poland Springs…and at places lacking any therapeutic pretensions at all, such as Newport, Palm Beach, Tuxedo Park, Louisville and Miami."
4. "Here the old Commodore delighted to repair in his two cars *Vanderbilt* and *Duchess* en suite, while at the head end of his special train, at first over tracks of the Harlem Railroad and then along the river on rails of the Hudson River Railroad. The engine, *Red Devil*, was in the talented charge of Jim Wood, a consummate throttle artist regularly assigned to the Commodore, who admired speed. Already established before the Civil War as a resort favored by planter aristocracy of the Old South, Saratoga Springs flowered as a mecca of society. Commodore Vanderbilt and his private cars made recurrent appearance there, during racing season, and after his death, successive generations of the family and their varnish were something with which to conjure at that upstate spa."

FIVE

CONCEPTS OF A WORKING ESTATE

When Mr. Vanderbilt returned to Asheville after his initial visit, he is said to have obtained horses from the Battery Park stables and ridden with his party down Church into Main, following along to the foot of the hill where he dismounted. If so, he was standing in the rural realm of Joseph Reed, a native son who until recently owned everything east and south as far as the eye could reach. The place might have been called Reedsville.

Immediately before the curious visitor's eye, land was flat and fertile. Filling of Blowgun Gulch, long a dangerous pitfall for the inebriated pilgrim, had been completed following arrival of the railroad. For now, its highest and best use was agricultural. In the immediate vicinity of city environs, prime farmland was at a premium, but commerce was beginning to create a different economic climate.

The Reed family had been around for a long time. Joseph was born at Cane Creek on May 7, 1827, six months after Mr. Smith began buying the hill northwest of this point, and first saw the light of day at his grandparents' home. Like Smith, he was strong and interested in acquiring land. On April 19, 1849, as the "merchant prince" was settling into life of a prosperous farmer, Reed married Katharine Miller. She was a descendant of Thomas Miller, governor of Albemarle (1677) under the reign of Charles II, and also Benjamin Harrison who came to Virginia in 1638 as progenitor of one of that state's famous first families.

They settled in the home of his parents on Gashes Creek where their seven children were born. Their homeplace extended over a large tract of land. After the war, when he was forty years old, he started purchasing more. First he bought Busbee Mountain south of town and then in 1870 acquired a 1260-acre plantation, abandoned by Low Country settlers. He added other small tracts hither and yon for ten miles east along the river and after the first line came in, a large tract (1883) on the north bank.

Upon the plantation lands, he built ponds, constructed sawmills, carding mills, and grist mills, and erected a new home for his family. He owned the first brick yard and the first meat market in Asheville and he was first in the region to cut, house, and sell ice. His office was located on the south side of the river and he figured this was a pretty good place for a new railway station, the existing one not amounting to much.

Recurrent flooding had deterred county commissioners from organizing here and in 1876, there was a serious flood. Nevertheless, Reed's resolve was reinforced by the fact that a second road was coming up the mountain from Campobello across the state line. And this seemed to be the best place for them to meet. If the rains don't fall and the creeks don't rise. When finally it became clear that plans of both were in line with his thinking, he decided to encourage intentions by building a brick structure a few yards east. He presented it for use as a sort of primitive union station arrangement, and after it was accepted, also built a brick store and hotel close by.

Joseph Reed did not live to see the connection. He died on August 22, 1884, when progress on the other line was still bogged down somewhere around Arden and Skyland. Just prior to death, however, he deeded six square miles around the station to his five sons and they divided it equally, Samuel, an attorney, receiving well over a hundred acres starting at the station.

**

The appearance of our primary subject on simple streets of the city must have been that of a wandering nomad in foreign lands of Babylon. His thin but full moustache, thick black hair, prominent aquiline nose, and dark complexion gave him the dramatic look of a Spanish nobleman.

Here was an accomplished linguist, even to ancient and classical languages. An experienced European traveler, he was an avid collector of books about art and architecture. After the Metropolitan Opera House was opened, he could sometimes be seen in his box there, every night for a week. A personality apart from the rough-and-tumble world of railroad business, this was an ideal person to build a house of exceptional merit because he understood and appreciated those who could create it. And his knowledge was not gleaned from books alone. From earliest childhood, he had been surrounded by things most people could only imagine.

George Vanderbilt lived on Vanderbilt Row, the finest collection of private residential buildings in America. There on what was known as Upper Fifth, it was a splendid series of mansions, scope of which was generally unknown. This realm of family and friends extended along the Fifties from 51st to Grand Army Plaza at the southeast corner of Central Park and eventually beyond.

Despite general eligibility, his grandfather's loud and somewhat uncouth manners on occasion had kept the family out of high social acceptance, specifically, approval from Mrs. Astor, social arbiter for the so-called Four Hundred. Regardless of merit, this prolific and vigorous clan was excluded from upper echelons because of a simple but incontrovertible fact. Its bombastic patriarch was unacceptable to her and her social director, Ward McAllister of Savannah, and as long as he was running the show and calling the shots for her by southern standards, mansions or no, they were o-u-t. *Outre.*

Then on the night of March 26, 1883, all this changed. Invoking the powerful patronage of Lady Mandeville, strong minded, iron willed Alva Smith of Mobile, now a Vanderbilt, staged the great ball of the century. One Southerner vs. another. As cordons of police held back curious mobs milling in the streets, the restrictive grip of the late Cornelius I and his unpolished image was loosened and now overnight Vanderbilts were in.

The socially inclined were in somewhat of a swivet but old C.V. never gave a tinker's damn about that. A man's man, with an eye for attractive women, he always thought most of these elegant, top drawer parties were for dainty, delicate dudes and dandies. Silly fops. Despite his reputation in some quarters, his word was good and he made his fortune the old fashioned way. By providing a needed service. General transportation. On the day that he died, January 4, 1877, his fortune exceeded cash reserves of the U.S. Treasury. He was 82 and the age of the so-called robber barons was still in the future.

During his lifetime, the "commodore" had sired some 13 children. He was critical and showed no particular affection for the eldest, William Henry, but he wanted his estate maintained intact. Thus for business reasons he left almost the entire fortune to him. The heir was as quiet and respectful as the father was overbearing and demeaning. He married a minister's daughter. He was honorable and dutiful, and he reaped the whirlwind along with the money. Through no fault of his own, he became embroiled in protracted litigation, brought by jealous family members.

Sensational charges were both vicious and mendacious. In a relaxed and informal conversation with newspapermen, he used a casual phrase to make a point about the principal competitor. The mighty Pennsylvania. It was taken out of context to make it appear that he was anything but what he was. Acting on cue from their bosses in the early days of yellow journalism, editorial cartoonists went after their prey like a pack of wild dogs.

Those who resented the father visited their animosity on the son. His thoughtful suggestions had led the senior capitalist to activities and decisions that converted him from the rich to the awesome rich. He had executed his tasks properly and treated those under his authority with tact and fairness. He had been a good husband and father, enjoyed mutual respect of colleagues, and shown affection for his children. In 1885, he was the richest man in the world...and father of George Washington Vanderbilt.

The heart of Vanderbilt Row was No. 660, home of George's brother, William. K., for Kissam, and it was one of the most opulent structures ever seen on this continent. Ranking along side it was No. 640, the triple palace of William H. and two of his daughters. All told, there were at least two dozen mansions, dominated by the Vanderbilt family, with a façade of splendor extending almost as far as the eye could reach.

Here and at other places like Pointe d'Acadie in Bar Harbor, George lived and grew up absorbing the spirit of his surroundings. Arriving at this spot at the foot of Smith's Hill was like reaching the Plains of Abraham from the palace at *Versailles*. If indeed he stopped there to study the situation and dismounted while his horse was facing south, steed and rider were standing on Reed property, surrounding them on three sides, east of the turnpike. To their right was Lone Pine Mountain in the distance, with its scrubby vegetation surrounded by one outstanding tree. Almost at his feet before him was the small brickyard waiting to be put to extraordinary use. One might wonder at the thoughts passing through his mind.

Whatever the exact progression of events, the Samuel Reed tract was acquired in due course and the brothers built substantial homes on their own shares to the south. The station hotel became full and another was built on the other (west) side. A railroad double sidetrack from the spur was established at the brickyard, which was converted to full scale operation. Among other things, a plant nursery was established as well.

Seldom had there been such a private project as this. By 1894, the headquarters building had been completed across the street. A new railway station was nearing completion, new church under scaffolding, post office starting. Along the south side of this new village, a compact row of a dozen temporary structures was providing homes for foremen, managers, and others holding supervisory positions during development. South along the road there were additional buildings known locally as "the red row of houses" and "the green row of houses."

Joseph Reed never saw this astonishing transformation. And visualization by that unlikely visitor only a few years before can merely provide one with material for a lively imagination.

***

While the country as a whole remained part of an agrarian society to the end of our epoch, manufacturing complexes centered around the Pittsburgh steel triangle were developing into a powerful industrial complex and this base was creating a spate of great fortunes.

Arteries of commerce were kept moving by a growing network of railway lines and while these involved hundreds of companies, engines of production were dominated by two mighty systems which controlled operations of a dozen lesser route structures. These two empires were the Pennsylvania and the New York Central. Officials of the former created fashionable Main Line communities from the Quaker City west to Paoli, under a series of authoritarian executives such as Alexander Cassatt, father of the late, great Pennsylvania Station.

Above the foremost street of wealth and power in the nation, magnificent Park Avenue, stood Grand Central, also magnificent, station and office tower, at the prime intersection with 42nd Street. As the fame and status of a hundred names rose, DuPont, Carnegie, Schwab, Frick, Armour, Cudahy, Rockefeller, Flagler, a different crusade was getting under way. Thoreau was its prophet, Whitman its poet. A philosophy coming from naturalists who combined scientific exploration with literary exposition. Among visionaries, John Muir, the Scottish born botanist and geologist, was at the forefront. At a time when natural resources were generally seen as inexhaustible, his lonely journeys from the South to the Arctic were beginning to show Americans a different path.

And some were drawn not only to the concept of public preserves but the idea of working enclaves in which large farms and commercial ventures could be brought together with planned residential communities. Some members of the extended Vanderbilt family were expending part of their considerable energies in that direction. One of George Vanderbilt's ideas was a working farm, along with that of forestry as a mainstay for maintenance of the estate. Scientific forestry or *silvaculture* was a European subject, centuries old across the Atlantic but generally unknown in this country. It consisted of professional woodlands management for the largest possible timber crop consistent with healthy future growth.

In much of this country, commercial logging consisted of little more than felling trees and leaving the landscape almost as barren and desolate as a crater on the moon. In this part of Appalachia, wide swathes had been stripped and destruction was continuing unabated. The situation called for just the right man. Mr. Olmstead had his eye on a promising young fellow who might be just the ticket. His name was Gifford Pinchot and he was studying this very subject. After graduation from Yale, he had taken a different route by enrolling in the Ecole Nationale Forestiere at Nancy. When he returned home, he seemed to be qualified for employment in a job that did not exist.

It so happened, however, that young Pinchot came from a socially prominent Philadelphia family whose house had been designed by none other than Richard Morris Hunt. Before long, this happy set of circumstances led to a triumvirate in which he was given the task of planning and coordinating a survey of devastated lands and then engaging in a large scale project of thinning, cutting, and replanting. He was also given the original Olmstead plan, a design that he greatly expanded. The forest was restored, Pinchot went on to success which led to widespread talk that he should run for President, but alas, the vision of a self sustaining situation at *Biltmore* never reached fruition.

***

With passage of time, the Pisgah of ancient days became the Pisgah of modern times. An emblem for the new city of tomorrow. And a Vanderbilt vision as well. Small parcel by medium parcel, it would become Vanderbilt territory. Vanderland. In an age of moguls, there was nothing quite like it to be found east or west.

Indeed its reach was so extensive that the public was left confused and would remain so for decades to come. Among stories and rumors of an empire stretching to neighboring state lines, tales compounded by the press, ongoing accounts distorted a situation of significance in its own right. Landscaped grounds immediately surrounded the mansion itself but vast forest lands, extending over into Haywood and Transylvania, were part of the master's master plan for creation of a working estate...economically self sufficient.

***

In the Eastern world, from the banks of the Ganges to the plain at Agra, a hundred treasures but only one *Taj Mahal.* An expression of compassion for celestial perfection on a scale beyond ordinary comprehension. And there were the Stately Houses of Britain. Some architecture is so rare as to be unique.

And in the New World, was there any privately owned residential creation to match *Biltmore?* Yes, the nation had produced its own level of excellence in plantation houses of the Coastal South. From the Eastern Shore of Maryland and Delaware to Galveston Bay. All with slave labor.

The Gilded Age might produce mansions more ornate, more heavy, more dense, but nothing to equal this achievement. It was the consummation of European artistic achievement, perfected in the best American manner. Inspirational in nature, classic in concept, superb in scope. Unique. Indeed it was sublime.

Observations

Thinking and motivation resulting in creation of *Biltmore* was idealistic, a rather romantic vision of a community in which various elements could work together in harmony for the good of all. It was an esthetic concept, however, rather than a political statement of theoretical ideology such as collectivism.

According to several undocumented reports, Mr. Vanderbilt abandoned mountain lodge ideas in favor of a colonial home, one that would probably have surpassed that of the famous Southern mansions. Slavery had been abolished a quarter century earlier and with it the economic foundation of plantation life, but there were appealing aspects that might be utilized to different ends.

As we have seen, the Charlestonians had brought their philosophy of life to the very doorstep of the place where this development would take place. So there was some precedent for such an experiment. On the other hand, the mountain way of life was altogether different and plantation operations had never really taken hold here. What small success had been realized, disappeared as a result of conditions existing during the Reconstruction era.

One might observe that European castles were equally foreign if not more so...and yet, there were historic relationships in background that would make the soil for this monumental project not inhospitable. The mediaeval structure of society in Britain and feudal villages associated with it were part of that tradition. And while they had been modified and altered over a century of national life, still there was not a basic ethnic clash such as that found between major racial divisions of the world.

If operations could be made profitable, the idea of a working estate might become practical... Agricultural crops, for example. Orchards. Cattle raising, dairy operations. Animal husbandry. Blacksmithing. Nurseries, fisheries, tanneries. Woodworking and furniture manufacture. Native crafts. Lumber yards, sawmills. Brick kilns. Florist shops. There were many possibilities.

Gifford Pinchot was brought in to supervise forests and natural lands, a forerunner of modern forestry in America. This was not the ambition of a frivolous social dilettante. Carl Schenck, student of the Black Forest, pursued a similar goal. Ravaged woods were turned into professional forests and a school of forestry established, a model for the environmental movement, at least for responsible members.

Beadle assisted Olmstead in planning and remained to supervise horticultural operations and develop small masterpieces of his own, at Biltmore and in other parts of the city. Following his mentor's death in 1901, Olmstead's two sons drew plans for an azalea garden of first magnitude. Beadle modified and augmented it. He, W.A. Knight, and Frank M. Crayton, an Asheville physician, with their chauffeur, Sylvester Owens, conducted a trans-American search for native varieties.

***

Information circulated about the estate was often fragmentary, sometimes distorted. There were approximately 23,000 volumes on the shelves. This was variously reported as 230,000 volumes, 320,000 volumes, a quarter million, half a million, and so on. Perhaps another two thousand were in transit. Again numbers were thrown around carelessly. The owner was a well educated man, an avid reader. While volumes were generally of first quality, many from holdings of noted collectors, this was intended primarily as a source of good books which could actually be read, not a spectacular display for entertainment value.

Other reports also were inaccurate. If facts were not readily available, fiction was substituted therefor. Others were written with heavy handed emphasis on statistical dimension, lumping it all together with the Brooklyn Bridge and other modern marvels and worldly wonders. Still others were hostile or envious. Shortly after it was completed, Thorstein Veblen became a member of the department of political economy at the unconventional University of Chicago.

Of Norwegian extraction, he reflected attitudes prevailing in a socialist movement then developing in Milwaukee and Minnesota from origins in Central Europe. Disturbed by growing affluence of wealthy industrial barons, he began writing about the subject, culminating in *Theory of the Leisure Class,* published in 1899. It was the source of a widely quoted phrase…*conspicuous consumption*…and among examples cited was that of great Vanderbilt mansions. Radical Brooklyn elements fulminated in similar vein.

As a new century dawned, there was ferment within socio-political circles of the European heartland. In 1903, the Social Democratic Workers Party…which was neither social nor democratic or even workers…split into Bolshevik (majority) and Menshevik (minority) factions, the former led by the diabolical V. Lenin. They advocated violent overthrow of established governments and seizure of private property for use by the party. Socialists generally agreed with their aims but rejected some violent methods.

On May 6, 1910, George Frederick Ernest Albert succeeded to the throne on the death of his father. He was crowned king of Great Britain on June 22, 1911, and his coronation as emperor of India took place at Delhi on December 12 of that year. Critics of the "age of the moguls" compared American owners of great mansion to foreign royalty, notably British. As ruler of the greatest mansion of them all, George Vanderbilt was one who drew ire, particularly since he was a son of W.H. Vanderbilt of the mighty New York Central, a man widely and maliciously quoted out of context as having said "the public be damned."

Those who knew George Vanderbilt thought it absurd when more caustic critics took to calling him George V…a double entendre combining the initial of his family name with the title of the ruling monarch. "He was anything but autocratic or imperial," one acquaintance remarked. Mental and emotional reactions to these pejorative words are unknown but there is no reason to assume that he was upset. In any event, no evidence is on record that he sought to retaliate. And sardonic comparison proved ironic, since the real monarch became one of the best loved of all modern British kings.

George Vanderbilt did not live to see the Great War. He died in Washington on March 6, 1914. On June 28, 1914 a violent fanatic shot the Archduke Ferdinand. And in the diplomatic turmoil that followed, the war broke out, one that brought Victorian and Edwardian eras to an end. A war during which the October Revolution brought a colossal experiment in government dictatorship. November 3, 1917. Nine days that shook the world and launched a maniacal campaign to control the earth.

Mr. Beadle quietly remained a landscape supervisor for 60 years, a dedicated and professional leader in the field of natural beauty. Mr. McNamee remained general manager at his estate office in Biltmore Village. Hundreds of other employees gave years of devoted service to ideals of the estate, many of them unsung workers known only to families and colleagues and friends. Their stories are legion but largely unrecorded.

Fact and fiction are not always kept apart, particularly in political journalism and revolutionary entertainment.

Endnotes

1. Oldtimers still called it Asheville Junction.
2. Originally this was called Gum Spring and the county had been organized here by Scotch-Irish pioneers.
3. In 1925, the permanent Hot Shot Café was established there to serve residents and railway passengers.
4. Begun as a sideline, the dairy operation was successful and helped save the entire venture in model building.

***

1. Several of the Reeds became lawyers and Samuel gained Mr. Vanderbilt as a client. Mark built down along the river, Clyde above the village to the south.
2. The business of accommodating visitors would grow & grow but few accommodations could match comfort & convenience of these well appointed properties. They were designed for permanence and would never need to be demolished.
3. By the time *Biltmore* was completed, Hunt was gone, his mental & physical health having collapsed. He took refuge in a sanitarium at Buckinghamshire, England, but was later committed to a hospital in Waverley, Massachusetts, his final resting place.
4. The church, station & post office were Hunt's only contributions to the village.
5. Brickyard was closed & replaced with an expansive village green, complete with gazebo-like shelter near the road. Located in front of the estate entrance, it was a scene of games & festivities in the community. Maidens danced around a gaily festooned maypole, where laborers had toiled at the kilns turning out millions of bricks & drain tiles.
6. For All Souls, Hunt used a combination of Norman & English Gothic detail, inspired by churches in the Cumberland district of northern England. At the front of the nave, the roof overhung to provide space for a bell but none was ever installed. Opalescent American glass windows were designed & executed by Maitland Armstrong of New York City, assisted by his daughter.

***

1. Guastavino was the recognized master of tile brick. Each was stamped with the name BILTMORE. There were two basic types, regular red extruded and a cream colored variety glazed on one side to repel moisture. The latter could be used for special purposes such as kitchen, laundry, gymnasium, indoor swimming pool.

2.   In 1901, Mrs. Vanderbilt established a school for craftsmen at the church. It was designed to maintain & develop skills of native workers.

3.   Although not so anticipated, the estate's dairy farm became the most profitable project, particularly following introduction of the famous Jersey herd of prize cattle from the British Isles.

4.   Whether Mr. Vanderbilt intended to use *Fernihurst* as a base is questionable. For obvious reasons, he liked the hill and residents did not want to give up the good life. They were content to look at the view of Biltmore, including house, village & forest lands, which some called Biltmore Forest while others referred to them as Pisgah Forest. The more cultivated acreage was often referred to as Vanderbilt Park.

✱✱✱

1.   When the socially elite Academy of Music refused to sell W.H. Vanderbilt a box, he and his sons got together with others so treated & organized the Metropolitan Opera Company, which built & operated the famous opera house.

2.   Three principal Vanderbilt mansions there were demolished for commercial "progress" prior to the end of our social chronicle.

3.   Muir's father, also named John, was a leading authority on Sanskrit and origin & history of people of India. The elder Muir was a brother of Sir William, a leading authority on life of Mahomet and history of Islam. Both were born in Glasgow, died in Edinburgh, and held leading positions at the University there, the latter becoming its principal. George Vanderbilt could also read Sanskrit. Both men died the same year. Among Muir's accomplishments was establishment of national parks at Sequoia & Yosemite.

4.   In due course, one of the street railway companies extended tracks to this point, stopping not because of the river, where a bridge could accommodate it, but because of the railroad tracks which posed a difficult and dangerous problem.

5.   The family's reign there is described by Lewis Auchincloss as "at least comparable to that of the Medici in Florence."

6.   The New York Central served many cities directly or indirectly, including Cleveland, Toledo, Detroit, Indianapolis, Grand Rapids, Omaha, Toronto, & Montreal.

7.   Not far up Main from this point near the river was a place where W.E. Breese was about to purchase three acres for a home site. Ground was broken in 1889. The banker had high level entertainment in mind. This charming house later became known as *Cedar Crest* but its owner encountered serious financial & legal difficulties long before.

8.   The Vanderbilt railroad led toward Lone Pine Mountain. The former right-of-way was later used for a road named for Mr. Vanderbilt leading to Cedarcliff Gate.

✱✱✱

1.   He visited the Battery Park on several occasions, including a trip with his mother who had been a widow since the death of William Henry Vanderbilt on December 8, 1885.

2.   After visiting in the summer of 1887, he returned to New York in the fall, keeping his own counsel. He did take into his confidence, however, his kinsman, Charles McNamee, a New York attorney.

3.   George Vanderbilt was born on the family farm at New Dorp, Staten Island, on November 14, 1862.

4.   He had in mind for McNamee to come to Asheville and, without using his name, supervise an acquisition program, i.e., begin buying hundreds of small tracts, individual parcels, and miscellaneous holdings around Lone Pine and west thereof.

5.   Once commissioned as chief Vanderbilt agent, McNamee began work (1888) to acquire land. It was time consuming and involved assistance of several confidential agents. McNamee later became mayor of Victoria.

6.   In October of 1889, the *Weekly Citizen* reported that a model of the house, five feet long & three feet high, had appeared in front of the Tribune Building in New York. This elegant structure (1873) was designed by Hunt and this was the first public display.

7.   The name "Biltmore" involved a combination of Bildt, the family's ancestral region in Holland, and "more," Old English for hill.

8.   At one point, Mr. Vanderbilt took over the Alexander house and used it as a residence.

9.   The G.W.V.R.R. was completed by May 23, 1890, with exception of some spurs to work stations & plants, including one some three-quarters of a mile in length to the main quarry. When a motor road named for him was later built from the village into a real estate development, it followed the right-of-way to Cedarcliff Road & Gate.

10. During the summer of 1890, the masonry firm of D.C. Weeks & Son began work and stone masons from around the western world were brought in to participate.

11. Other artisans from various places came to cut & fit Indiana limestone or execute elaborate carvings.

12. Asheville Woodworking Company supplied construction needs but could not handle them all and other customers at the same time. Owners did not wish to "hitch their wagon to a star" and then have everything come to a halt or slow down to a trickle in a few years. In 1893, Mr. Vanderbilt purchased it outright. Output was gradually diverted, honoring existing contracts, until total production was designated for the estate alone.

13. Among supporting facilities on the estate were brick kilns and tile making plant, using raw materials excavated there. Some 11 million bricks so produced went into the house alone; others were used in landscaping and ancillary facilities.

14. The Bradley & Currier Company of New York City alone spent eight months installing indoor tiling for baths, pools, gymnasium, hallways, fireplaces & other tiled surfaces.

15. After opening of *Biltmore*, leading hotels around the country began adding the word to their names, it having become synonymous with fashionable elegance. Thus the Whitehall might become Whitehall Biltmore.

***

1. Royal residences, like the *Louvre*, were also called chateaux, although in reality they were *palais* or palaces. A book on the subject, *Les Chateaux de la Loire* by Petit, was published in Paris in 1861, the year before Mr. Vanderbilt was born.

2. The *Rampe Douce* or gentle slope was modeled after a like construction at *Vaux le Vicomte* in France. Situated immediately in front of the house, it was on a lower level but beyond the main entrance mall or lawn known as the *Esplanade*. While these formal gardens followed the French pattern, the walled garden was of English design.

3. While not the first student, Hunt was the first graduate.

4. Dr. Carl Alvin Schenck served as forest assessor of the Grand Duchy of Hesse. He came to the United States from Darmstadt. He left in 1909 but continued to direct the school elsewhere. With outbreak of war in Europe, it was disbanded.

***

1. Macadamized paving, earlier invention of fine crushed stone by a noted Scottish highway engineer named J.L. McAdam, was introduced into the state on meandering roads of the estate, with addition of a petroleum based binder.

2. In 1893, he bought one half of Mt. Pisgah for hunting purposes and built *Buck Springs Lodge* there. He acquired the other half the following year, then owning 30,000 acres or practically the entire mountain, including the highly visible summit.

3. Over nearly six years of construction, Vanderbilt and associates traveled widely abroad to acquire the best furnishings & *objets d'art* for the purpose intended.

4. He continued official residence in Fifth Avenue, traveling to & fro by drawing room accommodations or his private car, *Swannanoa*, outshopped (delivered) early in 1891.

5. On July 28, 1895, Baron Eugene d'Allengh, the farm superintendent, died, followed 48 hours later by the architect-in-chief.

6. In the final year, Mr. Vanderbilt pushed to completion the new Biltmore railway station and with official designation as such, the old "Asheville Junction" station passed into oblivion.

7. Plans for a school of forestry were announced in the New York newspapers on October 19, 1895.

***

1. Some 40 housewarming guests remained to attend the Christmas celebration and stay for a fortnight thereafter.

2. At 11 o'clock on the morning of Christmas Day, the estate's initial 250 employees were invited to view the 40-foot tree cut on forest lands, and were later treated to a lavish "picnic." The event became an annual tradition.

3. Not long after the house was opened and then fully completed, his mother died (1896) and he gave up residence in Manhattan to take up full time residence at Biltmore. In later years, he made increasing use of drawing rooms for travel to New York.

4. In June of 1898, he married Edith Stuyvesant Dresser of Newport in a ceremony at Paris. Then 36, he brought her to Biltmore to live.

5. By 1905, the estate reached maximum size. Holdings extended as far as the eye could reach, even to Toxaway, forty miles as the crow flies. There were 600 employees and 24 regular domestic servants.

6. The estate included 15 highly developed farms operated by tenants.

***

1. Family name originated in province of Utrecht, derived from the basic Dutch word "van" meaning man or one, plus "der" meaning "of the" and Bildt, i.e., one of that section. Progression was from van der Bildt to van Derbildt to Vanderbildt to Vanderbilt.

2. A resident of the family farm on Staten Island, Cornelius acquired a harbor boat and thus became founder of the Staten Island Ferry, a steppingstone to bigger & better things.

3. The great era of modern bridge building coincided with this period. Brooklyn, Niagara Cantilever, Firth of Forth, Victoria Falls, Hell Gate Arch, Bear Mountain, Ambassador, Cooper River, George Washington, Sydney.

4. The four-track main line of New York Central was described in promotion of passenger service as "the water level route." It ran beneath the median park of Park Avenue and along the east bank of the Hudson to Albany & Buffalo, skirting shores of the Great Lakes on its way to Chicago and reaching many other cities.

5.   Veblen was a pioneer in development of modern American theory favoring utopian economic influence on the existing
      political system.

***

The triumvirate had many other accomplishments...

Olmsted planned the approach from Pennsylvania Avenue to the national Capitol, he was the first commissioner of Yosemite, and he was a leading member of the Niagara Falls Reservation Committee. He devised the system of parks & parkways in & around Boston. Important public works were conducted by him in Bridgeport, Trenton, Buffalo, Milwaukee, Montreal, Louisville.

Hunt was not present for the house warming at Biltmore, having died on July 31 of that year. His final work, designed shortly before, was a fitting achievement of extraordinary power & beauty. As the centerpiece for the village, All Souls Parish Church embodied his belief that the Byzantine form, following the short-naved Greek cross plan rather than the elongated Latin cross, was the most functional ideal for Protestant worship services. It was arranged so that everyone could hear & see proceedings.

Dominated by a large square tower at the crossing, the building centered on an apsidal chancel given equal prominence as an expansive cylindrical form under a sweeping conical roof. Nave reduced to an entry of the same depth as transepts, dark pebbledash accented by red brick quoins, crisply laid brick buttresses of the tower, and richly textured red tile in the flowing roofs. This church has been described as small but still monumental.

At the time of his commission, Hunt had recently become president of the Institute of Architects, of which he was one of the founders. Many prominent persons were his pupils. He was a knight of the Legion of Honor and a foreign associate of the Institute of France. He was the brother of William Morris Hunt, noted landscape, figure, and portrait painter, who also studied in Europe, returning to this country with him at the same time.

In 1898, the associated architectural & art societies of New York City erected a memorial to him in the peripheral wall of Central Park opposite Lenox Library. It was designed by Daniel C. French & Bruce Price.

At Biltmore, Mr. Vanderbilt went on to make benefactions felt throughout his adopted community. And at the suggestion of Olmsted, he developed an abiding interest in forestry. He brought in men like Pinchot, Schenck & Beadle and through them, a school of forestry, forerunner of efforts that many believe to be at or near the top in scale of physical priorities for protection & survival of man.

Many persons did not realize that the concept of Biltmore was more than a house. It was intended to be a self-supporting enterprise with business operations, including farming, dairying, landscape design, nursery, forestry, real estate, utilities, and other operations, most of which were put in service. Splendor of the entrance and perhaps a dozen principal rooms was so great that it obscured many purposes & uses of other sections, such as bachelor quarters wing, recreation rooms, and special sitting rooms & bedrooms of various sizes & descriptions.

Even as finishing touches were being applied in late November of 1895, most Asheville residents still had limited conception of its true proportions, its hundreds of rooms, stone stables with accommodations for about forty horses, and so forth. The *Daily Citizen* printed an article from the *New York Architectural Record* giving residents figures of size & scope, but numbers were so great that many still could not absorb their significance. A single span in the library alone, for example, was supported by a girder weighing more than 14 tons. The scale was just too vast for the average mind to understand the beauty.

An appreciative American observer saw this French inspired chateau simply & clearly as "one long tale of delight." "The proportions and scale, combined with details," he added, "fill one with the kind of peace that comes from artistic perfection." And for the appreciative, there was little more that needed to be said.

SIX

NEIGHBORHOOD ELIXIR

In yesterday's Asheville, residential neighborhoods were clustered around a dozen drug stores located at strategic corner car stops along eight lines of the central street railway system. In combination with a nearby grocery store or two, a "pharmacy" provided necessary goods and merchandise for everyday living in an easy going manner.

The neighborhood store was operated for the convenience of residents, not some headquarters in a distant city. You didn't need a big sign to find it and you could spend time walking in fresh air. No labyrinths of heavy traffic and sprawling parking lots. Home delivery and charge accounts available for regulars. Many items could be obtained for a nickel, dime, or quarter. And employees knew their business.

One of these was Grove Park Pharmacy. There Dorothy Dix, national paragon of popular advice to the lovelorn, might be sipping a soda slowly through a strawberry scented straw. Directly across the street, a rambling, shingle covered English inn stretched out along the hillside. Known as The Manor, it provided a pleasant social alternative to the downtown Battery Park in a quaint & quiet setting. Indeed the ambiance of Asheville was exemplified by Albemarle Park, the Manor grounds, and its charming little quirks of architectural detail & decorative design.

Built at the turn of the century by the House of Raoul, it was the centerpiece for a sprawling collection of perhaps forty substantial and inviting residential structures of English town styling. Each of distinctive name & design. In a similar fashion of shingled turrets & indentures, all were reached by twisting miniature roads leading from a pleasing & impressive formal gate house. In the shade of fine, large trees, practical walking paths led from one place to another. Children played around swings, merry-go-rounds, and large sandboxes with beads strung on narrow rods along the sides for games.

***

William Greene Raoul of Savannah was president of Central Railway of Georgia and later Mexican National Railways. Starting with our epoch in 1880, he brought his family to the mountains every summer to escape coastal heat, usually traveling by private railway car. C.R.R. No. 99. In 1881, they went to Hot Springs. They came for opening of the Battery Park and spent the rest of the summer in a large boarding house on Charlotte Street.

Boarding houses of that era were attractive but posed a problem in that they generally would not take many children and Mary Wadley Raoul was the mother of 11 active youngsters. Her husband bought a 42-acre farm nearby from Reuben M. Deaver. It was about two miles from the Square.

Born at Independence, outside New Orleans, W.G. Raoul was a grandson of Francois Guillaume Raoul de Champmanoir who left France around 1793 for the West Indies. William Morrill

Wadley, a prominent railroad executive, was director of railway transportation for the Confederacy. He brought his family to nearby Amite and the two families became close, went into business together, and in 1868, Mr. Raoul married Miss Mary Wadley. They led a good life in social circles of New Orleans, Savannah & Charleston.

Then a battle broke out between Southerners and New York investment bankers for control of the Central of Georgia and in the controversy, the Southerners lost and Raoul was ousted. He moved where his business was centered, first to New York and then Atlanta, and then went on to build the line from Laredo to Mexico City and from there to Vera Cruz. He continued to visit Asheville, however, and in July of 1897, retired to the city. He decided to build his own fine hotel, engaging Bradford L. Gilbert, a prominent architect in New York, for the purpose. His son, Thomas, became manager of the project.

In 1892, Helen Doyle came to the city from Washington, where her mother had been wife of an army officer. Five years later, Tom arrived as a somewhat tubercular youth but recovered fully. Educated as a civil engineer, played football for Georgia Tech but in the Southern tradition, was well versed in English literature. Reflecting a spirit of the age, he was unable to abide function without beauty. It had to run well and look good. He embraced the Arts & Crafts movement then rising in popularity and Asheville would become a mecca for scholars of that style.

In 1906, riding *Rex* in the Asheville Horse Show, she won the President's Cup. In 1910, they were married. She considered A&C a throwback to barbarism, however, and décor & furnishings reflected her preferences for Late Federal & Colonial Revival.

***

A few blocks back down the street was the traditional, ivy covered red brick building housing the Charlotte Street Pharmacy, with its comfortable apartments and casement windows upstairs. Here at the historic corner of Chestnut Street, flower pots added to a vaguely Old World image.

At this point, city street cars stopped on their short trip from the Square and steam powered railway cars departed for an eight-mile journey to the top of Sunset. This landmark neighborhood was once urban limits of the city proper and the start of what might be called a more suburban district.

Many guests walked to dinner parties on pedestrian arteries by shade covered stone walls and handsome, hand cut granite curbstones neatly fitted into place. After dark, city night crews came on duty to wash these streets down with power driven tank trucks, mounted spot lights, and strong men wearing yellow & black rubber slickers & boots, armed with heavy push brooms & spare shovels. A mark of responsibility & pride in neighborhoods where the sidewalk was your friend, not your enemy.

Across Charlotte on the other corner, a tall, tree topped lawn stretched up the slope to the pleasing white outline of the Parker house. Serene in its settled simplicity, it was known to several generations in the social atmosphere created by venerable homes, boarding houses, dining halls, tearooms, & residential hotels. Here Haywood Parker, a distinguished member of the bar, would sometimes ride the street car back from his office uptown...for punctual setting of the dining room table, almost within shouting distance of passersby at the friendly corner below.

Were one to entertain such a whimsical notion, he could organize a public progressive party, with trolley cars providing transportation from one location to another. Principal thoroughfares each contained a car line, with the flow east truncated by the mountain. Drug stores flourished at Biltmore, Kenilworth, Southside, Doubleday, Grace, Ramoth or Woolsey Dip, Montford, Society Hill, Oakley, Depot, Beacham's Curve, and out along Haywood Road.

Uptown drug stores were also popular, some at or near hotels. A social watering hole *par excellence* was Raysor's which held sway across from the post office until it was torn down at the end of the era. The younger set then moved to Goode's around the corner in Patton. Smith's on the southwest corner of the Square and Johnson's in the Oates Building on the northeast corner remained pillars of the central district.

Drug stores had high ceilings & wooden floors, cavernous basements, solid display cases, elaborate soda fountains with marble furnishings & heavy fixtures, carved wood & ornate glass, small tables with four little triangular chairs, interesting cardboard signs & pictures, merchandise of various descriptions. All in a friendly, relaxed atmosphere.

There were spacious doorways up front, usually side entrances as well, and ventilating ducts somewhere around the rear and mid section. Wafting out through the entranceway was a cool flow of air laden with a composite scent of unknown elements. Many a bold young man met many a comely young woman there beneath the sound of quietly whirring overhead ceiling fans.

Pack & Chestnut Hill

Inseparably linked with this ambiance was the name of George Willis Pack, who loved the place. An Ohio lumberman who came here on business because of the wealth of timber resources in the area, he stayed at the popular Swannanoa but then because of his wife's health, decided to make his home here.

Pack enjoyed mingling with townspeople at downtown drug stores and elsewhere and by the time *Biltmore* was opened, had made many friends. He was socially active in the Charlotte-Chestnut neighborhood and built a fine house at the Chestnut-Merrimon intersection, naming it *Many Oaks.* He enjoyed social conversation and listened with interest to constructive ideas for civic improvement. His own health was not always of the best and he was generous with contributions to medical facilities. When the hospital was founded, he was a primary benefactor. And he was enthusiastic about public parks, of which there was a shortage.

In due course, he became the city's greatest benefactor. Although generous, he felt strongly about seed money, rarely giving strictly on his own but providing matching funds, reserving some of the satisfaction in participation to others. He gave to the Young Men's Christian Association in time of need, provided a site for an early kindergarten near Hillside Street, and made it possible to establish public parks on Montford, at Aston, and at Magnolia. And by giving land upon which the Swannanoa Hunt Club established the first country club & golf course, became a factor in the rise of fashionable Asheville.

It was in the historic heart of town, however, that his foresight left such a lasting memorial. In 1893, the small city library collection next to the Swannanoa Hotel was transferred into a one-story red brick building between the Presbyterian & Episcopal churches, on the grounds of the former. In 1899, Mr. Pack acquired the First National Bank Building on the Square and gave it, under deed of trust, to the Asheville Library Association.

He contributed to an effort that resulted in erection of a granite memorial obelisk to the memory of Zeb Vance. Construction took place at the center island of the Square. And later, he provided land on College for the seventh courthouse just around the corner, and made possible expansion of the Square itself. He sometimes felt weak, however, and his doctor advised him that air pollen was contributing to his deteriorating bronchial condition so he felt he should leave the city.

Locke Craig, who later became governor, said Pack "made gifts that were all the result of his own generous impulse." After word came of his death, the fire alarm bell was tolled slowly for an hour as leading clergymen attended a public memorial service. Schools and merchants closed their doors. Speaking on the occasion, Mr. Craig said "his exemplary character and unfailingly courteous demeanor won the admiration of our citizens." A proposal to name the Square in his honor seems to have met no objection.

Endnotes

1. So-called "discounters" later drove them out, then raised prices.
2. Largely ignored by city fathers at a time when their interest might have made a difference, Chestnut provided direct access to connect the Princess Anne Hotel on the east with Pearson Drive on the west. It would have provided a shuttle for the transit system, crossing, as it did, trolley lines at Charlotte, Merrimon, Broadway, & Montford.
3. The area diagonally across the street led into the grounds of Camp Patton, where men were trained for the Confederate Army.
4. As completion of Biltmore drew near, a slight rise north of downtown provided a site for upscale residential expansion. Situated between Charlotte & Merrimon, it extended along East Chestnut, which was widened to accommodate development, and out North Liberty to Hillside. It became known as *Chestnut Hill*.
5. Some of the city's leading architects and residents were involved. Several houses were designed by J.A. Tennent, who had laid out the Second Empire style courthouse (1876) and later designed the City Building in front of it. J.M. Westall was the builder of choice. Design ranged from simple vernacular dwellings to sophisticated renditions of Queen Anne, Colonial Revival & Shingle styles.
6. Some of the talent from *Biltmore* came to work here. The first result was *Beaufort Lodge* at No. 61 North Liberty Street, completed (1895) in luxuriously detailed Queen Anne style for Theodore S. Davidson, the state attorney general. The architect was A.L. Melton, whose Drhumor Building was completed downtown that same year. The year following, R.S. Smith designed one of his larger shingle & pebbledash structures for Dr. H.S. Lambert on Chestnut. (Liberty Street was Libby Street until early in the 20th century.)
7. In 1884, Mrs. Connally of *Fernihurst* had bought most of the north side of Chestnut between Liberty & Washington Road. She had the land subdivided for sale and it was acquired by Mr. Pack, whose home was nearby. It had remained vacant all this time when Dr. J.E. David bought it in 1897 for rental property. He commissioned Mr. Smith to design five "cottages," all constructed before the turn of the century, with prominent gables & inset porches. (Nos. 138-160.)
8. At the turn of the century, the charming, multi-gabled Annie West house was finished at No. 189, another Smith design, and then in 1904, a house was completed at No. 223 for Mr. Tennent as his own residence, with Queen Anne style elements and a striking Steamboat Gothic entrance hall. It was later sold to Sen. Jeter C. Pritchard, who succeeded Zeb Vance in Congress. Smith also designed a 12-room house for Pritchard in Marshall.
9. In the deed to Dr. David, Mr. Pack stipulated that he not build within fifty feet of the street, thereby assuring the "residence park" quality of the streetscape. Dr. David planted a row of fine sycamores along his frontage and landscaped the lawns as well, an example followed by others.
10. Mr. Pack's house was located at the northwest corner of Merrimon & Chestnut, across from the site on which the Jefferson was built. At the Merrimon intersection, the Jefferson Apartments building was a product of the Twenties with a horseshoe plan and Spanish style detailing. A car stop at the door added to appeal of convenience. Only four blocks in length, Central Avenue also provided convenient connection between the center of the district and downtown at Woodfin & Spruce.

***

1. William Raoul was a founding director of the Central of Georgia and an organizer of Mexican National.
2. At the entrance, the gate house was named *The Lodge*. Tom Raoul lived there as a bachelor.
3. Sub-titled *The Journal of Society*, the *Asheville News & Hotel Reporter* provided relevant information.
4. In 1898, another prominent hotel was the Arcadia. Half a million visitors were coming to the city at that time.
5. British investors were active in railroad construction world wide during that era.

6. The Raoul houses were filled with silver trophies. *Manzanita* & *Milfoil* cottages on the Manor Grounds and *Raoulwood* on Vanderbilt Road.
7. Mr. Raoul became first president of Biltmore Forest Country Club, directly across the golf course from their house. Jane Raoul married Samuel Bingham.
8. *The Family of Raoul*, Mary Raoul Millis.
9. *The Manor & Cottages*, Jane Gianvito Matthews & Richard A. Matthews. (1991)
10. *Landscape of Albemarle Park*, Chas. A. Birnbaum. (1991)

***

1. The intersection at Doubleday became Five Points for north & south Broadway, east & west Chestnut, and Mt. Clare, formerly East Street. It was connected to Montford by a viaduct over a nearby ravine.
2. Probably the best known business enterprise at Grace was Grace Supply, consisting of three connecting stores, grocery & meat market, hardware & building supplies, and dry goods & ready-to-wear. A subsidiary, Grace Fuel, was operated at the railhead at Newbridge, in Woodfin. J.L. Parks, owner.
3. The association operated the property until 1926 when the city acquired it and built a handsome structure there.
4. The monument is the point from which all distances from the city are measured.
5. Mr. Pack died (1903) at his home in Southampton, L.I.

SEVEN

REAL SIGHTS & SOUNDS

While the many civic periodicals and numerous promotional publications were pouring forth their contrived flow of artificial rhetoric in stilted language of the day, Tom Wolfe was drinking in real sights and sounds of actual life around him.

Following his fictionalized account of diverse characters arising from slumber, last of which deals with nuns and girls at St. Genevieve's, he takes on the new city market. Where hacks might have concentrated on some questionable statistics or glowing accounts of how much operation was of benefit to commercial progress, the literary genius of Wolfe brought us to reality...

"Below, tree-hidden, in the Biltburn bottom, there was a thunder on the rails, a wailing whistle cry.

"Beneath the City Hall, in the huge sloping cellar, the market booths were open. The aproned butchers swung their cleavers down on fresh cold joints, slapping the thick chops on heavy sheets of mottled paper, and tossing them, roughly tied, to the waiting negro delivery-boys.

"The self-respecting negro, J.H. Jackson, stood in his square vegetable-stall, attended by his two grave-faced sons, and his spectacled businesslike daughter. He was surrounded by wide slanting shelves of fruit and vegetables, smelling of the earth and morning—great crinkled lettuces, fat radishes still clotted damply with black loam, quill-stemmed young onions newly wrenched from gardens, late celery, spring potatoes, and the thin rinded citrus fruits of Florida.

"Above him, Sorrell, the fish and oyster man, drew up from the depths of an enameled ice-packed can dripping ladlefuls of oysters, pouring them into thick cardboard cartons. Wide-bellied heavy sea-fish—carp, trout, bass, shad—lay gutted in beds of ice.

"Mr. Michael Walter Creech, the butcher, having finished his hearty breakfast of calves' liver, eggs and bacon, hot biscuits and coffee, made a sign to one of the waiting row of negro boys. The line sprang forward like hounds; he stopped them with a curse and a lifted cleaver. The fortunate youth who had been chosen then came forward and took the tray, still richly morselled with food and a pot half full of coffee. As he had to depart at this moment on a delivery, he put it down in the sawdust at the end of the bench and spat contemptuously upon it in order to protect it from his scavenging comrades. Then he wheeled off, full of rich laughter and triumphant malice. Mr. Creech looked at his niggers darkly.

"The town had so far forgotten Mr. Creech's own African blood (an eighth on his father's side, old Walter Creech, out of yellow Jenny) that it was about ready to offer him political preferment; but Mr. Creech himself had not forgotten. He glanced bitterly at his brother, Jay, who, happily ignorant of hatred, that fanged poison which may taint even a brother's heart, was enthusiastically cleaving spare-ribs on the huge bole of his own table, singing meanwhile in a rich tenor voice the opening bars of "The Little Gray Home In The West."

'...there are blue eyes that shine. Just because they meet mine...'

"Mr. Creech looked venomously at Jay's yellow jowls, the fat throbbing of his jaundiced throat, the crisp singed whorl of his hair.

"By God, he thought in his anguish of spirit, he might be taken for a Mexican.

"Jay's golden voice neared its triumph, breaking with delicate restraint, on the last note, into a high sweet falsetto which he maintained for more than twenty seconds. All of the butchers stopped working, several of them, big strong men with grown-up families dashed a tear out of their eyes.

"The great audience was held spellbound. Not a soul stirred. Not even a dog or a horse stirred. As the last sweet note melted away in a gossamer tremolo, a silence profound as that of the tombs, nay, of death itself, betokened the highest triumph the artist is destined to know upon this earth. Somewhere in the crowd a woman sobbed and collapsed in a faint. She was immediately carried out by two Boy Scouts who happened to be present, and who administered first aid to her in the rest-room, one of them hastily kindling a crackling fire of pine boughs by striking two flints together, while the other made a tourniquet, and tied several knots in his handkerchief. Then pandemonium broke loose. Women tore the jewels from their fingers, ropes of pearls from their necks, chrysan-themums, hyacinths, tulips and daisies from their expensive corsages, while the fashionably-dressed men in the near-by stalls kept up a constant bombardment of tomatoes, lettuces, new potatoes, beef-tallow, pigs' knockles, fish-heads, clams, loin-chops, and pork-sausages.

"Among the stalls of the market, the boarding-house keepers of Altamont walked with spying bargain-hunting eyes and inquisitive nose. They were of varying sizes and ages, but they were all stamped with the print of haggling determination and a pugnacious closure of the mouth. They pried in among the fish and vegetables, pinching cabbages, weighing onions, exfoliating lettuce-heads. You've got to keep your eye on people or they'll skin you. And if you leave things to a lazy shiftless nigger she'll waste more than she cooks. They looked at one another hardfaced—Mrs. Barrett of the Grosvenor at Mrs. Neville of Glen View; Mrs. Ambler of the Colonial at Miss Mamie Featherstone of Ravencrest; Mrs. Ledbetter of the Belvedere———

" 'I hear you're full up, Mrs. Coleman,' said she inquiringly.

" 'O, I'm full up all the time,' said Mrs. Coleman. 'My people are all permanents, I don't want to fool with the transients,' she said loftily.

" 'Well,' said Mrs. Ledbetter acidly, 'I could fill my house up at any time with lungers who call themselves something else, but I won't...' "

***

One circulating the rounds of high society on circuits from Southampton to Hot Springs to Asheville to Aiken & Palm Beach might lose sight of some of the basic changes being wrought. But one who walked down Water Street from the Grand Central would quickly find himself in a world where lack of change was more obvious, a place often jammed with wagons, mules, livestock, farm-ers, drummers, and shoppers.

Here it was easier to imagine life on turnpikes of old. Or to visualize the plank road of thick oak boards that had been completed to Greenville in 1851...only to be abandoned shortly before the war.

One might readily visualize in his mind's eye those progenitors of modern hospitality stretch-ing out from point to point along the eight routes of history. James M. Alexander and his 1816 hotel on South Main and then his inn down river toward Hot Springs. Vance Inn beyond, Barnett's stand, Barnard Inn, and Patton's Place near the Tennessee line. R.D. Alexander's Inn at Swannanoa. The Smathers place to the west or Joseph Reed's to the east. Sherrill's Inn down toward Hickory Nut Gap. South to Forster's Inn, Fletcher Tavern, the McDowell Hotel, Farmer Hotel. Tabor's Place. A stream of hogs turning into a torrent, with human travelers sometimes jostling for position here & there along the way.

From earthy to ethereal, resort clientele was undergoing change as well. Frame hotels, as previously observed, were fortunate to survive if located outside the immediate radius of organized fire stations. The Hot Springs Hotel built by John G. Baker, abandoned to modern competition, had then gone up in smoke. Far up in mists of The Roan, The Cloudland had met a similar fate. The Belmont. And now the magnificent Kenilworth came to a fiery ending on the night of April 14, 1909. It would later be rebuilt along neo-Tudor lines during America's participation in the coming great war, and survive to the end of the epoch in that form...but no one could foresee that now.

Yes, as the man said, the times they are a changin'...and a dramatic sign was visible in the motor car. A plaything for the affluent or a challenge to the entrepreneur. Pioneer Sawyers were the earliest and most prominent of automobile owners & dealers. Their home was on Haywood Street when it was still residential but there were several others. Coxes, Rumboughs, Costons, Alexanders. A Locomobile actually appeared in 1898 but virtually nothing was purchased until after the turn of the century, and during the first decade only a handful then.

Livery stables were still a prominent feature of the town but here and there a horseless carriage appeared. These were generally primitive. A two-cylinder Brennen, a Locomobile steam surrey, a Centaur Electric. A White Steamer. Frank Coxe bought a one-cylinder Cadillac passenger touring car. After the war came a profusion of models, however. Including Pierce-Arrow & Peerless. Rambler & Roamer. Marmon & Maxwell. Oldsmobile & Studebaker. McFarlan & Stutz. Lincoln & Chrysler. Not to mention a few exotic species of British or Continental extraction. The ladies were said to have difficulty keeping the names straight and with good reason. Some two thousand makes were produced at one time or another and some luxury name plates were seen by a particular individual only once.

In those early days, Mr. Grove brought one from St. Louis that would be hard to top, even by the Vanderbilt garages at Biltmore. It was an expensively crafted, four cylinder Pope-Toledo of unknown potential, estimated to be somewhere between 30 and 40 horsepower. Driven by a competent chauffeur.

EIGHT

R.S. SMITH'S BROAD LEGACY

A talented Englishman who came to town to supervise construction of *Biltmore* remained to leave his mark on appearance of the city, from the gate house for the estate to the largest downtown hotel to residential suburbs on all sides of town. His ideas influenced other architects and builders.

A versatile and authoritative designer, Richard Sharp Smith created a range of works from cottages to mansions, log lodges to fine homes, small stores to large office buildings. When his supervisory task was completed, Mr. Vanderbilt, who had come to trust him implicitly, persuaded him to remain and begin his own private practice. He designed the Paragon Building at One Haywood Street and established his office there.

Educated and trained in London, Smith was almost 21 when he emigrated to New York, where he was employed by B.L. Gilbert. He also gained experience working in Chicago. After Mr. Hunt began creating plans for the great estate, he entered the offices of Hunt & Hunt, junior and senior, the following year to assist in their development. He proved to be a natural for the task and later the senior Hunt sent him to Asheville as supervising architect in charge of work on site.

He continued in that role for the entire six years that the historic project was underway, making his home in the city during that time. When he was able to turn things over to one of his assistants for a short time, he took on various small projects in the Biltmore area himself. After the house was completed, he designed most of the structures for Biltmore Village, a model community contemplated for some time. He also was responsible for *Vernon Hill*, a special section just above on Smith's Hill, founded by another Smith, no relation.

According to his daughters, Smith was the epitome of an English gentleman. Former member of the Grenadier Guards, he dressed immaculately in custom tailored suits of English tweed. His bearing was military, his manner very British. A cane was an integral part of his attire. Because of long hours seated at the drawing board, he kept a second suit in an alcove off the living room at home. Suits included two pairs of trousers, attire complemented by matching English walking caps.

According to Nancy Brower, popular social columnist for the local newspaper, Smith attended the round of parties that marked opening of the big house. "At these events," she wrote, "he became acquainted with a young Scotswoman of the household staff, a member of Clan Cameron. Her name was Isabel. She was slim and pretty with an extraordinarily beautiful complexion. They were married and he designed a country home for her at the head of Chunn's Cove. Called *Stoneybrook*, the stone house (and barn) still stands. There he lived like a country squire, coming to his office in the Drhumor Building..." (Across from the Paragon.)

Smith designed famous Lodge Gate, the main gate house, an entrance used from a point in the village along the Swannanoa. It was built of brick and roof tile made on the estate. Once past the gate, a visitor found himself on a road winding through carefully landscaped grounds in a deep natural forest with pools, streams, and springs. Around the last turn, he passed through iron gates and pillars topped by early 19th century French stone sphinxes, and thence into the expansive court of the house.

In front of the gate, Hunt laid out a village in the old English manner and following this master plan, Smith set to work designing a school, post office, and railway station. Stores and office buildings. Throughout the village, there were some sixty houses and cottages. And at the turn of the century, in a pleasant neighborhood of Victoria, he designed some handsome places where important visitors could stay for an extended period of time when they did not wish to take up residence at a hotel.

Created under influence of the reign of Queen Victoria, the village of Victoria was incorporated on Smith's Hill in 1888. The nucleus of *Vernon Hill* was five houses completely furnished except for silver, linen, and blankets. Each with its own stable. One of the first was Washington Cottage at 335 Victoria Road, ten rooms with reception hall and coach house adjacent. The term "cottage" could mean something quite different in that era. Near confluence of the rivers, the site commanded good views of the valley of the Swannanoa below.

Several hundred black laborers had worked on construction. Mr. Vanderbilt wanted to do something, not only to show appreciation for their efforts but to provide a community center for young men and others of their race, a place where they might develop mentally and spiritually on the road to responsible citizenship. An opportunity to prepare themselves for trades and occupations in which they could earn a good living for their families. A block east of the Eagle, behind the hotel where black business was developing on Market, a choice piece of property was acquired and Smith drew up plans.

Inspired by the Young Men's Christian Association, it was called the Young Men's Institute and it became known as the Y.M.I. Of English derivation, this typically Biltmore style building was begun in 1892, the same year that the new city hall and post office were being completed nearby. After its formal opening the following year, it soon became a permanent home of social and civic activity for that vibrant community just south off the Square.

As for the Paragon, he could not have chosen a better place to display his wares. By the turn of the century, this intersection was becoming a hub of the city. All passersby had to do was glance at his work. It was not a show stopper but it spoke to the idiom and vernacular of the city's emerging style. There followed a series of commissions in that business district, starting with the Medical Building in the middle of Battery Park Place across the way. The Miles Building, several times remodeled, diagonally across the street.

On the Square, the Legal Building in the middle of the south side, and the Oates Building at the eastern end of the north side. The Technical Building at #108 College and adjacent buildings. The Majestic. The Langren. The Loughran. In 1914, the Elks Lodge on Haywood and the Eagles Home on Broadway. And then a few doors down on the opposite side, the prime work in this category, the Scottish Rite Cathedral & Masonic Temple at the corner of Woodfin.

Smith also designed St. Mary's Church and rectory at the little park where Macon began its ascent of the mountain in Grove Park. The stone chapel at Grace. A new building for St. Genevieve's and later St. Joseph's. He found time to do several county schools. And his residential work was attracting increasing attention. Montford began slowly with a cluster of houses and other structures around the Rumbough property on a knoll at the head of Montford Avenue and eventually reached a peak of 700 houses. Of these, 14 were later identified as his and several others attributed to him.

Smith drew on a variety of resources to produce pleasing effects. According to studies by the preservation society, "he was sophisticated and knowledgeable about national architectural trends as well as English precedents, combining a variety of style, motif, and material for clients. Among his favorite (forms) were gambrel roofs, hipped gables, heavy porch brackets, pebbledash or stucco walls, shingles, stone foundations, half-timbering, and simple Colonial Revival detail. Two of his most important works are the Frederick Rutledge House at 209 Cumberland, featuring a broad gambrel roof and stuccoed walls, and the Ottis Green House at 288 Montford, with an irregular Queen Anne exterior, including asymmetrical porch and corner turret."

This versatile Englishman was also a pioneer in use of reinforced concrete. The Haywood Building (1917) was the first commercial office building combined with garage in the downtown district. Under commission from a member of the famous Roebling family, builders of the Brooklyn Bridge and other great spans, it was a project of Smith & Carrier, which performed most of his later work. This structure proved to be an exceptionally sturdy linchpin for what came to be the widely known street of fashion, dominating as it did the central section across from the Walnut intersection.

In the days when Biltmore Village was something out of an English book, he was captain of the cricket team that played matches there. He was also an outdoorsman, hunting birds while riding on the estate and keeping a pair of English setters to flush game. Hunting regalia included a hunting horn and a silver bird whistle. On more formal occasions, he wore an English derby but when driving to building sites in his pony cart, he wore one of his walking caps. The cart was pulled by a small chestnut horse named *Rowdy* while his hunting horse was a big bay.

In his younger days, he liked to hunt raccoon and opossum with friends, following that up with an invitation for all to enjoy an English dinner prepared by his wife who, among other accomplishments, was an excellent hostess and cook. Her dapper husband walked with a spring in his step and a lilt in his stride. Some speculated that it was enhanced by that, as well as the vigor and good natured activity of his daughters, who shared his love for the outdoors and were proficient in handling horses, milking cows, and other such pursuits, learned from him.

Among others, he enjoyed the confidence of Frank Loughran, widely known innkeeper and purveyor of spirits in the days before they were restricted under the federal constitution. At No. 165 North Main, he designed for him a residence described as "one of the best built houses in this section." A dozen rooms and large reception hall, trimmed in hardwood with tile vestibule and fireplaces, large verandahs, clapboard and shingle siding, slate roof.

When Lt. Lawrence Loughran died in the world war, Smith designed a monument for the grave at Riverside. And then in 1921, when the father foresaw the future role of Haywood Street, they sat down to plan a building as its capstone, a classic composition in white glazed terra cotta of soaring vertical pilasters and crisply-cut paired windows. Opened the following year, it was home to Denton's, newest and for a time most fashionable department store in town.

Now his remarkable career was winding toward a close. His influence had modified the city's appearance. Where only a few years before, heavy brick Italianate and Romanesque Revival styles predominated, with brick and stone masonry, now Renaissance Italian *pilazzi*, combined with Spanish Mission and Tudor Cottage elements, was in ascendancy. And a distinguishing characteristic was strong emphasis on vertical and horizontal planes in windows, an essential ingredient in personality of a particular structure.

For Mr. Vanderbilt, he had designed Clarence Barker Infirmary, which in the Twenties became Biltmore Hospital. Near his half-timbered post office were buildings containing several stores, including grocery, druggist, meat market, retail furnishings and so forth, with four, five, and six rooms to flats on the floor above. Exterior walls were English half-timber, roofs composition, streets macadamized and sidewalks paved with brick. Street lamps, identification signs, markers and other accoutrements were of the best materials and design.

Downtown were small Smith touches wherever he went. Like the little log "mountaineer" restaurant in the midst of shopping bustle or the *Halthenon*, a low cottage style structure designed for Dr. Paul Pacquin who pronounced it to be "the most complete arrangement of therapeutic baths in the South." A small urban reminder of the city's social origins in days of the spa.

On the Square stood Vance Monument, emblem of the city, surrounded by many of his works and up Haywood was the Auditorium, built not long afterward, gathering place for the community. But two decades later, these were changing days. Some called it the age of movies. The Emporium fire left a void in front of the Pack Theater and his firm was called upon to design a new, more expansive public entrance. Work progressed without a hitch but by the time completion was approaching, this proper and conscientious architect was ill. A gentleman in the English sense from first to last, he maintained his manners and poise but his physical condition grew worse.

On Friday, February 8, 1924, at two o'clock in the morning, he died in his room at the Meriwether Hospital, which he designed. Funeral services were conducted at three o'clock the following afternoon in Lewis Funeral Home, a mortuary which he designed less than two years before. Next door to the courthouse, new and old, it was his last commercial building commission.

Two weeks later, on Washington's Birthday, the remodeled theater was reopened with its elaborate new entrance. Smith and his times were gone, public attention shifted in a new direction. A few hundred yards from the mortuary, a soaring, shining shaft rose from the darkness below, a skyscraper signal for the new age. The Jackson Building had arrived. And attached to its lofty penthouse was a powerful searchlight that would comb the skies, a symbolic sweep into space.

Below, the buildings of Richard Sharp Smith would stand their ground, however, tangible evidence of a gracious and personable era whose qualities would linger in the minds of thoughtful Ashevillians for decades to come. Fifty years afterward, one of his daughters remarked, "He was exacting. He wanted things right, but he was fair. And he trusted everybody."

Endnotes

1. The Swannanoa Gate entrance to the estate was located near the western extremity of the site.
2. A nicely designed little brochure, intended for interested persons who might wish to acquaint themselves with the situation, describes it like this:
3. Situated at the western extremity, *Spurwood* derives its name from a copse at the rear of the house. It has one view to the west, looking toward Mt. Pisgah, a second to the east, up the valley of the Swannanoa, toward the Craggy and Black Mountains.

A little higher up, to the east, is *Westdale*. Still further east, on the summit of the ridge, is *Sunnicrest* while on a spur just below is *Ridgelawn*. These three command substantially the same view, looking at right angles across the valley toward Busbee Mountain, Hickory Nut Gap and Cedar Cliff, while to the left may be seen the range of the Craggies. *Hillcote*, the smallest, is situated at the head of a cove on a lower slope. Its view is south and west, including the Pisgah range and panorama of Biltmore Estate.

4. Dark pebbledash with red brick and tile were used in a building containing gymnasium, meeting rooms, and stores, with many entrances, imparting an urbane presence to this prominent, sloping site. *N.C. Architecture*, Chapel Hill, 1991.

5. *My Sketch Book* shows a variety of homes. French Broad Press, 1901, copyright Samuel J. Fisher, Asheville.

6. When a resident passed on, his widow or other relative often helped maintain the house by accepting boarders of good social standing, persons who could provide companionship. A comfortable arrangement, one often lamented in later years after the motor car had fragmented social life, with many stranded in its wake of noise and fumes.

7. Down the central artery there, his works included No. 192 for Dr. Harmon Miller, 214 for Mrs. Leon Mitchell, 296 for Dr. Charles Jordan. A beautiful ten-room house with a tin shingle roof for Mrs. Ex. Norton and a house for William F. Randolph, the newspaper publisher.

8. *Book of Montford*, Historic Preservation Society. (out of print)

9. His first venture in reinforced concrete was the Legal Building, planned to sit next to the courthouse. By the time it was built, the courthouse had been moved but only around the corner.

***

1. The prolific Smith was able to produce such a stream of work by virtue of his disciplined character which resulted, among other things, in early rising habits. Although he often worked past midnight, his daughters told Nancy Brower that he was up at five. "We used to quarrel about this," said one, telling him that he was not getting enough rest. His reply was to quote Napoleon as saying, "When a man has to turn over, it's time to get up."

2. Acquired from Mayor Melvin Carter in 1869, the Penland House property on Battery Park Hill extended south from Hiawassee some 10-12 acres between Haywood & Water (Lexington).

3. In 1880, the Rev. Louis M. Pease, a Presbyterian minister, was attracted to the city by arrival of the railhead at Azalea. He purchased 31.45 acres along Smith's ridge west of lower South Main and established his residence there. On June 16, 1887, he deeded the property to the Home Industrial School (for mountain girls) of which he became superintendent, and on October 5th, first classes were held.

4. In 1882, Alexander Garrett came to the city from St. Louis with tuberculosis and purchased the Smith-McDowell House. June 28, 1888, marked the Silver Jubilee of Queen Victoria and in honor of the occasion, he built a luxurious hotel nearby to rival the Battery Park, naming it *Victoria Inn*. He began developing adjoining land and on October 2, 1889, the area between Main and McDowell's Street was incorporated as the Town of Victoria.

5. Robert U. Garrett, son of the founder, deeded the property to the Presbyterians in 1891. By 1898, Governor Steadman had converted it to the Oakland Heights Hotel but before long, demand caused conversion to a temporary sanitarium.

6. A decade later, Mr. Vanderbilt founded his enclave north of Lodge Gate to accommodate guests. His business manager, Charles McNamee, acquired central acreage, established his own residence, and began construction of other houses. For promotional purposes, the Biltmore Estate office referred to "model cottages or villas in Vernon Hill."

7. In time, they became rental properties and subsequently were made available for sale. Other houses were built and it became a fashionable neighborhood, centered around St. Dunstan's Circle. The more developed area of Victoria was extended all the way north to Choctaw Street. The Oakland Heights section was developed by the Garretts, doing business as Oakland Development Corp.

8. In 1909, it was re-opened as a resort hotel under the original name but after being damaged by fire, was sold to The Sisters of Guadalupe Hermosa. Converted for use as a girl's school, it became widely known as St. Genevieve-of-the-Pines.

9. The hotel's extensive storage tanks supplied water for all of Oakland Heights.

10. The history of Victoria is the most complex and confusing in the city, stretching as it does from Mr. Smith across a century and more. After the Presbyterian school was closed, the site would become a great medical center, nationally recognized, with approximately fifty buildings involved.

NINE

ARRIVAL OF MR. GROVE

While the names of Coxe and Vanderbilt are linked inseparably with social history of Asheville, the prime mover in development of the modern city was Edwin Wiley Grove. A successful pharmaceutical manufacturer, he came to the city from St. Louis, where he had amassed a fortune after starting in business in southwest Tennessee.

As we have seen, Asheville had become widely known as a health resort, starting with visitors from Southern coastal areas. The primary scourge of these low lying regions was fever, a variety of diseases that left victims debilitated. Notable among them was the one known as *malaria*. Like Yellow Jack, it was feared around the world in days before advent of modern medical miracles.

A typical attack or *paroxysm* was characterized by three well defined stages, all of which left victims helpless to function normally. The *cold* stage was preceded by headache, yawning, and general malaise. Gradually, the patient began to shiver and, in the height of chill, shake violently. Temperature then rose to 102 or even to 105 or 106 degrees, a stage lasting from ten minutes to an hour, followed by the *hot* stage, during which surface coldness disappeared and skin became flushed.

In about 30 minutes, the *perspiring* stage usually set in, lasting three or four hours. Beads of sweat appeared on the forehead and then the whole body became soaking wet. Gradually, fever & headache disappeared and within an hour or two, the patient sank into sleep and the cycle was over. In ancient times, some students of the subject believed it was caused by swamp vapors arising from contaminated soil. In mediaeval Italy, it was blamed on bad (mala) air (aria) and thus the name *malaria* was so derived.

The germ theory of disease, fully developed and generally accepted by about 1873, led scientists to search for parasites and in 1880, while railway service was being established at Asheville, they were found in French North Africa by Charles Louis Alphonse Laveran. Over the next 18 years, complete solution to the mystery was attained.

***

Born on a small plantation between Bolivar & Whiteville, Grove was ten years old when his father left to join the Confederate Army for service under Nathan Bedford Forrest, the legendary tactical genius. The lad stayed home with his mother, doing all he could to help her in the struggle to keep their place going.

Following war's end, the father returned home and when he was about 18, young Grove went over to Memphis on his own to study pharmacy and learn business across the river in Arkansas. As Reconstruction was coming to an end, he learned that a position was open in Paris, Tennessee. He went there (1874) to pursue it and became a clerk in Caldwell's drug store, later pharmacist as well. On his own, he began experimenting with new products and four years later was developing his first formula.

In the coming year, having saved some capital, he told Dr. Caldwell that he would be interested in purchasing the business.

**

E.W. Grove was familiar with the fevers and with public need for medicinal relief. In Memphis, he had also heard stories about the effects of herbal medicines developed in the Smokies and other Appalachian areas, the numbers of lowlanders visiting the Land of the Sky for reasons of health, and the mystique of the great Battle of Chickamauga.

For more than three centuries, treatment of malaria depended on an extract from *cinchona* or *calisaya* bark from the Peruvian Andes. Known as *quinina* or *quinine.* By the middle of the 19th century, it was being dispensed by pharmacists in drug stores. As our era began in 1880, two things transpired. Early in the year, aging Dr. Caldwell decided to retire and when Grove became the store's new proprietor, he renamed it Grove's Pharmacy. On November 6th, the malaria parasite was identified.

Quinine was effective and reasonable in price but it had a definite drawback. It tasted terrible. Users made awful faces when the bitter effect took hold. Where it was available, the powdered form of cinchona bark was bought as a necessity, nothing more. While it took several forms with varying characteristics, there was a general pattern. The material was soluble in alcohol, not very soluble in water.

Devoting spare time to experiments in pharmacy & chemistry, Grove succeeded in evolving a formula that could produce it in suspension, i.e., suspend it in liquid form. He then found that iron would help disguise the taste. And with sweetened flavorings such as lemon, he was able to offer a more palatable potion. Satisfied that he had the answer, he wanted to try it out on the public. And now that he had his own pharmacy, he was ready to act.

After bottling his concoction, he labeled it *Grove's Tasteless Chill Tonic.* Almost immediately, he found a ready market. Contents of a bottle were not actually tasteless but a lot closer to it than raw bark of a tree. And it would not destroy the parasite, but once in the bloodstream, quinine would hinder its growth and thereby reduce chills & fever. To prevent onset or recurrence of the disease, wise Dr. Grove advised taking "four tablespoons full daily for a period of eight weeks or during the entire malarial season." A lot of medicine.

By the time the Battery Park opened, demand was so great that he organized Paris Medicine Company to manufacture it. By 1890, the market was still expanding and he moved both offices and laboratories to St. Louis, where railroad facilities were extensive. Several variations were developed. Then he struck upon the idea of a cold tablet. Cold remedies were on the market but no tablets. The convenience factor was appealing. He commissioned the fledgling Parke-Davis company to produce his new product, called it *Grove's Bromo-Quinine,* and another success story was in the making.

When it came to promotion, Dr. Grove was no shrinking violet either. A wag called it Grove's Bromo-Promo. Patent medicine salesmen were becoming notorious but he had a legitimate, bona fide product, and he was one who didn't mind using his own name. Advertising for *Grove's Tasteless Chill Tonic* began to appear through a variety of channels, newspapers, street signs, posters, handbills and the like, until it had reached a flood. The Paris Medicine Company was becoming a medicinal money making machine. By 1894, he had become a millionaire, at a time when a factory worker might earn ten dollars a week. He could well afford to take a vacation.

Summertime in the Mississippi River basin was sweltering hot. Memphis. St. Louis. Stories of the mountains lingered in his mind, particularly refuge taken by denizens of Charleston & Savannah. One early fall day, his secretary booked a drawing room on the Asheville sleeping car and before long he was alighting with his wife at Biltmore Station, where a carriage from Kenilworth Inn was there to meet them, along with the hotel luggage wagon. The entrepreneurial doctor liked everything he saw there, and the inn appealed to the nature of his Scottish ancestry.

Biltmore was nearing its final year of construction. He visited the Battery Park. He loved the beauty of the mountains and many readily available carriage rides. He went on the popular day trips around the city. Victoria, Montford, Sulphur Springs, Beaver Dam, Riverside, Lookout, Beaucatcher & Sunset. Upon his return to St. Louis, he again plunged into his work with determination. Another Presbyterian imbued with traditional facets of that ethic. He saw goals to be reached, tasks to be completed along the route.

Somewhere along the way, however, the intense pace began to take its toll. He started experiencing occasional bouts of exhaustion, which eventually led to collapse. In 1896, he was advised by physicians to seek a change of environment & setting, and because of its reputation, Asheville was suggested. No persuasion was necessary. Accompanied by his wife and assistants, he came back to the city for a rest. Stayed at Kenilworth again. As his strength returned, he took walks on the grounds. The great house across the way had just been completed and he went for carriage rides in Vanderbilt Park.

He rode trolley cars up South Main. Enjoyed cuisine of the Battery Park and admired views of the celebrated western exposure. Rode out Charlotte to Edgemont. Went on the day trips. And he attended services at the Presbyterian church where young Dr. Campbell was attracting attention with his Calvinist inspired sermons. He talked to him and others about what climate had done for their health. And he was attracted to the gently rolling section around the end of Charlotte Street.

St. Louis was a fine city, one of the best in the country. The German character, from manufacturers to braumeisters, had made it a model for the vast area once known as the Louisiana Purchase. But Grove had personal matters on his mind. His young wife had died in 1884 while they lived in Paris. Of their four children, only Evelyn survived infancy. He remarried and a son was born but a third child died of diphtheria after the family moved to St. Louis.

With branch manufactories in Toronto, London, Sydney, Rio & Buenos Aires (good airs) his small town drug store had become a multi-million dollar corporation. Grove's tonic was becoming practically a household word, particularly in the South where mosquitoes thrived. And the South was home to bottled beverages.

Dr. Grove followed the success of Dr. Pemberton and Asa Candler of Coca-Cola with interest. He had come to see Atlanta as a place to succeed in business, and the South as a place to relax. He bought land on the outskirts of the city. Other acreage back in Arkansas. He began to acquire land holdings in the Gulf Hammock section of northern Florida, on Tampa Bay, in Chihuahua, Mexico. By now he was beginning to suffer other ailments, however, among them bronchitis & chronic insomnia. And increasingly his thoughts turned to a place that lingered in his mind, the undeveloped lands beyond Charlotte Street.

Later in the year of his Asheville sojourn, he went to the headquarters of Parke-Davis at Detroit to discuss a problem that had arisen in manufacture of tablets. There he met a fellow who had risen from clerk at Johnson & Johnson to a position as head of tablet manufacturing for this leading company. The man was Frederick Loring Seely and he was only 25 years old. Grove was impressed.

Seely had already distinguished himself by inventing a machine to compress tablets. The older man saw in him something of himself. And when Seely solved his problem, a relationship was formed. He began to entertain in a quiet way and one of his first guests was Fred Seely. They saw the sights together, with Grove acting as guide. Mutual admiration extended to Grove's only daughter, Evelyn.

Introduction led to courtship and the following year, they were married. October 24, 1895. The groom's father-in-law established a branch plant near the Depot in Asheville, naming it The Tasteless Quinine Company. Seely became manager, learning intricacies of operation at ground level, both manufacturing and sales. This talented versatile young man had hitched his wagon to a star. "Tonic Water" or "Quinine Water" had already reached the capstone of commercial success, outselling Coca-Cola in many areas.

At the turn of the century, Grove sent his son-in-law on a round-the-world trip in search of new sources of quinine. A combination of increased competition and dwindling supply from the slow growing cinchona tree was threatening the future of their business. He and Evelyn Seely left in October for San Francisco, where they boarded a steamer for Java, the only place where these trees were grown commercially. They were gone five months. Despite many setbacks, he was able to negotiate a contract that secured a steady supply for the next 42 years.

After their return, Seely went into management at headquarters and Grove established temporary residence at The Manor in one of the substantial new cottages there. He continued to entertain quietly and the Seelys were frequent visitors on the St. Louis sleeper. Grove & Seely saw the sights together, with Mr. Raoul sometimes acting as guide. In due course, Grove bought land to establish second residence. He did not have to look far. A block north of fashionable Chestnut, he began building his house. In early summer of the next year, it was completed and he and his wife, Gertrude, moved in with their young son, Edwin Junior. There they were happily situated, where he could look out toward the Sunset slopes.

In St. Louis, Seely set out to bring the company into the 20th century in line with modern manufacturing methods. Significant new products were made ready to come on stream. Sales rose dramatically. The modest Paris medicine man was free to turn the focus of his creative energies into real estate.

***

In the world of Wolfe, Grove was Park, and a park was what he set out to create. The city had Battery Park & Kenilworth Park & Vanderbilt Park & Riverside Park & now Albemarle Park. He envisioned something of his own imagination, and a new perspective to go with it. Like Mr. Vanderbilt, his early acquisitions were carried out through unidentified agents.

In 1903, people were talking about meeting in St. Louis next year for the big world's fair and in time for its opening, a new railway passenger station for Asheville was opened. Folks from all over town were using the station and now there was this exciting attraction. Grove was one of the fair's sponsors but it did not divert him from his purposes. He correctly saw the new station as a signal for things to come.

The quinine king had walked the Kimberly lands and become increasingly familiar with them. Before the fair closed that fall, he had built a formal little park, the E.W. Grove Park, at the point where Mr. Howland's right-of-way began its ascent from Charlotte to the mountain top. Around this triangular green space, he began planning a residential area of the highest physical and aesthetic standards. He proceeded slowly, more or less as an interesting hobby, naming the streets for his wife and seven children, living & deceased. It was something new for him but it appealed to his basic instincts. At the south end, he built a small, temporary wooden structure for his on-site office.

The slopes were still largely wooded with few houses but the turn of the century had brought with it some developments being reflected in social life. In early July of 1899, the country club had been moved from nearby Ramoth into quarters in a lodge at Edgemont, made available by Mr. Pack, a fellow member. Grove also became a member. Then on New Year's Eve and New Year's Day, Mr. Raoul and company celebrated the actual turn of the century with a festive opening at The Manor. Plans for expansion of Albemarle Park were being discussed.

Mr. R.S. Howland, publisher of the *Providence Journal,* came to the city that year (1900) and on Sunset nearby purchased a 325-acre tract from Mr. Pack, establishing residence in a new house called *Dolobran* there above the Pack summer place. Adjoining the previous site of the club house, new *Winyah* (sanitarium) was established. Christ School and the Asheville School would be opening with start of the fall term.

The Charlotte Street car line was extended to the Manor Gate House. Mr. Grove replaced his office with a permanent structure. From there, Mr. Howland built an electric car line to Locust Gap where an art studio and other amenities were established at *Overlook.*

Spurred on by activity of Grove's small staff, the club constructed (1905) a new house on the south slope, changed the name from Swannanoa to Asheville, and extended the golf links. Also designed by Smith, this old fashioned wooden structure soon became a landmark in the middle of lower fairways. Mr. Grove saw it as a good step in the right direction and top flight golfers in America began entering tournaments there.

The two lines were then connected and the city car line was extended to the club, this becoming known as the Charlotte Street Extension. A cable car system was planned to run directly between the club and *Overlook.* And Asheville Rapid Transit Company was incorporated for purposes of connecting Grand Central with the Golf Club and thus to *Overlook.*

The heart of fashionable Asheville was now shared between Battery Park Hill downtown, and Montford and Charlotte Street, connected by Chestnut, a mile or two out. While the great fair was in progress, the city as a whole was stirring as well. After the new depot was opened, it was announced that the long awaited second railroad was coming, via Burnsville & Woodfin. W.T. Weaver began operating a new electric generating plant at Craggy Station on the river. Officials were preparing to open Riverside Park. And the Southern, with other lines, was promoting the town far & wide as a resort destination.

Late in 1905, Grove & Seely launched the *Atlanta Georgian.* Meanwhile, plans were drawn for the area between the Manor Grounds and the club. The Grove concept was one with views & open space, trees & sidewalks, and restrictive covenants & building limitations. He vowed that no property would be sold until "every modern convenience" had been provided. Successful from the start, the development process would continue until the end of the era.

Not long after Kenilworth Inn was gutted by fire, Mr. Grove began talking with his real estate manager, W.F. Randolph, about the possibility of building a new hotel. The big inn went up in flames on the night of April 14, 1909, and concerns about institutional fire, aggravated by the Belmont and the Auditorium, were stimulated anew.

The city's reputation as prime place for consumptives was also something to consider. What effect would that have on travelers? Would it be wise to launch a major project with hundreds of rooms for the general run of tourists or would it be better to plan for the carriage trade with visitors to Grove Park and environs in mind. Learning of these talks, Mayor J.E. Rankin, a highly respected banker, was asked to lead a delegation of businessmen to St. Louis, where Mr. Grove was then in residence. It was late in 1910.

The club car was full and good Cuban cigars in evidence. Discussion included reminiscence of early days at Battery Park & Manor and other exciting events of the past 25 years. Hope was expressed for even closer ties with Palm Beach & St. Petersburg. Optimism for the future of the Auditorium, now that the City was taking it over. Next morning, they met with Grove at his offices. The mood was buoyant. Some had been to the fair and congratulations were in order. That night they had a formal dinner at his home and again found him receptive and seriously interested. Their mutual concerns were civic rather than commercial, and conversation cordial and constructive.

Early the next year, Grove authorized Randolph to begin solicitation of architectural sketches. Structural elements were analyzed in nearly a dozen hotels across the country. Nothing definite developed, however. One day Mr. Grove's secretary handed him a brochure she had just received. The title was *The Hotels of Yellowstone Park*. It struck both Grove and Seely as suitable for the city's setting. Photographs & sketches of Old Faithful Inn and Grand Canyon Hotel were turned over to the architects for review. Again, nothing was produced that met Grove's expectations.

From his office at the newspaper in Atlanta, Seely was corresponding directly with Robert G. Reamer, the Yellowstone architect. Built during the winter of 1903-4, the inn there was of massive log construction. Seely pondered every aspect of the situation. Then on April 15, the indestructible *Titanic* struck an iceberg on its maiden voyage and public safety was again foremost in people's minds. During the following month, Seely provided Grove with a sketch of his own. He explained the source of his ideas as to appearance but suggested something far more substantial. Boulders from their own lands could be employed.

With an actual plan in hand, Grove responded with characteristic dispatch. The two met at his house for lunch, then went to Sunset and walked the slopes, talking about their vision. As Seely later wrote, "the idea was to build a big home where every modern convenience could be had, but with all the old fashioned qualities of genuineness. No sham…all attempt at the bizarre, the tawdry, and flashily foolish omitted."

Mr. Seely was wearing several hats. A native of the Garden State, he was an admirer of Mr. Wilson as governor and as president of Princeton. Now he was engaged in his campaign for President. And to cap the stack, Mr. Hearst was interested in the newspaper for his national chain. Seely agreed to sell out late in the year so that he could then turn his full attention to this mammoth project. Mr. Grove agreed. The price reportedly included a substantial profit.

The plan conceived for these verdant slopes was monumental in scope but one that would not scar the mountainside with a multi-winged monster. No conventions or commercial conclaves.

Instead it was visualized as originating in nature, pleasing in harmony, a part of the fortuitous surroundings in which it would rest. Although inspired by Yellowstone, this proposition was as original as its location. A setting on the hills, with clear view of the city. Panorama to the west. It was unique.

"After a long walk one evening, at the sunset hour, scarcely more than a year ago, I sat down here to rest, and while almost entranced by the panorama of these encircling mountains and a restful outlook upon green fields, the dream of an old time inn came upon me...an inn whose exterior, and interior as well, should present a home-like and wholesome simplicity, whose hospitable doors should ever be open wide, inviting the traveler to rest a while, shut in from the busy world outside." So Grove later wrote.

As Seely later wrote, "all the old fashioned qualities of genuineness...no sham."

About 400 men in various categories were hired as laborers. With perhaps a hundred mules available, and one steam shovel, they set to work leveling the site. Gradually a great ledge began to form in the side of the mountain. Mule powered drags excavated the broad foundation for a six-story structure. Massive wooden scaffolding rose steadily on all sides. Clearly this was not the beginnings of an ordinary hotel.

Meanwhile, a remarkable operation was taking place nearby. With pulleys & ropes, granite rocks & stones were being collected from mountainsides, some weighing as much as ten thousand pounds. Mule teams dragged the boulders onto wooden sleds and pulled them down to the road. The Grove company owned several Packard trucks. About 14 wagons would be strung together to form a train, each towed by a truck to the sire.

By mid-June, they were about ready to start construction. By now, plans were starting to get their finishing touches. On the Fourth, the Langren was opened on the corner just north of the Square and advertised as fireproof.

On July 9, groundbreaking ceremonies were held. As reporters converged on the site, it was announced that the following July 1 had been set as scheduled date for completion. Only a year's time for the foremost resort hotel building project in the world. Not for current fashion or style of tomorrow but something more permanent. They had set out to erect an indestructible mountain monument. Here they would build for the ages.

***

Stone was not a unique building material but this project was based on the natural environment. As Mr. Seely later explained...

"The men worked under instructions that when the Inn was finished, not a piece of stone should be visible except it show the time-eaten face given it by thousands of years of sun and rain...on the mountain side. These great boulders were laid with lichen and moss on them just as they were found."

By February, weather permitting, Mills was ready to start pouring the roof over the Great Hall, highest of five individual roofs. Atop wooden forms, a steel web of half-inch reinforcing rods was woven. Up to 35 feet long, square, twisted rods intersected at six-inch intervals, horizontally as well as vertically. This added more than 90,000 pounds of weight, roof being supported by massive granite walls and six concrete pillars extending through the main lobby and into the basement.

Once all this was in place, men began pouring more than five inches of concrete over forms in a continuous, round-the-clock operation. On March 24, Mills wrote to his family back home. "I had to come back to the hotel tonight," he told them. "They are pouring the roof and sometimes working all night. I came down (from up there and have) taken these few minutes to write you all. Up top, the wind is blowing like fury. I can see all over Asheville, but Good Lord how one peep of Dear Old Atlanta would stir the latent blood in my veins."

When the concrete had cured, each roof was sealed with five layers of hot asphalt & felt. On top of the final layer, they laid red tile shingles, a foot long, half a foot wide, 3/8 of an inch thick. Around dormers, they were arranged in an irregular pattern to provide a desired English thatch-like appearance. Recognizing general public antipathy to hard, angular, slice-like lines, it had been decided that there would be no angles anywhere in roof lines, only lazy, graceful slopes, as one reporter put it.

Meanwhile, workmen had turned (March) to finishing the interior. Water pipes for guest rooms were attached to concrete pillars in the lobby and then stonemasons covered them with granite. At each end of the 120-foot room, a massive fireplace rose. Some 36 feet wide, each required 120 tons of boulders to construct. Hammered iron andirons, weighing 700 pounds apiece, would carry 12-foot logs in its giant firebox.

To protect guests from noise, Seely cleverly concealed elevators by design within the huge fireplaces. For the same purpose, he housed machinery far away in cavernous basement areas. Phonographs were prohibited and airwaves were still virginal. Anyone with carnival abandon or conventioneering debauchery in mind would do well to jettison any such bacchanalian ideas or select another resort destination.

As the deadline approached, it became apparent that it could not be met. Some things were not quite finished. No major details stood in the way, however. A Seely drawing of how it would all look when landscaped was reproduced in the form of a personal invitation from Mr. Grove and sent to a list of prominent men. In part, it read: "On the night of Saturday, July 12th, we expect (to open) the Grove Park Inn to the public. We have built what we believe we can honestly claim is the finest resort hotel in the world, and on that night we shall be honored by the presence of the Secretary of State, William Jennings Bryan, who will make the principal address.

"I believe that it is generally known that this enterprise was not born of purely commercial motives, but was an outgrowth of a movement set afoot by Mayor Rankin and a number of prominent businessmen who finally called on me at St. Louis and placed the matter before me. After deciding to act upon their suggestion, I did what I could to build a hotel worthy of these wonderful mountains.

"I sincerely trust, therefore, that you may be present at seven p.m., Saturday, July 12th, to view the building before the banquet, which is to be at eight o'clock."

Dressed in full formal attire, the four hundred were greeted by an army of grey-coated attendants. Most guests could hardly imagine the confusion that had prevailed at the end of the month. Some finishing touches remained but tonight confusion was gone. An elaborate banquet was served to perfection. Mr. Seely acted as toastmaster. After dinner, he introduced the speakers.

The distinguished audience listened to Mr. Grove with quiet & respectful attention when he said, "A man never grows too old to build castles and dream dreams. Standing here tonight in the midst of friends and guests, I find a dream realized and a castle materialized.

"It affords me more gratification than I can express to have in my immediate family an architect and builder, one who by artistic conception and untiring zeal has studied out the most minute detail, making this dream a reality and accomplishing what, in so short a time, seems almost beyond human endurance."

The speaker was followed by Mr. Bryan, a man he first met at Dr. Campbell's church downtown. America's greatest & most famous orator said: "Today we stand in this wonderful place, not built for a few, but for multitudes that will come and go. I congratulate these men. They have indeed built for the ages."

Mayor Rankin rose to the occasion with some impressive statements of his own, praising the city's adopted son without reservation. "By his brilliant fellowship, broad enlightenment, and gracious hospitality, he has endeared himself to (us) and this magnificent structure will remind those who follow of his foresight and accomplishment. Here we see a triumph of architectural skill mingled with the splendor of nature's handiwork, the whole blending in one great harmony never before equaled in annals of the builder's craft."

The Roeblings had built the Great Bridge, Cunard the Great Ship. Even then, Goethals was still building the Great Ditch. In New York, the great railway tunnels had been built beneath the rivers. And up at Croton, the Great Dam with its vast reservoir for the city was finally complete. Now Mr. Grove had finished the great resort hotel. An inn worthy of the mountain behind it, not to mention a castle on the far side of town.

***

A year later, the guns of August were being put in place. Among other things, the inn would be used as a secure place for foreign diplomats and other government officials during wartime.

Mr. Seely leased the property and under his regime, it was run with needs & comforts of guests foremost in mind, rich & famous and lesser lights as well. After ten in the evening, for example, talking was restricted to low tones & whispers. One place where tired & weary, but not sick & infirm, would find comforts & pleasures without having to go to a small hotel or inn. Unhampered by contrary ideas and carelessness of others.

After the war, as things returned to the popular "normalcy" of President Harding, George Stephens came to Asheville and bought Biltmore Village from Edith Vanderbilt, first staying at The Manor. And then that same year, the builder of Grove Park bought Albemarle Park, Manor included, from Mr. Raoul. Before the decade was over, there would be 500 houses in the Grove Park area. Not cookie cutter copies. Each a real home of individual design.

At the start of the decade, development in the northeast part of the city was nearing completion and Edwin Wiley Grove had become one of the largest landowners. He was ready to turn his attention in the other direction. There the grand old lady on the hill was still the city's foremost landmark and from massive terraces of the inn…it was a natural target of opportunity. His sights were set on that familiar outline in the distance.

Downtown Asheville would never be the same.

Endnotes

1. In the Andes, Indian tribes had known for centuries that chewing bark of the "fever tree" could ward off disease.
2. In 1894, Patrick Manson published an explanation of his theory that they were transmitted by mosquitoes.
3. On August 20-1, 1897, proof of Manson's idea came when Ronald Ross found malaria parasites of man growing as cysts on the stomach wall of *Anopheles* mosquitoes.
4. On the Fourth of July in the following year, he observed *sporozoites* of bird malaria in a *Culex* mosquito's salivary glands.
5. Born in Almora, India, Ross was a British ship's surgeon who entered the Indian Medical Service in 1881. Of Scottish extraction, Sir Ronald was awarded the Nobel Prize for work in etiology.
6. A graduate in military medicine, Laveran was a French army physician & bacteriologist. In 1878, he went to Algeria where he discovered the blood parasite that causes malaria. He also received the Nobel Prize.
7. Since most female anopheles took blood every other night, resting on walls & ceilings before and & after feeding, resting places were sprayed with chemical poison. Because mosquitoes bred in stagnant water, drainage procedures were employed and petroleum used to destroy larvae in season.
8. In the tropics, a pernicious form of malaria produced sudden, violent attacks of intense cerebral disturbance, either delirium or coma, generally fatal.
9. .The term "yellow jack" originated with a flag of that color used to announce presence of contagion in naval hospitals and quarantined vessels.
10. A neighborhood developed along Charlotte Street between Sunset Parkway & Edgemont Road was known as Proximity Park, so named to indicate that is was close to town.

***

1. In 1885, John Pemberton, an Atlanta pharmacist, registered a trade mark for *French Wine Cola—Ideal Nerve & Tonic Stimulant*, a brew he developed in a three-legged pot stirred with an oar in his back yard. Since the stimulant is said to have contained cocaine, along with wine and a few other ingredients, the name may be seen as appropriate.
2. About a year later, he removed the wine from his recipe, added caffeine and extract of kola nut. His partner and bookkeeper, Frank Robinson, changed the name to *Coca-Cola* because he thought the two Cs, written in a Spencerian script popular at the time, would look good in advertising. Asa Candler bought sole rights in 1889 and began to sell the syrup, along with shapely little glasses.
3. Candler sold the parent company in 1919, then the largest business transaction in financial history of the South.

***

1. The business was owned by two of the town's most prominent citizens, Dr. Samuel H. Caldwell, a battlefield surgeon of the Civil War, and A.B. Mitchum, a banker.
2. Grove named his original compound *Feberlin*. Because of a high level of quinine, dangerous in high dosage, it could be sold only by prescription.
3. Yellow fever epidemics had spread along the Mississippi from New Orleans to St. Louis. By the turn of the century, an estimated half million deaths had been reported. The last major epidemic occurred in New Orleans in 1905.
4. With some 25 roads converging from Mexico to Canada, St. Louis was one of the great rail centers of the world, not only manufacturing but a distribution center for products representing the entire country.
5. One of the company's popular products was known as Bromo Laxative Quinine. Along the river in Arkansas, a freed slave gave it to one of her seven children, who completely recovered from chills and fever. In grateful recognition of its efficacy, she named him Laxative Bromo Quinine. He lived into healthy manhood with a nickname of "Laxy"
6. Grove met Pack and admired what he had done for the city, as well as his business acumen in timberlands. Pack died in 1906 and Grove started buying small tracts of timberland east of the Kimberly farmland.
7. Dr. Campbell had recently conducted funeral services for Zeb Vance, an event many saw as passing of an epoch in city life. He was talking to a man who would come to represent its modern phase.
8. In his journal, Seely later noted: "I think we felt nothing short of lonesome. 14,000 miles from home. I believe there were six or seven men who had been Americans at some time in their lives. Evelyn was the only American woman."
9. At one time, he owned 11,000 acres of prime land between St. Petersburg & Tampa. He also acquired substantial coal properties in West Virginia.

***

1. The wedding ceremony was held at King's Highway Presbyterian Church, where Grove was an elder.
2. The property was situated at the northeast corner of Liberty & Broad.

3. He reorganized the business from clerical departments to advertising to manufacturing.
4. Drawing upon experience, he invented a machine that would form, count & box tablets, which Grove had been first to foresee as the most popular future form of cold medicine. As incidence of malaria receded, these improvements would enable the company to adjust for a changing market and become a world leader in the field of cold remedies & medications for respiratory & digestive disorders.
5. Starting from Albemarle Park, he made his first acquisitions in a northerly direction.
6. Designed by R.S. Smith, it was built of rubble rock with tile on gable roof. Also small but practical, it continued as a place of considerable activity.
7. Plans called for a funicular counterweight like the one at Lookout Mountain, Chattanooga.
8. Plans called for the Clinchfield to be extended from Huntsdale to a new Asheville depot on the river at North Main and then by electric line via Hickory Nut Gap to Rutherfordton and Charlotte. The Howland lines extended from Sunset and the club across Kimberly lands to Grace, Newbridge, Craggy Station, Coleman's Boundary & Weaverville and part of its right-of-way would be used to make connections. (Reported 4-17-04 & other times.)

***

1. Seely was publisher, Grove principal stockholder. The first issue appeared early the following year. The newspaper succeeded where other publishing ventures had failed. Seely's strong editorials pushed for civic reform and helped abolish the chain gang. They also tended to create a climate that paved the way for adoption of prohibition.
2. Using Asheville as a base, they also started *Fortified Hills*, a residential subdivision on ample land holdings there. The name was intended to indicate strength & success and was an oblique reference to the burgeoning beverage business in Dixie.
3. Centered on Lawrence & Gertrude Place, Block A was offered in 1908 and soon expanded to include Edwin Place.
4. Raymoth was named for Col. Jas. M. Ray, commander of the celebrated 60th N.C. Regiment. It extended for perhaps a mile north of Hillside. He lived there at the time.
5. In 1900, the city boundary was extended to the river and the mountain.
6. St. Louis had been the capital of Upper Louisiana. The Louisiana Purchase Exposition was planned for 1903 to commemorate its centennial but was delayed a year. It was open from May 1 to December 1. There were nearly 20 million admissions and for many, it was their favorite fair.

***

1. Mr. Pack died in 1906 and Mr. Grove started buying small tracts of timberland east of the Kimberly farmlands.
2. The Sunset Parkway areas became available by 1914, sections of Macon by 1916, and lower Kimberly, along the golf course, by 1923.
3. He wanted local financial institutions to organize a syndicate and issue bonds to finance construction. Because of bank failures in 1897, the attitude of bank officials was still negative.
4. Among active business leaders of the day were H.W. Plummer, F.M. Weaver, E.C. Chambers, J.P. Sawyer, George Powell, Clarence Sawyer, W. Vance Brown, Fred Stikeleather, J.C. Pritchard, D. Harris, J.M. Chiles & S.P. Burton.
5. On November 6, 1911, Randolph wrote to Grove: "We have photographs and interiors sent by Mrs. Williams and regard them as the finest we have seen. We are glad to have material of this kind in view of the similar development you propose here."
6. The secretary of the Board of Trade wrote (12-12-11) to Grove, confirming a telegram sent earlier in the day. It referred to a decision by bankers not to finance the project but reaffirmed full support from the business community.
7. The Sunset Mountain Autoway, one of the first of its kind in the nation, was opened by Mr. Grove about this time.
8. Beginning February 26, 1912, each firm was given notice that plans did not meet with Mr. Grove's approval and he did not desire to continue competition.
9. The following month, Seely explained the situation to a friend: "We did not succeed in getting a satisfactory plan...and for that reason I undertook it myself and, strangely, made a plan that suited Mr. Grove."
10. Unlike a proposal for the mountaintop, this lower site would not put them at the mercy of the elements.

***

1. They spent the month of June developing the plan. Mrs. Grove turned the first spadeful of earth.
2. Some Italian stonemasons had worked at Biltmore.
3. Wagons were supplied by T.S. Morrison & Co. of Asheville. The automobile train attracted nationwide attention.
4. The project represented one of the largest continuous-pour concrete roofs in the world. The famous red tile was supplied by Murray Roofing Co. of Cloverport, Ky.
5. Four hundred rugs were woven on special order in Auvergne, France.
6. Lighting fixtures & equipment throughout were produced by Roycrofters. Its custom shops turned out two or three table

lamps for each of the 156 guest rooms and a copper ceiling light suspended on iron chains. Hallways & public rooms had custom ceiling lights, including eight copper & mica fixtures in the dining room and a dozen in the lobby.

7. In addition to more than 700 lighting fixtures, approximately 2,500 hammered copper drawer pulls were commissioned with Roycrofters for installation on bedroom tables & dressers manufactured by White Furniture Company at High Point.

8. A superb orchestral organ with 7,000 pipes was built by Ernest Skinner of Boston. It was sold in 1927 for a substantial sum.

***

1. Grove met Donald Ross at the opening. They were two of a kind and Grove was one of those who urged the Scottish golf master to concentrate on golf course architecture and start by redesigning the Asheville links. (See country club.)

2. After the inn went into full operational status, Mr. Randolph retired and was succeeded by W.R. Campbell. Randolph lived across the street from the little real estate office.

3. Consumptives were specifically cautioned not to seek entry.

4. At 2¼ miles, the Inn Gate and the Lodge Gate were equidistant from the monument on the Square.

5. Northeast of Charlotte Street Extension, his mountain lands were estimated to be in excess of 20,000 acres. On certain portions, he and associates engaged in cattle & sheep raising.

Grove Park Inn

George Vanderbilt Hotel

Battery Park Hotel

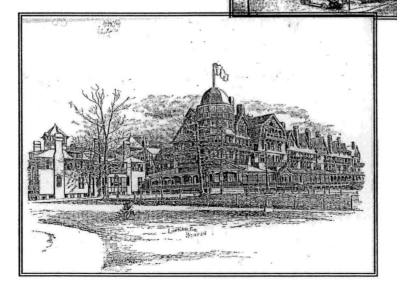

Biltmore

Old Country Club

Club Room, Biltmore

Biltmore Club

Billy Campbell House

Zealandia

Von Ruck Terrace

Top: Fred Seely's residence, *Overlook*

Right: Coxe family residence, *Klondyke*

Left: A typical Montford residence

Right: Von Ruck's *Winyah*

Bottom: A typical fashionable boarding house

Top: J.E. Rumbough

Left: Dr. F.A. Sondley

Right: Dr. Karl Von Ruck

Bottom: G.A.G. Westfeldt

PART THREE

SPECTRUM OF STYLE

ONE

A FAMOUS BOARDING HOUSE

SPEND YOUR SUMMERS AT
DIXIELAND
In Beautiful Altamont
America's Switzerland
Rates Reasonable—Both Transient and Tourist
Apply Eliza E. Gant, Prop.

"He writhed as he saw himself finally a toughened pachyderm in Eliza's world—sprucing up confidently, throwing his shoulders back proudly, making people "think he was somebody" as he cordially acknowledged an introduction by producing a card setting forth the joys of life in Altamont and at Dixieland, and seized every opening in social relations for the purpose of 'drumming up trade.'

"He hated the jargon of the profession, which she had picked up somewhere long before, and which she used constantly with such satisfaction—smacking her lips as she spoke of 'transients,' or of 'drumming up trade.' In him, as in Gant, there was a silent horror of selling for money the bread of one's table, the shelter of one's walls, to the guest, the stranger, the unknown friend from out the world; to the sick, the weary, the lonely, the broken, the knave, the harlot, and the fool."

Look Homeward, Angel

In the mid-Twenties, Tom Wolfe was usually in New York, teaching and composing the mountainous manuscript for which he would become famous. Released in series, it had a profound impact on the literary world and in time the last great volume would be titled *The Hills Beyond*.

Look Homeward was his first major work, published by Scribner's in the crucible of 1929. Chapter seven contains a memorable passage, describing the return of Gant the elder to his home town. It begins with these words: "This journey to California was Gant's last great voyage. He made it two years after Eliza's return from St. Louis, when he was fifty-six years old. In the great frame was already stirring the chemistry of pain and death."

Therein may be found an account of what is transpiring in the weary traveler's mind. Tormented by melancholy thoughts and rambling images of distant experiences leading up to the shock of stark reality upon his arrival back in Altamont…while interspersed briefly is a factual description of the familiar route home from the railway station.

Seeking inner meaning of life while exploring outer experience to the utmost degree was the author's never ending quest. In microcosm, this passage exemplifies that search. The date was

March 17, 1906. Street railway lines were burgeoning, new routes being proposed to all the outlying areas as far away as Burnsville & Rutherfordton. During warm weather, some 25 cars & more were running full & overflowing to Riverside on holidays & special occasions.

This was the raw cold of winter, however. Not a time for joy rides…or tourists. For another point of view, a different side of life in the same town…Come take a true trip on the "Toytown" trolley with Tom…

"This was the final flare of the old hunger that had once darkened in the small gray eyes, leading a boy into new lands and toward the soft stone smile of an angel.

"And he returned from nine thousand miles of wandering, to the bleak bare prison of the hills on a gray day late in winter.

"How looked the home-earth then to Gant the Far-Wanderer? Light crept grayly, melting on the rocky river, the engine smoke streaked out on dawn like a cold breath, the hills were big, but nearer, nearer than he thought. And Altamont lay gray and withered in the hills, a bleak mean wintry dot. He stepped carefully down in squalid Toytown, noting that everything was low, near, and shrunken as he made his Gulliverian entry. He had a roof-and-gulley high conviction; with careful tucked-in elbows he weighted down the heated Toytown street-car, staring painfully at the dirty pasteboard *pebbledash* of the Pisgah Hotel, the brick and board cheap warehouses of Depot Street, the rusty clapboard flimsiness of the Florence (Railway Men's) Hotel, quaking with beefed harlotry.

"So small, so small, so small, he thought. I never believed it. Even the hills here.

"'I'll soon be sixty.'

"His sallow face, thin-flanked, was hang-dog and afraid. He stared wistful-sullenly down at the rattan seat as the car screeched round into the switch at the cut and stopped; the motorman, smoke-throated, slid the door back and entered with his handle.

" 'Where you been, Mr. Gant?'

" 'California,' said Gant.

" 'Thought I hadn't seen you,' said the motorman.

"There was a warm electric smell and one of hot burnt steel.

"'…A land of life, a flower land. How clear the green clear sea was. And all the fishes swimming there. Santa Catalina. Those in the East should always go West. How came I here? Down, down—always down, did I know where? Baltimore, Sydney—…

" 'Jim Bowles died while you were gone, I reckon,' said the motorman.

" 'What!' howled Gant. 'Merciful God!' he clucked mournfully downward. "What did he die of?' he asked.

" 'Pneumonia,' said the motorman. 'He was dead four days after he was took down.'

" 'Why, he was a big healthy man in the prime of life,' said Gant. 'I was talking to him the day before I went away,' he lied, convincing himself permanently that this was true. 'He looked as if he had never known a day's sickness in his life.'

" 'He went home one Friday night with a chill,' said the motorman, "and the next Tuesday he was gone.'

"There was a crescent humming on the rails. With his thick glove finger he pushed away a clearing in the window-coated ice scurf and looked smokily out on the raw red cut-bank. The other car appeared abruptly at the end of the cut and curved with a skreeking jerk into the switch.

" 'No, sir,' said the motorman, sliding back the door, 'you never know who'll go next. Here to-day and gone to-morrow. Hit gits the big 'uns first sometimes.'

"He closed the door behind him and jerkily opened three notches of juice. The car ground briskly off like a wound toy.

"In the prime of life, thought Gant...

***

"But westward now he caught a glimpse of Pisgah and the western range. It was more spacious there. The hills climbed sunward to the sun. There was width to the eye, a smoking sun-hazed amplitude, the world convoluting and opening into the world, hill and plain, into the west. The West for desire, the East for home. To the east the short near mile-away hills reeked protectively above the town. Birdseye, Sunset.

"A straight plume of smoke coiled thickly from Judge Buck Sevier's smut-white clapboard residence on the decent side of Pisgah Avenue, thin smoke-wisps rose from the nigger shacks in the ravine below. Breakfast. Fried brains and eggs with streaky rashers of limp bacon. Wake, wake, wake you mountain grills!

"A paper-carrier, number 7, finished his route on the corner of Vine Street, as the car stopped, turned eastwards now from Pisgah Avenue toward the town core. The boy folded, bent, and flattened the fresh sheets deftly, throwing the block angularly thirty yards upon the porch of Shields the jeweler; it struck the boarding and bounded back with a fresh plop. Then he walked off with fatigued relief into time toward the twentieth century, feeling gratefully the ghost-kiss of absent weight upon his now free but still leaning right shoulder...

"The car still climbing, mounted the flimsy cheap-boarded brown-gray smuttiness of Skyland Avenue.

"America's Switzerland. The Beautiful Land of the Sky. Jesus God! Old Bowman said he'll be a rich many some day. Built up all the way to Pasadena...

"The car paused briefly at the car-shed, in sight of its stabled brothers. Then it moved reluctantly past the dynamic atmosphere of the Power & Light Company, wheeling bluntly into the gray frozen ribbon of Patton Avenue, running gently up hill near its end into the frore silence of the Square.

"Ah, Lord! Well do I remember. The old man offered me the whole piece for $1,000 three days after I arrived. Millionaire to-day if——-

"The car passed the Tuskegee on its eighty-yard climb into the Square. The fat slick worn leather-chairs marshaled between a fresh-rubbed gleaming line of brass spittoons squatted massively on each side of the entry door, before thick sheets of plate-glass that extended almost to the sidewalks with indecent nearness.

"Many a fat man's rump upon the leather. Like fish in a glass case. Traveling man's wet chewed cigar, spit-limp on his greasy lips. Staring at all the women. Can't look back long. Gives advantage.

"A negro bellboy sleepily wafted a gray dust-cloth across the leather. Within, before the replenished crackle-dance of the woodfire, the night-clerk sprawled out in the deep receiving belly of a leather divan.

"The car reached the Square, jolted across the netting of north-south lines, and came to a halt on the north side, facing east. Scurfing a patch away from the glazed window, Gant looked out.

The Square in the wan-gray frozen morning walled around him with frozen unnatural smallness. He felt suddenly the cramped mean fixity of the Square: this was the one fixed spot in a world that writhed, evolved, and changed constantly in his vision, and he felt a sick green fear, a frozen constriction about his heart because the centre of his life now looked so shrunken. He got very definitely the impression that if he flung out his arms they would strike against the walls of the mean three-and-four-story brickbuilt buildings that flanked the Square raggedly.

"Anchored to earth at last, he was hit suddenly by the whole cumulation of sight and movement, of eating, drinking, and acting that had gathered in him for two months. The limitless land, wood, field, hill, prairie, desert, mountain, the coast rushing away below his eyes, the ground that swam before his eyes at stations, the remembered ghosts of gumbo, oysters, huge Frisco sea-steaks, tropical fruits swarmed with the infinite life, the ceaseless pullulation of the sea. Here only, in this unreal-reality, this unnatural vision, did life lose its movement, change, color.

"The Square had the horrible concreteness of a dream. At the far southeastern edge he saw his shop: his name painted hugely in dirty scaly white across the brick near the roof: W. O. Gant— Marbles, Tombstones, Cemetery Fixtures. It was like a dream of hell, when a man finds his own name staring at him from the Devil's ledger; like a dream of death, when he who comes as mourner finds himself in the coffin, or as witness to a hanging, the condemned upon the scaffold.

"A sleepy negro employed at the Manor Hotel clambered heavily up and slumped into one of the seats reserved for his race at the back. In a moment he began to snore gently through his blubbered lips.

"At the east end of the Square, Big Bill Messler, with his vest half-unbuttoned over his girdled paunch-belly, descended slowly the steps of the City Hall, and moved soundingly off with country leisure along the cold-mettalic sidewalk. The fountain, ringed with a thick bracelet of ice, played at quarter-strength a sheening glut of ice-blue water.

"Cars droned separately into their focal positions; the carmen stamped their feet and talked smokily together; there was a breath of beginning life. Beside the City Hall, the fireman slept above their wagons: behind the bolted door great hoofs drummed woodenly.

"A dray rattled across the east end of the Square before the City Hall, the old horse leaning back cautiously as he sloped down into the dray market by the oblique cobbled passage at the southeast that cut Gant's shop away from the market and 'calaboose.' As the car moved eastward again, Gant caught an angular view of Niggertown across this passage. The settlement was plumed delicately with a hundred tiny fumes of smoke.

"The car sloped swiftly now down Academy Street, turned, as the upper edge of the negro settlement impinged steeply from the valley upon the white, into Ivy Street, and proceeded north along a street bordered on one side by smutty pebble-dash cottages, and on the other by a grove of lordly oaks, in which the large quaking plaster pile of old Professor Bowman's deserted School for Young Ladies loomed desolately, turning and stopping at the corner, at the top of the Woodson Street hill, by the great wintry, wooden, and deserted barn of the Ivy Hotel. It had never paid.

"Gant kneed his heavy bag before him down the passage, depositing it for a moment at the curbing before he descended the hill. The unpaved frozen clay fell steeply and lumpily away. It was steeper, shorter, nearer than he thought. Only the trees looked large. He saw Duncan come out on his porch, shortsleeved, and pick up the morning paper. Speak to him later. Too long now. As he expected, there was a fat coil of morning smoke above the Scotchman's chimney, but none from his own.

"He went down the hill, opening his iron gate softly, and going around to the side entrance by the yard, rather than ascend the steep veranda steps. The grape vines, tough and barren, writhed about the house like sinewy ropes. He entered the sitting-room quietly. There was a strong odor of cold leather. Cold ashes were strewn thinly in the grate. He put his bag down and went back through the wash-room into the kitchen. Eliza, wearing one of his old coats, and a pair of fingerless woollen gloves, poked among the embers of a crawling little fire.

" 'Well, I'm back,' Gant said.

" 'Why, what on earth!' she cried as he knew she would, becoming flustered and moving her arms indeterminately. He laid his hand clumsily on her shoulder for a moment. They stood awkwardly without movement. Then he seized the oil-can, and drenched the wood with kerosene. The flame roared up out of the stove.

" 'Mercy, Mr. Gant,' cried Eliza, 'you'll burn us up!'

"But, seizing a handful of cut sticks and the oil-can, he lunged furiously toward the sitting-room.

"As the flame shot roaring up from the oiled pin sticks, and he felt the fire-full chimney-throat tremble, he recovered joy. He brought back the width of the desert; the vast yellow serpent of the river, alluvial with the mined accretions of the continent; the rich vision of laden ships, massed above the sea-walls, the world nostalgic ships, bearing about them the filtered and concentrated odors of the earth, sensual negroid rum and molasses, tar, ripening guavas bananas, tangerines, pineapples in the warm holds of tropical boats, as cheap, as profuse, as abundant as the lazy equatorial earth and all its women; the great names of Louisiana, Texas, Arizona, Colorado, California; the blasted fiend-world of the desert, and the terrific boles of trees, tunneled for the passage of a coach; water that fell from a mountain-top in a smoking noiseless coil, internal boiling lakes flung skywards by the punctual respiration of the earth, the multitudinous torture in form of granite oceans, gouged depthlessly by canyons, and iridescent with the daily chameleon-shift beyond man, beyond nature, of terrific colors, below the un-human iridesence of the sky.

"Eliza, still excited, recovering speech, followed him into the sitting-room, holding her chapped gloved hands clasped before her stomach while she talked.

"I was saying to Steve last night, 'It wouldn't surprise me if your papa would come rolling in at any moment now'—I just had a feeling, I don't know what you'd call it," she said, her face plucked inward by her sudden fabrication of legend," but it's pretty strange when you come to think about it. I was in Garret's the other day ordering some things, some vanilla extract, soda and a pound of coffee when Aleck Carter came up to me. 'Eliza,' he said, 'when's Mr. Gant coming back—I think I may have a job for him?' 'Why, Aleck,' I said, 'I don't much expect him before the first of April.' Well, sir, what do you know—I had no sooner got out on the street—I suppose I must have been thinking of something else, because I remember Emma Aldrich came by and hollered to me and I didn't think to answer her until she had gone on by, so I called out just as big as you please to her, 'Emma!'– the thing flashed over me all of a sudden—I was just as sure of it as I'm standing here—'what do you think? Mr. Gant's on his way back home.' "

"Jesus God! thought Gant. It's begun again.

"Her memory moved over the ocean-bed of event like a great octopus, blindly but completely feeling its way into every seacave, rill, and estuary, focussed on all she had done, felt and thought, with sucking Pentlandian intentness, for whom the sun shone, or grew dark, rain fell, and mankind came, spoke, and died, shifted for a moment in time out of its void into the Pentlandian core, pattern and heart of purpose.

"Meanwhile, as he laid big gleaming lumps of coal upon the wood, he muttered to himself, his mind ordering in a mounting sequence, with balanced and climactic periods, his carefully punctuated rhetoric.

"Yes, musty cotton, baled and piled under long sheds of railway sidings; and odorous pine woodlands of the level South, saturated with brown faery light, and broken by the tall straight leafless poles of trees; a woman's leg below an elegantly lifted skirt mounting to a carriage in Canal Street (French or creole probably); a white arm curved reaching for a window shade, French-olive faces window-glimmering, the Georgia doctor's wife who slept above him going out, the unquenchable fish-filled abundance of the unfenced, blue, slow cat-slapping lazy Pacific; and the river, the all-drinking, yellow, slow-surging snake that drained the continent. His life was like that river, rich with its own deposited and onward-borne agglutinations, fecund with its sedimental accretions, filled exhaustlessly by life in order to be more richly itself, and this life, with the great purpose of a river, he emptied now into the harbor of his house, the sufficient haven of himself, for whom the gnarled vines wove round him thrice, the earth burgeoned with abundant fruit and blossom, the fire burnt madly.

"What have you got for breakfast?" he said to Eliza.

"Why," she said, pursing her lips meditatively, "would you like some eggs?"

"Yes," said he, "with a few rashers of bacon and a couple of pork sausages.

"He strode across the dining-room and went up the hall.

"Steve! Ben! Luke! You damned scoundrels!" he yelled. "Get up!

"Their feet thudded almost simultaneously upon the floor.

"Papa's home!" they shrieked.

"Mr. Duncan watched butter soak through a new-baked roll. He looked through his curtain angularly down, and saw thick acrid smoke biting heavily into the air above Gant's house.

"He's back," said he, with satisfaction.

"So, at the moment looking, Tarkinton of the paints said: "W.O.'s back."

Thus came he home, who had put out to land westward, Gant the Far-Wanderer.

Endnotes

1. Cars awaiting railway passengers stood on the switch or passing tracks in front of the main entrance on Depot Street. From there, a car moved over Lyman's Crossing (freight sidings) and up the hillside slope where the right-of-way cut through the woods into company property at Mud Cut.

2. Pisgah Avenue was South French Broad, Aston Park at the first corner. Turning eastward, Vine was Hilliard, Skyland Asheland, Hatton Patton and the Tuskegee the former Grand Central, now the deteriorating Berkeley. Shields were Fields, the leading jewelry store, then in the Drhumor Building.

3. Upon entering the Square, cars passed over the noisy & confusing switching web or grid of the central track exchange on their way to the north side terminus where passengers were discharged directly to the sidewalk near the fountain & monument.

4. Heading northeast, the car now became a part of the Charlotte Street line, winding around the little gooseneck of Market into Academy (College) and then across the one-block length of Ivy (Oak) to the corner of Woodson (Woodfin) where it again followed one block before turning into Charlotte and continuing straight to the end of the line at the golf links & club house.

5. There were two routes to the station. Depot via Southside was the original trip. The second was provided by excavation of Mud Cut in 1900-1. After completion of Grove Park Inn, through cars ran from Old Toll Road there to Brevard Road (Dunwell Avenue) via the new bridge.

6. The Manor Hotel (not the Manor) was on the southwest corner of the Square. The Western was owned by Dr. McBrayer, who became state health officer.

7. Earlier cars had a motorman and a conductor; later Birney cars had only a motorman, with a fare box.

TWO

THE BINGHAMS

While Wolfe was setting the standard for skillful writing about the family boarding house, the epitome of social standards and mores in the community was represented by the Bingham School and the famous family that operated it for four generations. It also had a profound effect on public education.

The cadets were a part of social life in Asheville through a variety of activities ranging from churches to parades and other public events to tea dances. The young ladies were invited to events at the school and in turn the cadets were participants in social functions all over town.

The Bingham name itself was a badge of distinction. During August of 1918, the headmaster's son, Robert Worth Bingham, purchased the *Louisville Courier-Journal* and thereby established another dynasty that would be the subject of journalistic scrutiny and speculation for decades to come. It was called the "royal family" of Kentucky.

A pillar of North Carolina education, the Bingham Military School was founded in 1873 when a group of Wilmington men, traveling in Scotland, had looked into the university while visiting Glasgow. They were favorably impressed, and with so much enthusiasm that they wanted to engage the services of a faculty member to come to America and establish a school for their sons.

The young man selected was carefully chosen for his character and ability. He was the Rev. William Bingham. He arrived at Wilmington, Delaware, for reasons now obscure, but was finally able to reach North Carolina after a long and arduous journey. While the Scotch-Irish came down the Great Wagon Road, the Scots themselves came in numbers to the Cape Fear River and thence up its waters to the place where they founded Campbelltown, renamed for the Marquis de Lafayette following his visit there.

This school was established in Wilmington along Scottish lines and principles but shortly thereafter was moved out into the countryside of the county. For reasons similar to those which impelled the founders of the University of North Carolina to select Orange County as a site for the first state university, the school was moved there, at Mebane near Chapel Hill. Activity in Asheville in the late Eighties attracted wide attention and a decision was reached to move the school to the social and physical climate of the Land of the Sky.

The 250-acre site was one of the finest in the city, a majestic bluff overlooking the French Broad, adjacent to the estate Richmond Pearson was in process of creating. Across the river, the Montford community was just getting started. On the bank, a rustic park had been established for recreational purposes of a casual nature. And plans had been considered to extend the street car line to a new terminus there at Pearson's Bridge.

The academy commenced relocated operations effective with the 1889-90 term. Standards were based on uncompromising Presbyterian principles that gained it a wide reputation for integrity and merit. Its graduates held high commissions and fought at the front in every war in which the United States participated. America's leading diplomat during the First World War, Walter Hines Page, was a "Bingham boy." He served throughout, 1913 to 1918, as United States ambassador to the Court of St. James's and played the key diplomatic role in Allied opposition to the Kaiser Wilhelm.

Born at Mebane, Robert W. Bingham was an instructor on the faculty of the school in Asheville. His political career took him to Kentucky and from there to the top. By the end of the epoch, he was regarded as one of the foremost social, political, and diplomatic personalities in America, and this led to his appointment in the same role as his predecessor. An Independent Democrat, he was not appointed to high office under the Hoover administration but when Mr. Roosevelt took office, he was ready to appoint him as secretary of state.

An Anglophile, Bingham was regarded by many as an ideal choice for the top diplomatic assignment in London. Immediately thereafter, Roosevelt chose him for that position and instead named Cordell Hull as secretary of state. He remained there until his death, becoming a part of British social life. Honored by the monarch, granted honorary degrees by Oxford and Cambridge. With war clouds then darkening on the horizon, he found himself in a similar position to that of his earliest predecessor and he sought to follow honorably in his footsteps.

Along the way, Bingham married into several of the most wealthy and prominent families in America, notably Kenan, Flagler and Morgan. His marriage on May 20, 1896 to Eleanor E. Miller of Louisville ended with her death during a controversial automobile accident in 1913. On November 15, 1916, he married the former Mary Lily Kenan, widow of Henry M. Flagler, father of modern day Florida. A former partner of J. P. Morgan and John D. Rockefeller. She died just eight months later, leaving him an extensive fortune.

The Binghams of Asheville remained on Bingham Heights. His father was in command of the school, instrumental in establishment of compulsory public education. A distinguished captain of Confederate infantry during the war, Col. Robert Bingham was deeply concerned over the plight of education in the Tar Heel state, once described as that "vale of humility between two mountains of conceit." As a result of extreme poverty, the public school system was virtually non-existent. Those who could afford it were educated by private tutors or small academies. Except in a few large towns, the rest generally had to fend for themselves.

Bingham led an intellectual and moral crusade for improvement which led to many reforms, including compulsory education, a system of normal schools for the establishment of minimum standards, a woman's college at Greensboro, and an agricultural and mechanical school at Raleigh which evolved into North Carolina State University. The educational renaissance at the turn of the century under Governor Aycock followed Bingham's repeated exhortations in a classic vein.

Colonel Bingham served as head of the school from 1873 until becoming headmaster emeritus in 1920, when his son-in-law became commandant. A firm influence for right causes and principles to the last, Bingham passed away quietly on May 8, 1927. Funeral services were conducted by Dr. Campbell the following day. As in 1914 when word was received of the death of George Vanderbilt and earlier that of George Pack, flags of city and suburbs were flown at half staff. Some saw it as a symbol of possible social change as well.

Throughout travels of Colonel Bingham's illustrious son, the Binghams of Asheville remained on Bingham Heights and he was a frequent visitor to the city, where he maintained many ties. In spring of the year following, Col. S. R. McKee, speaking for the administration, announced plans for construction of a major new building that fall. Later there was another announcement, the school would be closed during construction. It never reopened. The road of progress was being closed down with barriers and detour signs, the economic bridge about to be washed out, and it went down with the rest. After four generations starting with the ambassador's great-grandfather, the school was out of business.

Unlike his staunch Presbyterian forebears, Robert W. Bingham became a devout Episcopalian and an active participant in the Anglican Communion of Britain and America. The family in Asheville included his sisters, Mrs. S. Reid McKee and Mrs. Robert Temple Grinnan, affectionately known in the community as Sadie, and the McKee children, Robert B. McKee, Miss Martha McKee and Miss Sadie Temple McKee.

In later years, remaining members lived in one or two of the almost deserted old buildings standing on the bluff. An old fashioned family carrying on where this distinguished and venerable institution had been a vital factor in the life of the city. A social influence since it was founded in the year Louis XVI lost his head during the French Revolution.

As the corps came into rigid formation for its closing review along the old courtyard, tears fell from some who watched those ranks with many emotions.

Endnotes

1. On August 20, 1924, he married Aleen (Muldoon) Hilliard of Louisville in London. She survived him.
2. He received degrees from the University of North Carolina, the School of Law there, the University of Louisville, the University of Michigan, and honorary degrees both in America and Britain. (He was graduated from the family school in 1888.)
3. Mary Lily was the sister of Wm. Rand Kenan, Jr. Under terms of a hotly contested will, the famous Kenan fellowships, scholarships, and professorships were established at the University of North Carolina and the Kenan and Morehead families became the university's leading benefactors. Bequests were suggested by Mr. Bingham.
4. Some accounts describe Colonel Bingham as father of compulsory education in the South.
5. .5. Bingham and Hull were born (1871) a few weeks apart, the latter in Overton County, Tennessee, south of Louisville.
6. In August of 1918, he bought a two-thirds interest in the *Courier-Journal* and the afternoon *Times*. Remaining shares were acquired the following year. It became one of the most important regional newspapers in the country. He also established WHAS, the first radio station in Kentucky.
7. Bingham was succeeded in London by Jos. P. Kennedy, founder of a different dynasty.

THREE

A FASHIONABLE WORLD

In 1904, when Asheville still retained characteristics of the previous century with respect to natural scenic qualities, many ordinary citizens intended to go to the great world exposition in St. Louis. Wolfe's family left on the train...

In his first published novel, we read early on: "He was vaguely appeased. The train jerked, and moved off slowly. He kissed her clumsily. 'Let me know as soon as you get there,' he said, and he strode swiftly down the aisle.

" 'Good-by, good-by,' cried Eliza, waving Eugene's small hand at the long figure on the platform. 'Children,' she said, 'wave good-by to your papa.' They all crowded to the window. Eliza wept."

***

"Eugene watched the sun wane and redden on a rocky river, and on the painted rocks of Tennessee gorges: the enchanted river wound into his child's mind forever. Years later, it was to be remembered in dreams tenanted with elvish and mysterious beauty. Stilled in great wonder, he went to sleep to the rhythmical pounding of the heavy wheels."

***

While a smell of raw lumber, steel, and dynamite was rising in Spruce Pine, the odor of fresh paint and plaster was in the air of late May on Depot Street as remains of the old station came down, and news from New Orleans was starting to make headlines here and across the country.

Spring excursions had been bringing in 300, 500 and 700 visitors at a time, second sections ran on some trains, and the Board of Trade was predicting a banner year. Private carriages and public hacks were lined up as excited drivers and starters competed with trolley cars for passengers.

Those arriving in time for the summer season found a fine new passenger station there to accommodate them and civic representatives, male and female, there to greet and welcome them. The station's style was influenced by Spanish and Indian architecture of the Great Southwest, a region coming into popularity. With its large central rotunda and circular dome, it created a somewhat exotic impression in a city not otherwise noted for such. But reports from the Crescent City related to entirely different matters.

Another epidemic of yellow fever had broken out and thousands were leaving for Chattanooga and Asheville, some stopping at Highlands or going up to Roan and other high elevations. The Queen & Crescent Route between Cincinnati, Chattanooga, Birmingham and New Orleans was running extra sections and although new sanitation measures at Memphis had brought things under control there, many were leaving that cotton trading center anyway to be on the safe side. At Mobile, a similar situation.

In the fall, this traffic slackened but by then, other traffic was rising and during the following year, there was as much activity at midnight as at noon, with crews and staff handling more than 30 regularly scheduled passenger trains a day. Special excursion trains were advertised for Atlanta, Chattanooga, Charleston, Washington, Norfolk, and other destinations, including special events such as the Kentucky Derby, first run in 1875.

The Depot was a cool and comfortable sanctuary, comparatively speaking. Huge oak benches were provided for waiting passengers, some wearing white linen suits and Panama hats, beneath a ceiling that stretched high into the dome atop the building. New electric fans whirred and personal straw fans were offered for sale at modest prices, usually a few cents or a nickel. Water coolers boasted of mountain reservoirs as source of supply. An office of the Travelers Aid Society was open, with licensed nurse on duty. A barber shop with manicurist and "shoe shine" attendant.

A small but spacious formal restaurant beckoned and the usual cigar stand offered high grade Cuban stogies and newspapers from leading Southern cities, a few Eastern centers as well. Charlie Mascari, the Italian born fruit vendor up on Patton, had a small stand with premium grade fruit, a family member in charge. Iced tea, lemonade, and Coca-Cola vendors manned their white carts and uniformed porters moved about, ever ready to handle luggage and baggage for any purpose, with an easy, friendly smile. Few passengers were trying to get anywhere in a hard rush. Those who did were usually called Yankees, regardless of origin.

For *crème de la crème*, there was the *Toxaway Special* from Asheville into Sapphire Country. This had nothing like the traffic to popular destinations such as Mitchell but those who thought going to the mountains meant going into the mountains found it highly desirable, even if routing was circuitous. This was for Pullmans. Even with all-Pullman trains. Even all-drawing room cars. And, yes, like Palm Beach, even with private sidings for those arriving in private cars. And logging trains added substantial revenues to some of these same lines.

At the turn of the century, as the Manor was being opened, the idea of an exclusive resort in the heart of the mountains had been explored, accessibility provided along the route of a leading logging road. Some 20,000 acres of prime gameland were acquired in Transylvania County on the South Carolina border. With cooperation from Louis Carr, J. Francis Hayes of New Castle, Pennsylvania, organized the Toxaway Company, which built the Toxaway Inn, Mt. Toxaway Lodge with individual lodges on Mt. Toxaway, Sapphire Inn on Sapphire Lake, and Fairfield Inn on Fairfield Lake.

During the 1890s, several attempts to build a rail line from Hendersonville to Brevard ended in bankruptcy but it was finally completed and in 1903, with advent of the new enterprise, extended to Toxaway in time for opening of the inn. To bring passengers in, a regular train schedule from the East was established. The *Toxaway Special.* Passengers boarded at Penn Station in New York, Philadelphia, Wilmington, Baltimore, and Washington. In Asheville, motive power was changed for a run to the land of waterfalls. At its peak, there were 14 trains daily in each direction.

The *piece de resistence* was Toxaway Inn, a five star, five story hotel with deluxe accommodations for five hundred guests. Open year round, Sapphire Inn could handle 50 guests on a lesser basis. The Charleston trade, including Savannah, Columbia, Aiken & Augusta, generally came in by traditional ornate private carriage although some used the *Carolina Special.* The so-called Eastern Establishment came by rail. The influx of "rich millionaires" made it something to behold. Some made stopovers in Asheville, most remained aboard for direct passage.

Passenger lists read like a gold plated, blue ribbon directory of American business, starting with Mr. Vanderbilt. R.J. Reynolds, Dukes of Durham. Nunnallys of Atlanta. Flaglers of Florida. Rockefellers of New York. Wanamakers, Pews, and other leading families of Philadelphia. Residents of the Main Line. DuPonts of Wilmington. Mellons and steelmakers of Pittsburgh. Braumeisters of Milwaukee and St. Louis. Astors of Manhattan and Armours of Chicago. Successful textile magnates and others of the New South. High financiers from Jekyll Island.

***

These were poignant images that drew the appreciative to the region for reasons of beauty and then for matters of health, but when the dreaded scourge known as consumption began to spread across country, the significance of Asheville as a place name took on a new dimension. Smiles vanished. The health resort of Asheville would emerge as the leading center in the United States for treatment of the disease.

Although many did not realize it, tuberculosis was an ancient disease. Some of the earliest human skeletons to be unearthed show evidence of its course. One of the commanding infectious plagues of the world, it had reached epidemic proportions in Europe and America during the 19th century, thereby gaining the soubriquet of "great white plague." Those suffering a massive spread of infection were said to be in the throes of "galloping consumption."

A massive body of medical study, research, and opinion failed to produce a cure. Furthermore, professional opinion sometimes seemed to be in a state of flux. Therefore, "T.B." was a disease of fear and mystery, a condition exacerbated by secrecy. People tended to whisper or lower their voices about who the next victim might be and all sorts of characteristics were ascribed to patients, generally centering around their supposed intensity of physical, mental, and emotional creativity and drive. For an actual certainty, however, nobody seemed to know much.

The original "old tuberculin"…O.T.…a term embracing various preparations of protein, was developed in 1890 by the illustrious Robert Koch. At the Tenth International Congress of Medicine in Berlin that year, he announced his creation as a substance that could protect against tuberculosis, probably even cure it. His statement was electrifying. News spread rapidly and consumptives from all over stormed into Berlin, seeking this healing agent. He would not divulge the nature of his "remedy," however, until forced to do so by ethical pressures. Not long afterward, claims were discredited. Meanwhile, more patients were probably killed than helped.

In 1882, Koch discovered the causative microorganism and brilliantly demonstrated that it was essential to development of the disease, thereby making possible its exact experimental study. In that same year, Carlo Forlanini of Italy introduced nitrogen gas into the pleural sac that envelops the lung, thus permitting the lung to deflate upon itself. The idea came from the fact that since 1696, it had been observed that soldiers suffering from T.B. sometimes showed improvement following a penetrating wound of the chest which brought about collapse of the lung. It provided an alternate method of treatment to excisional surgery.

As a result of these and other advances in the art and science of medicine, interest in treatment was renewed, rather than consideration of serious patients as essentially hopeless cases. There was confusion, however, as to proper conditions under which patients should be kept. In the absence of proven fact, many authorities felt that it was a good idea, physically and psychologically, for them to be confined to areas of pure fresh air, and beautiful mountain settings, free from impurities, became destinations of choice.

The concept of a mountain town like Asheville as a good place for upper class patients may have come to mind in part because of the first meaning of sanatorium. A health resort, a locality selected as a retreat because of its salubrity; specifically, a high altitude summer station in a tropical country for European troops, officials, or residents. As Darjeeling in India. British writers and culture were popular in that day. And the concept of fashionable Asheville was based largely on British standards.

As the city became known as a center for tuberculosis, there was confusion over names. Most included the word "sanitarium." In practice, however, the words were sometimes published interchangeably as <u>sanitarium</u>, <u>sanitorium</u>, <u>sanatarium</u>, <u>sanatorium</u>. One long time resident remarked: "Lord only knows what the doctors call it...and some of the patients aren't ever goin' to get well anyway...so they might just as soon call it a moratorium." The *Asheville Spectator* suffered a spate of difficulties getting various customs of resorts and nomenclature straight, in the process eliciting the appellation of *expectorator* from some detractors.

To some, there was a stigma attached to it. The subject made people cautious or uncomfortable. No one knew how contagious the ghostly, ghastly disease might actually be. With hundreds coming and going, there was always a question of where the line was drawn between tubercular and others. The city's reputation was attracting an increasing number of knowledgeable persons but ordinary citizens knew little of clinical history.

The area around Asheville was becoming a national center for boys and girls in summer camps. A girl was the only child from Asheville enrolled at a fashionable camp some distance from the city. During parents visitation, one mother was heard to inquire in clearly audible tones, "Oh, isn't that the one, you know, the child from that T.B. place?" Such comments may have lacked tact but cause of concern was understandable.

Local newspapers, which carried little hard news of a regional nature, compounded the situation by keeping "T.B. stories" out of their editions. Much of their local coverage was semi-fictional and so regarded by the more sophisticated readership; many influential subscribers wanted more of it to boost the town and encourage "progress and prosperity" out of its previous condition of "backwardness and regression." Accordingly, the policy was generally accepted.

When truth is stifled, however, circuitous communication and direct word-of-mouth reporting takes on primary credibility. Social goings-on and T.B. doings were the talk of the town. Only too happy to report bad news emanating elsewhere, local press turned a blind eye to such within its own boundaries. With freedom of the press comes a constitutional right to stifle the news. And emergence of the city as a center for medical treatment contributed to its rise as a cosmopolitan center in general. Architects, artisans, actors, academics, authors, and attorneys. Many who recovered remained to play major roles in life of the city. Although seemingly an anomaly, the two were compatible.

***

As we have seen, emergence of Asheville as a health resort and medical center did not come about overnight. Before the white man arrived, the Cherokee had reserved a neutral territory near

Hot Springs, one to which they could bring their sick and wounded, aging and ailing. Bishop Asbury himself was consumptive.

The idea of mountain therapy originated in studies of Alpine life, particularly among German speaking people. In 1821, Dr. J.F.B. Hardy, a Presbyterian layman, came to Asheville from South Carolina as the city's first physician, cured himself, and remained to practice medicine for 61 years. His stature and reputation was an influence in establishment of the colony at Flat Rock.

***

Like Mr. Pack, Dr. Battle stayed at the Swannanoa until the Battery Park opened. A widower, he lived as a highly visible and valuable member of society. According to Robert Latham, editor of the *Asheville Citizen* who had won the Pulitzer Prize as editor of the *Charleston News & Courier,* "he was a gifted speaker on any occasion. Diction was polished, phraseology carefully chosen. A sparking and pungent wit, he was at his best as an after-dinner speaker, and a raconteur blessed with an unusually retentive memory."

"Distinctively individual in all things, Dr. Battle was particularly so in his attire. He never followed fashions; he set his own, and no matter what he wore, it always seemed a part of him, rather than an external decoration. Outside of the formal evening silk *topper,* his favorite headgear was a soft felt hat of the wide-brimmed variety. In winter he wore a cape, reaching almost to his knees. A white flannel suit, with a black silk sash in lieu of a waistcoat, was his usual summer attire. In evening clothes, of masterful cut and fit, he was in truth the glass of fashion and the mold of form. Always he carried the small rattan cane so popular with English and Indian army officers…

"Dressed with meticulous care, pointed mustachios, carefully trimmed Vandyke, and a military air withal. With cape and cane swinging as he came down Battery Park Hill, across Haywood and up the avenue, it was little wonder that fellow members sitting in the windows of the Asheville Club watched him with admiring interest." An alter ego to proprietor of the hotel on the hill. Dr. Irby Stephens described him as the very essence of Southern aristocrat. "Courtly, elegant, and strikingly handsome, endowed with irresistible personal charm."

After graduation from Virginia, he studied medicine in New York City and attained a medical degree from Bellevue there. He embarked on a career as a naval surgeon but was forced to retire because of injuries incurred while on sea duty. Interested in tuberculosis, he was a firm believer in the theory of climato-therapy and made his own geographical studies before selecting Asheville as the ideal area for pulmonary treatment.

Following opening of Winyah sanitarium, he delivered a paper before the medical society. In it, he made special reference to merits of the Asheville plateau. His enthusiasm was unreserved. There is "nothing like it east of the Rockies," he stated. The climate is "tonic, invigorating, and bracing." He attributed an almost antiseptic quality to the air, in that "conditions which seem to favor germ propagation and prolong species of the genus *bacterium* do not exist here," noting that as a rule, natives were not afflicted.

And his field of influence was not limited to that of the dread disease.

Second Section

Seen through the eyes of Martha Rumbough, the world of Dr. Battle was certainly significant but the realm of society came into much sharper focus. One involved the other. Where traces of one were found, the other would not be far away. And in this peacetime era, the symbiosis might be exemplified by neighbors on a rise near the end of the Montford district.

Montford was a counterpart to Hot Springs, in its own way as much a part of the social scene as Sulphur Springs. The place along the French Broad River where Pattons built their 200-room Warm Springs Hotel, one of the South's finest resorts. With its great colonial colonnade of 13 white pillars, each representing an original state, it was a stately structure rivaling the city's best. Woven into social fabric of the time.

Here was an attraction to prominent visitors from every state, with facilities to accommodate them in style, including a dining room seating 600 persons and the second largest ballroom in the Old North State. A place where the legendary Wade Hampton, one of the South's wealthiest men, had built his own "cottage" next door. The hostelry in which Zeb Vance had worked as a young man. And the tranquil spot that had inspired Christian Reid to write *The Land of the Sky* while she was a contented guest.

Situated in a park with a 100-acre expanse of river bottom between turnpike and river, it was a prime destination. During the war, a stagecoach operator purchased it for his own. The buyer was James H. Rumbough of Greeneville who settled his family in Hampton Cottage there in 1862. Because of his successful role in transportation and hotel operations, he had received a commission in the Quartermaster Corps of the Confederate States Army.

By 1873, the hotel was being advertised all over the country and before long, business was strong. With arrival of the railroad from the east, Colonel Rumbough's son, James Edwin, came to Asheville. With a close eye on the railroad situation, he kept his father informed of developments and two years later, when the line from Asheville reached that point, they were ready for passengers with an elegant 350-room hotel. All to have it go up in smoke just two years later from "a fire of undetermined origin."

Dismayed, Colonel Rumbough "sold the rubble" along with two family mansions and much of the village to Southern Improvement Company, a northern syndicate. In 1886, as the Battery Park was going up in Asheville, they built the Mountain Park as a friendly competitor. A spring of higher temperature was discovered, prompting a change of name from Warm Springs to Hot Springs. The state's first golfing club was organized here, with its beautiful landscaped upper lawn and lower lawn, and a bathhouse of 16 marble pools.

Young Rumbough was in a business where the prospect of railway service meant exciting new opportunities. He placed himself in a position to monitor them. A year earlier, the first warehouse for flue-cured tobacco in the city was opened in time for the fall market season. Impressed by rapidly rising activity, he took rooms at the Swannanoa, in the center of the auction district, where he could look down on proceedings, and entered the business. It proved highly profitable.

Thus he was on his way to becoming a successful entrepreneur at a time when native capitalists were few. A bachelor, he had time to travel back and forth along the banks of the river between the resort downstream…the river flowed north…and his seasonal business interests in the city. In a sense, an early business commuter. With a new Depot car stop at the door.

***

Meanwhile, another aspect of these social relationships was developing in Philadelphia where the house of John G. Baker at Kensington, a neighborhood sometimes known as Northern Liberties, became birthplace of an admired only child.

Martha Elizabeth Baker was the apple of her father's eye, a thoughtful and observant girl who would become increasingly interested in literature, theatre, and travel. Her memory was vivid and over the years she became a repository of family and social history. What others forgot, she remembered.

To broaden horizons, her father began taking her on annual trips to social watering holes, beautiful gathering places for affluent northern and western sections of the city. Watkins Glen. Ausable Chasm. Niagara Falls. Catskills, Adirondacks. Lake George, Lake Champlain. Thousand Lakes region of Canada. Rock bound coast of Maine from Camden to Bar Harbor. Kennebunkport.

Annual trips soon became quarterly. Along the way, she eventually became familiar with the best hotels of Manhattan. "The Astor House, down near Wall Street and Trinity Church, was the first hotel I had ever visited," she recalled. "Our rooms faced out over the old church cemetery. Father had taken Mother and me to see the great city of New York. I was about 12 years old and I wanted to ride around in the old horse car belt, so we did that too. We went to the Stock Exchange. And we saw the great Brooklyn Bridge." Built between 1872 and 1883, it was under construction, then about half way to completion.

"I stayed at the St. Denis with friends once en route to my first voyage to Europe. It was on Broadway at about 10th Street. Father liked the Brevoort House on Fifth Avenue. It had the best restaurant and wine cellar, and all the *bon vivants* from miles around were to be seen there with their congenial cronies. One of my (later) favorite shopping luncheons was lobster patty with shrimp sauce, followed by a trip over to Maillard's for French chocolate ice cream. There were many wonderful *chocolatiers.* Henri's was fine, later Sherry's, and much later came Page & Shaw, but Maillard's was my choice of them all.

"The Waldorf-Astoria was a great place for Southerners to meet. They all liked *Peacock Alley,* as someone dubbed it, a hallway with a double row of high backed, carved King Charles chairs, very becoming to the average well dressed woman. In after years, it was a thoroughfare, a meeting place for all sorts and conditions of people, so it lost its charm. And then much later, of course, they tore it down to build the world's greatest skyscraper, but everyone remembers Oscar, the head waiter.

Martha's father was a successful inventor, according to the newspapers. Well, not exactly an inventor. To his way of thinking, he was something better. Where basic inventors had devised something interesting but impractical, he acquired the patent rights and turned it into a practical product, commercially profitable as well. Like a meat chopper. He made an easily workable grinder out of it. For home use or butcher shops. Coffee grinder and mills. Tobacco knives, cheese slicers, sausage stuffers, cherry stoners, fruit presses, general food choppers.

Mrs. Potts sad iron with a cool, detachable handle. A useful machine to set saw teeth, which made a fortune for somebody else. He was a practical genius with a good, steady disposition and out of his talent, more than eighty converted products and patents poured forth in pleasing profusion, the sort of thing that gave American ingenuity its reputation.

La femme de boulanger, Mrs. Baker was of a domestic disposition, satisfied with home pursuits and related matters, but Martha and her grandmother were of a different bent. She loved the theatre and knew all of the leading players, their special quirks and characteristics. Maude Adams, the great interpreter of Peter Pan and other memorable roles. John Drew, the popular leading man. John Jefferson, the old character player. Ethel Barrymore. And one of her favorites, the famous Edwin Booth.

The situation was ideal for a man of means who took pleasure in seeing what the world had to offer, with an appreciative daughter who took it all in. Mr. Baker began these trips before 1880 and four years later went alone on his first trip to Florida, a place he found somewhat primitive but full of potential. A place of discovery for the right capitalist.

For now, the established lake and river resorts appealed to him more. Grand Union at Saratoga. Profile House, Edgewood Park, Appledore Island, White Mountains. Montpelier, Burlington. Blue Mountain Lake, Scroon Lake. Lake Mohawk, Lake Hopatcong. Good meals and comfort by the water. By 1887, the reputation of Asheville and Hot Springs had become well known in Philadelphia circles and Baker, perhaps under an impression that the climate was comparable to Pinehurst and eastern sandhills of the state, wrote to Hot Springs for reservations after the Christmas holidays.

They stopped in Asheville en route and spent a few days at the new Battery Park. Hotel carriages and wagons brought the party up the hill, and back when it was time to leave for the short trip down the river. All in style. At Hot Springs, Martha soon found the owner's bachelor son to be a romantic flirt with all the young ladies, including her. Pleased by their general experience, the Bakers engaged space for the coming summer season. Martha wrote to friends about the two attractive new hotels and the pleasing summer climate of 1888 and Father booked rooms for the coming year.

When the Baker party returned for the following season, young Martha decided that J.E. Rumbough, still the lively charmer, was worth more than a summer flirtation. Now 28, he was popular with both genders…agreeable manners, accomplished on the dance floor, expert on horseback, and fond of hunting and available sports. He had just won the gold medal in a major tennis tournament at Knoxville, where he had entered the tobacco manufacturing business. They fell in love.

In late fall, he and one of his sisters visited the family in Philadelphia to pay his respects and somewhere along the line, an engagement was announced. On October 23, 1890, they were married in a large wedding at the family home. An Episcopal priest conducted the ceremony and the father of the bride fascinated some of the guests with an informal demonstration of a few special kitchen gadgets. After a honeymoon trip to Mexico via the West Coast, bride and groom went to Knoxville but Martha wanted to return to Asheville and so they did.

For the time being, they made the Battery Park home while the new groom scouted around for a house. Walking across Chestnut Street one day, he found a nice one for rent at No. 209. They settled in and were soon content there. He resumed activities in the bright leaf tobacco market and gave up the manufacturing business, rise of the tobacco trust having hampered progress.

Martha got to know Anna Dandridge Rumbough better, the sister who had spent time in Philadelphia and who now came and spent the month of August there on Chestnut. It was a pleasant life in the city's most comfortable neighborhood, made even more convenient by recent arrival of the electric car line at the corner of Charlotte. That first car was now leading to establishment of a citywide system.

Before long, Martha's intimate knowledge of fine stores and hotels and theaters in Philadelphia and New York led her to ask her husband to accompany her there. Broadway productions often "tried out" at Walnut Street Theater in the Quaker City or one of the other historic theatrical houses there. In New York, there were good hotels that she was eager to try. She knew all the many fine stores in Philadelphia and could describe each in detail, from Strawbridge & Clothier to Sharpless Bros. to Bailey, Banks & Biddle and the smaller establishments as well.

For his part, he was agreeable but pressed for time. Mr. Baker was pleased with the whole business. He liked his son-in-law and he thought Asheville was wonderful. The feeling was reciprocal. A lot was going on in the younger man's life during the course of a single year. He was reported to be as busy as a bee, or a beaver. The Swannanoa had been a comfortable and convenient place to stay as a bachelor but the Battery Park had given him a new vista, and an interesting dimension.

As the previous year had begun, exciting things were happening. During 1889, Messrs. Vanderbilt, Carrier, Pearson and others had started building fine homes, the street railway began its historic operation, and evidence of social luxury such as the opera house opened their doors. Banks were in an expansive mood and Rumbough would soon be elected a director. Hotels, boarding houses, railway cars and theaters were full to overflowing in season. And a dozen new stores opened along Patton and Main.

At Hot Springs, the hamlet had become a small town, and Presbyterians started another of their flourishing schools, but the syndicate had overextended itself financially. The younger Rumbough was still monitoring the situation in Asheville and closely advised, Colonel Rumbough acquired the property once again. And once again operated it successfully.

Endnotes

1. The founder of Hot Springs was William Neilson from Ayrshire, Scotland. On March 19, 1791, he purchased 200 acres, including the springs, and established a hotel & tavern. Methodist Asbury said Presbyterian Neilson, unlike some others, "treated me like a minister, a Christian and a gentleman."
2. A health resort since the turn of the century, it was bought by James Patton in 1831 and he and his two sons built a brick hotel that burned down six years later. They then built the great Warm Springs Hotel.
3. After the war, guests included Gen. Braxton Bragg, Cardinal Gibbons, and the families of Gen. T.J. Jackson & Jefferson Davis. President Johnson's son, Frank, met Bessie Rumbough here. In 1907, O. Henry spent his honeymoon at Mountain Park.
4. He received the Scott Medal (bronze) for a rotary blower to circulate air in mines and other remote places.
5. She said of her father, "I think of him as being European in appearance, of perhaps northern Italy or Spain." In other words, tall, dark & handsome.
6. Other favorites included Sheperd's for linen & blankets, Porter & Coates for books, Darlington & Runk for imports, Deweese for dry goods.
7. Also on her Philadelphia itinerary was Steinway & Sons. On a later trip to Europe, she met Mr. Steinway aboard ship and he offered to obtain a grand piano for her on the Continent, having it shipped directly to Asheville without involvement or profit by his firm.

***

1. Martha was in Buffalo at the Pan-American Exposition when McKinley was shot. She could describe in detail every aspect of the entire event.
2. They lived at the Battery Park throughout the first quarter of 1891, having taken a small suite for three months.
3. An avid reader of classic & contemporary works, she had collected nearly a thousand fine volumes, mostly deluxe editions, and now she filled them in around the upstairs hall, between bedroom doors, wherever they fit the bookcases. The east bay window made things light & airy. A Brazilian Lily and other plants grew there amid dark green palm, her dark mahogany desk nearby.
4. Even before they moved in on February 6, 1902, the house was a scene of lavish musicales, with special guests from many places.

5.   During this period, the Rumboughs made several hundred real estate transactions. She became owner of the building that housed M.V. Moore & Co. and commercial property at the southwest corner of Main & Woodfin.

***

1.   The daughter of Col. Joseph Montfort, a patrician of old Halifax, married the father of Samuel Ashe, for whom the city was named.
2.   In 1898, Frank Coxe built the crowning castle on the district with construction of *Klondyke*. Groundbreaking took place during start of a "gold rush" to Alaska, its objective being the Klondyke, an 800-square-mile region in the Yukon Basin.
3.   In reverse order, the lake was built after the hotel was finished.
4.   *Treasures of Toxaway*, by Jan C. Plemmons. Pub. Jacksonville, 1984.

FOUR

THE MANTRA OF MONTFORD

The plans of 1889 also included other northern capital. As we have seen, the Gazzam interests in Philadelphia announced their intentions to build a great hotel across from the entrance at
Biltmore. Learning of this, Mr. Baker first became interested in the area, and others were coming
to the city on that basis as well.

There was talk of building a great hotel on the eastern side of town. At Haw Creek or north of
Azalea on beautiful, rolling farmlands there near the Swannanoa. And to the north near Nicholas
Woodfin's horticultural farm & gardens, a place now becoming known as Woodfin, on the French
Broad.

If plans materialized, this would give the city a major hotel at the central core, and one on each
side. For a young bridegroom, this was intriguing business. From Battery Park, land running north
for a mile or two was clearly visible and attracting interest, with several additional houses having
been erected here & there. A road led down from the hotel grounds out through this area. With
his new status, Rumbough joined with other investors to form the Asheville Loan, Construction &
Improvement Company, chartered that same year.

Along this gently sloping saddle, the new organization purchased several of the large estates
and divided them into lots, laying out streets and then running a street railway line down the central
thoroughfare, known as Cumberland Avenue. The result was an early spurt of interest, followed by
a slackening. When prospects did not improve, the enterprise was brought under the direction of
Mr. Pack, whose business acumen turned it into a lasting success.

The railway was moved over to Academy Street which became known as Montford Avenue, the
principal thoroughfare. Over the course of time, nearly a thousand structures were erected between
the hotel grounds and the river, and of these, more than 600 would remain as testimony to the
architectural diversity & sophistication represented therein.

***

Meanwhile, at the other end of the street, S. Westray Battle was having great success. With
connections all along the Eastern Seaboard, he was able to bring in enterprising persons. Mrs.
W.H. Vanderbilt, suffering from chronic malaria acquired on her travels, came to the city under his
care, according to Dr. Irby Stephens, a leading medical historian. Accompanied by her son, George.
Troubled by a bronchial complaint, Mr. Grove was one of his patients.

At the turn of the century, there were 55 boarding houses catering to persons with tuberculosis. By 1910, the number had reached 137 and would remain at that level for the next two decades.
Common to all was the ubiquitous open-air sleeping porch, so obvious to tourists and townspeople
of that day. In 1908, Merriwether Hospital, a general facility, was opened at 24 Grove Street, just
below Battery Park.

For J.E. Rumbough, it was a banner year. Things were stirring. Final plans for Biltmore were in draft stages. He rode the new electric cars, saw the possibilities for expansion into a city system, and was elected a company director. The family regained possession of the Mountain Park.

His financial ventures were doing well. He was elected a bank director. He got married. He gained an affluent father-in-law. He moved to another hotel. He got himself a nice house. In the city tobacco market, business was good. He visited Philadelphia & New York. And he was involved in a promising new venture.

Martha was interested in the house Charles B. Leonard, a prominent contractor, was building for Mr. Breese on a three-acre tract at the entrance to the driveway of Kenilworth Inn. As a Philadelphian, she had a natural connection to that great hostelry. Later named *Cedar Crest*, the new house was going up in opulent style with a prominent turret, expansive side & rear porches, and interior woodwork of remarkable elaboration. It would become a focal point for wealthy society and she could visualize something comparable next door.

Before long, Mr. Baker decided to build it for her. Naturally he wanted to please her but at the same time, her husband was involved in this promising new venture in Montford and he showed his father-in-law a prime tract in the most desirable section. Some 16 available acres on a pleasing wooded knoll overlooking the city from a point near the end of Montford & Cumberland avenues. Views of Sunset & Beaumont. Another little mountain park.

Martha posing no objection, he bought the main section of the property on April 16, 1891, from the A.L.C.&I. Company, with title registered in her name. Like the product designer that he was, he began designing the inner workings of a house, a mansion worthy of its setting on this pleasant promontory. Gas lighting fixtures of the latest design and highest quality. Parquet flooring, wainscoting & doors of solid oak, highly polished. Dumbwaiters for the servants. Even a miniature post office with its own regulation grilled window. He could see it all in his mind.

Leaving everything to her father, Martha persuaded "Teddy," as she had affectionately nicknamed him, to make Pullman reservations from the little station below *Cedar Crest* and soon they were off on a romantic journey back up north.

This was the first of many such trips as she showed him around her home town. "On the northwest corner of Broad & Chestnut," she recalled, "was that classic circular building of the Girard Trust Company in white marble. To me it was always the most imposing of all the downtown buildings." The City Hall at Market & Broad gave her problems. "It proved to be a very large and ornate building, and created a great traffic inconvenience." They went to Wright, Tyndal & Mitchel near Chestnut & 11th Street, a fine china store. Across the street to Drekas fine stationery store, also hand tooled & gilded leather goods and high grade desk accessories. Curry's for luggage. Specialty grocers sandwiched in between.

In New York, they stayed at the Marlborough with its wonderful painting of the Great Duke at Blenheim. "The horses in that battle picture were stunning," she exclaimed. "I have often wondered whatever became of it. It was so large that it covered the entire east side of the dining room." At some point, they stayed at the Manhattan and came to know all the maids & clerks. Liked it so well, they returned repeatedly. "We had a friend from the South who took over the Woodward at 55th Street & Broadway. He had been with Mr. McKissick at the Battery Park, then at the Mountain Park, and later at the grand Jefferson in Richmond.

"He gave us a large & luxurious suite so we went there year after year. So convenient to the street cars. It had an elegant appearance with heavy velvet draperies of emerald green and a writing room done in the style of Louis XVI with glass mirrored walls as in Marie Antoinette's boudoir at Versailles. Really a good family hotel though and everyone knew us. Large marble pillars and a couple of steps separated the family part from the more formal front part, with a nice balustrade that made it rather foreign looking." The manager was Thomas D. Green of Columbia, South Carolina, generally regarded as able, affable & attentive.

Meanwhile, Mr. Baker had brought in an architect, S.S. Gotley from Cincinnati. He stayed in the city for varying periods of time, riding the *Carolina Special* from his home office, and he developed some other business from the commission. On one of these trips, he stopped off at Mountain Park for vacation. The two men had plunged into the design process right from the start. The ceiling of the second floor foyer was opened to the first below, elegant chandeliers & stained glass windows included. The frame was built like a battleship. Climate did not seem to call for it but they were taking no chances.

When they returned to spend the summer at Chestnut Street, there was an accumulation of things for motherhood and the house. Arriving at the Depot, she was handed down the vestibule steps with care. Given by her father to her husband as if at the wedding or church steps. Waited on by attendants, including nurse & maid, baggage porter, and drivers for private carriage & luggage wagon. Not to mention the ubiquitous Pullman porter close at hand.

Steamer trunks loaded securely, the party moved up Depot Street, later Clingman, to Patton to Battery Park to Montford to Chestnut. A year later, they would proceed straight down Montford's length to the first curve and turn into Zillicoa. For now, they went across Doubleday to Chestnut. On September 4th, Martha observed her own Labor Day there in the master bedroom of that substantial house, in the middle of that closely knit neighborhood, characteristic of the city's social enclaves.

In early fall, Colonel Rumbough offered the Russian Demens house. With excitement and some misgivings, they set up housekeeping there. "It was finished with hardwood," she said, "in very odd designs." A big rambling place, difficult to furnish. Over the stairway, there was a sort of canopy with fancy grille work. In the dining room, the ponderous oaken sideboard was large enough for a hotel...and had a square center compartment that might have been meant for a big samovar. The sides could easily keep off a draught of air from the charcoal fire they used under those water heaters in Russia.

"Teddy's brother, Jack, kept us company and there were occasional guests but generally I was lost in it. John Broderick was there from Brooklyn with his wife & step-daughter. Every now & then he would get drunk and start to beat them up. I would have to scold and threaten to have him turned out. There was a large salon parlor with a nice deep Axminster carpet. On the second floor above it was a very large bedroom along with four smaller bedrooms. Downstairs a sort of chamber and a library. The kitchen was in the basement with a regular passenger elevator to bring up food and haul freight."

For entertainment, they took long carriage drives around town and in the evening, often went to Kenilworth Inn, the Battery Park, and the opera house. The Patton Avenue car line had its terminus at the foot of the street and they could change at the Square for Charlotte Street. All in all, not a bad life but, of course, they were looking forward to the new house.

***

By the following spring, it was finished & ready for the summer season. Artisans from Biltmore had helped perfect the detail work. A matching carriage house complemented the house itself while an ornate iron fence enclosed the lawn, along with a perfectly crafted stone wall.

Some of the family came up from Hot Springs and an elaborate dinner was planned, complete with the hotel orchestra. A full staff was on hand and the street railway company ran a special car from the Depot with a stop at the Square and at Battery Park. Arriving in her own carriage with coachman, breathless Martha derived from the festive approach an idea of riches in store...

She found the door flanked by twin oval, beveled windows. Doorknobs of carved silver, hinges in hammered silver. A few final touches. Her dream house had been finished down to the last detail. With a squeal of delight, she raised a gloved hand and placed it on the dark silver hand that served as a door knocker...

***

An avid reader of both classic and contemporary works, Martha had collected over the years nearly a thousand fine volumes, mostly deluxe editions. All around the upper hall, between bedroom doors, she filled the bookcases. The east bay window made everything light & airy. A Brazilian Lily and other plants grew there amid dark green palms, her dark mahogany desk nearby.

She had a fine brougham with an extra folding seat inside for children, all in blue leather with blue silk curtains and silver trimmings such as locks & handles. In the winter, the colored coachman wore a high-back goatskin cape that she had purchased in St. Paul, Minnesota. "It kept him good and warm, covering him to such an extent that just his high hat showed over the top." She also had a victoria in green broadcloth with matching coachman's livery. "These turnouts I bought myself in Philadelphia. They were just right.

"The brougham had been made for a lady whose husband got into financial difficulties as a result of the panic and I got a good bargain. I had the initials changed on the harness and enjoyed many a good afternoon's drive with friends. I sometimes wonder that I did not tire of everyday drives...but I didn't. Shortly after teatime, we started out and usually did not return until about 5:30 or six. After telephones were installed, it was easy to make a date."

Surrounding the house on three sides was a spacious porch, a seat affording a spectacular view of city and surrounding countryside. Within a few months of settling in, J.E. and Locke Craig got together with another resident, formed a commission, and early in 1893, organized the community under the name it had been called. Rumbough was elected mayor and *Hopewell Hall* became capstone of the district, "a unified neighborhood of varied and lively character and a rich combination of influences," as Sarah Upchurch, an authority on the subject, succinctly put it.

It mirrored "in subtle ways Asheville's cosmopolitan character," she observed. And in 1896, influenced by his good friend, Dr. Cheesborough, Mayor Rumbough built a six-hole golf course as a pleasing touch. Design influenced by Mountain Park, it spread neatly across the lower levels of his property between outer reaches of the two primary avenues. Something to complement membership in the new country club, of which he was a founder.

Combined with Battery Park, the Rumbough line between Society Hill and *Hopewell* became a triangle, linked to Charlotte Street by Chestnut, Haywood leading to Main not far distant, with Montford boasting far more residences. Among them, many of Asheville's most fashionable settled in for their lifetimes.

Endnotes

1. With the two Rockefeller brothers, the other two partners were Samuel Andrews & Stephen W. Harkness. Flagler married Harkness' sister.
2. In addition to aesthetic qualities, the Ponce de Leon housed 16,000 gallons of water for fire protection.
3. The Alcazar provided a range of entertainment, as well as healthful diversions, including choice of Roman, Russian & Turkish baths.
4. After J.P. Morgan died, Mr. Baker gradually became the most powerful man in Wall Street. Many believed he was the prime mover in igniting the stock market. When he died on May 2, 1931, he was succeeded as chairman by his son.
5. The younger member became chairman of the syndicate that produced *Enterprise*, successful defender of the Americas Cup against *Shamrock V*, the yacht entry of Sir Thomas Lipton. In American nautical racing circles, it was a primary part of the stellar event of the century.
6. The Ormond was located on the river a few miles above Daytona.
7. Although smaller in size, the Royal Palm had 450 guest rooms and was otherwise somewhat similar to the Poinciana.
8. Hotel Biscayne opened (1896) in Miami that same year.
9. Miami Electric Light & Power Company got its "juice" from the great power plant at the Royal Palm there.
10. Among guests on the private upstairs floors at *Whitehall* were members of the Kenan family.
11. In 1897, the Saffords were presented at the Court of St. James's in London by Whitelaw Reid, Special Ambassador to Queen Victoria's Jubilee. Mr. Reid later became ambassador. Three decades later, Martha could describe her attire down to the last small detail.
12. .The Waddells came to America with early Scotch-Irish migrations. The Waddell brothers married two Cameron sisters of Scottish ancestry. The insurance business became known as Waddell, Sluder & Adams, the city's leading firm.

***

1. The prime event throughout the Flagler System was the annual Washington's Birthday Ball, limited to guests.
2. Founded in 1886, Carrere & Hastings designed buildings for both Houses of Congress, Royal Bank of Canada, N.Y. Public Library, and many other magnificent structures.
3. Flagler was a trustee of Union Theological Seminary and other eleemosynary institutions. His anonymous philanthropies were immense.
4. The Bingham, Kenan, Morehead, Flagler, Carnegie, McCormick, Grove, Phipps, Stotesbury & Reynolds families were major contributors to the Presbyterian church & its agencies, as were most Rockefeller associates. The Harkness fortune was one of the largest ever amassed in this country.
5. E.T. Stotesbury was the Philadelphia equivalent of J.P. Morgan. Indeed they were partners in Drexel, Morgan & Co. After Mr. Drexel died, the New York operation became the more familiar Morgan firm.
6. Mr. Stotesbury knew the Baker family and visited Asheville in his private railway car. He stayed at Kenilworth Inn, owned by Philadelphia capital, Mountain Park at Hot Springs, and visited Grove Park Inn for the opening. He was a guest in private homes and his car was coupled with the *Toxaway Special*. While in the city, he acquired the former Demens properties.
7. Stotesbury's second wife (1912) later ruled Palm Beach society from their mansion on the ocean boulevard. They were among organizers of the famous fancy dress balls there.
8. As a progressive empire builder, Flagler was classed with Commodore Vanderbilt, Collis P. Huntington, Frederick Weyerhaeuser & J.J. Hill.
9. As an organizer of a colossal business, he had the power to part the waters of the sea, in the Gulf of Mexico, but nature could not be denied. On September 17, 1926, a monster hurricane, most powerful in history, blew it all to kingdom come.

***

1. Martha looked up "marroon" in her Oxford Concise Dictionary and found it described as meaning a runaway slave.
2. The following year, they went to Jamaica again, this time sailing from New Orleans after Mardi Gras.
3. In Charleston, they stayed at the historic Mills House, by then the St. John. Once the South's most elegant hotel. Built circa

1801, a reminder of the saying that for Charleston, one moves the centuries back a notch. They liked houses down near the water, to which they were referred by friends in Fletcher & Flat Rock.

4. Charmed by the authentic antiquity, Douglas Ellington stayed at the St. John after he left Asheville. Half jokingly, he used to say that his real reason was the antique city fire station directly across Meeting Street.

5. Rumboughs & friends enjoyed spending an afternoon at the classic Charleston Museum, once the exposition's main building.

6. Mary Lily was a strong part of the family. Years later, Martha sometimes said that she could "almost hear her hearty laugh now."

7. Ethel Brownsberger was known to several generations of families, first as companion & nanny, then as a registered nurse. One of the original houses in Biltmore Village served as a medical office & residence.

8. Martha Rumbough purchased property at Fletcher and Miss Brownsberger's brothers established Mountain Sanitarium there.

❊❊❊

1. The Craig residence was located at 169 Montford Avenue.

2. For a century, he was the only governor from the Asheville region.

3. In 1915, he established the first state park at Mt. Mitchell. After the great flood of the following year, he was long remembered for having brought effects of the disaster under control.

4. After his term ended, he returned to his law practice and later retired to his home on the Swannanoa River. He died in Asheville near the mid-point of the Twenties.

FIVE

THE DEMENSCHEFF DEVELOPMENT

As hallucinogenic as it might seem, the best conceptual projection for Asheville as a center of progressive development came not from its own civic planners but from influential circles in the court of imperial Russia. The winter palace of the Romanoffs and the Tsar in old St. Petersburg, the Venice of the North.

A young Russian nobleman by birth, Pyotr Alexeitch Demenscheff was a member of the Imperial Guard, an aristocrat whose authority was derived from family and ability. He was on close terms with the most powerful elements. Over a relatively short time span, however, he became a political exile. He joined our epoch at the beginning. In 1880. And paths of his journeys would cross with the Rumboughs.

Like many a political observer across Europe from England to Western Russia, Demenscheff sympathized with the Confederacy. Such persons saw the Sunny South as an agrarian victim of crass commercialism by New England Yankees, with abolitionists the very descendants of those who had brought the slaves to America in the first place.

Southerners were ready to free them in orderly fashion as the British had done, but had been overpowered by a greedy cobra of profit. It was clear that the Confederate army was superior on the field of battle but ultimate victory had gone to the side with superior *materiele*. And that was made possible by the blockade, something Rhett understood but Scarlett did not.

A string of eight major ports in Dixie, Hampton Roads, Wilmington, Charleston, Savannah, Mobile, Biloxi, New Orleans, Galveston, from the Chesapeake to the Rio Grande, strangled by industrial output like an octopus around an innocent dolphin. They wanted the King of Great Britain to join with the Czar or Czarina of all the Russias, Romanoffs and Windsors, as it were, to break the blockade by naval force. After all, Brittania ruled the waves and Russia covered a massive portion of the earth from Central Europe to the Pacific.

Now that was history and Appomattox could not be undone. Ports were open once again. But the future lay along the railroad track and if the South could build a network on ribbons of steel, connecting all river & ocean ports, competitive with that of erstwhile foes, a bright future was possible. Atlanta & Chattanooga could be the Chicago & Cincinnati of the South.

The situation in Russia was fluid. Pyotr was in favor with Czar Alexander II and his ministers but there were outbreaks of violence by anarchists and other marxist revolutionaries. To ameliorate conditions, the secret police organization was abolished and reforms proposed. For a time, the atmosphere seemed improved but he sensed danger, even within government, and mobility began to take on greater significance than nobility. He decided to make a break.

His particular interest was in forestry, woodworking, & building. Forests in the St. Petersburg region were extensive and he was told there were similar areas in the South. In 1880, this young man with good credentials quietly left the Gulf of Finland aboard a freighter bound for Charleston. There he explored the city about which he had heard so much, starting with The Battery. He made friends easily and in social circles, he learned about the Little Charleston of the Mountains.

Later that same year, Mr. Pack made his first visit to Asheville. Demencheff heard about it and contacted him to learn more about lumbering in the Appalachian forests around the city but rail service had not yet been established and he decided to go south instead. Boarding a train for Jacksonville, he was ready to explore. North of Winter Haven, he found what he wanted at Longwood, near Sanford.

Shortly after setting up shop, word came from New York by telegraph that on March 13, 1881, the Emperor (czar) had been a victim of terrorist activity. While on his way to the Winter Palace at *Tsarskoe Selo* in St. Petersburg, a bomb was thrown by one of a group of conspirators and he was killed by force of explosion. There were other lesser assassinations.

Because of difficulties with transportation, the Longwood operation did not fully live up to expectations and Demenscheff went over to the Tampa Bay area. This time he put rail connections first. Built a narrow gauge railroad from Lake Monroe to Lake Apopka, which became headquarters for the Orange Belt Railroad serving a series of produce collection stations for the many small plantations.

Gen. John C. Williams of Detroit was buying up a great deal of acreage on the west side of the bay there and in him Demenscheff found a willing collaborator. They agreed it was a great place for a city, port & resort, composed of persons from both sides of the Mason-Dixon line. Together, they organized the Orange Belt Investment Company and built houses around a neighborhood centered on Ninth Street. Soon they founded a town and he gave it a natural name. St. Petersburg.

And he simplified his own name. Perceiving pronunciation and the Russian reputation for violence as impediments to communication, he simply translated Pyotr to Peter and shortened Demenscheff to Demens, after deciding that it would not become confused with demons or dementia.

The climate there was cooler than in most parts of Florida and this helped start the town on its way to becoming an urban center, as residents began moving from other areas. Health, climate, & disease were popular subjects of discussion. This led to some familiarity with Asheville and Mr. Demens came by train via Charleston to visit the new Battery Park Hotel.

He began talking to civic leaders about promoting Asheville & St. Petersburg as opposite ends of a health resort and recreational destination. Hearing from Mr. Pack and other lumbermen about heavy logging operations in the Land of the Sky, he went to Washington to gather more information. From the Depot, he saw a bustle of activity and found a nearby site on which to build a substantial woodworking plant.

On April 1, 1888, his railroad reached Pinellas Peninsula, on the 20th the edge of town, and on June 28th, the first passenger train pulled into the middle of town. It connected St. Petersburg & Asheville for the first time. Demens became a regular visitor, talking with Dr. Battle, engaging in social life of Battery Park and homes of the sophisticated, such as *Richmond Hill*. A guest when Mr. Vanderbilt and his mother came to visit and obtain medical advice. Among those with whom he came in contact was Colonel Rumbough, an Asheville property owner.

Demens was a pioneer in helping promote the practice of spending spring & summer in Asheville, fall & winter in St. Petersburg, to one degree or another. Thousands of persons followed this migratory pattern. As the Flagler System came into being, this was extended along its operations on the Florida East Coast. With Colonel Coxe and Southern Railway officials in Washington & Atlanta, he & Williams established a mutual promotion of hotels in both cities through first class hotels in Philadelphia & New York, as well as Atlanta & New Orleans.

Peter Demens was impressed with plans for the street railway system to connect Battery Park and Belmont via the Depot, and commercial development of the southern boundary of Battery Park Hill. His entrepreneurial eye drawn by possibilities, he discussed with civic leaders their idea of building an imposing new post office & federal court on a triangular piece of land just below the Coxe properties at the foot of that hill.

From the plant, he admired the neighborhood on the bluffs directly above. The main street there was called Park Avenue after lawns & fine trees abounding. At the time, it was called Society Hill because homes were perhaps the finest in town, ranking at least on a par with large ones on Main & Haywood. Built following Reconstruction, they commanded a splendid view of the river & lands beyond, all the way to the western mountains in the distance.

After learning that the Patton Avenue car line would be extended from Haywood, he purchased a large lot at No. 31 and determined to build a large house, perhaps the biggest in town. The result was a spectacular structure, under construction in 1887.

With some experience in the subject, he served as his own architect. Drawing on knowledge of Russian Byzantine, he added conventional Western Classical touches, along with new Victorian ideas. The result was a massive brick structure that startled the neighborhood with a unique projecting bay, surmounted by a two-tiered tower capped by jerkinhead gables above a broad, bracketed eave.

It was unique but the interior was just as surprising. Designed not only to accommodate his large family but to serve as a showcase for his business wares, it was richly wooded and it approached the effect of something known as Steamboat Gothic. Elaborate woodwork reached its zenith in the entrance hall with intricate parquet flooring, paneled wainscoting, patterned ceiling. An ornate millwork mantel with mirrored overmantel, a heavy cornice punctuated with pendants & medallions.

As if this were not enough, a baroque closed-stringer stairway displayed turned balusters, heavy molded rail, and heavy turned posts joined by an arched spindle frieze defined by a focal landing. The city had not seen anything quite like it, nor was it likely to do so again. In the summer of 1889, as ground was bring broken for *Biltmore* and social life was getting organized at *Richmond Hill,* he moved his family in from the Battery Park.

From the beginning, he had taken part in philanthropic efforts, as well as contemporary cultural activities, which were held in leading hotels & private homes. Many felt that an auditorium was needed and now he became an enthusiastic founding patron of the opera house, opened on the evening of October 3, 1890.

The Demens manner & style attracted the attention & interest of J.E. Rumbough. The future mayor of Montford called on Mr. Demens at his office in the woodworking plant below, inviting him to be his guest at the resort hotel down the river. And hearing of the Russian émigré's intention to leave for Florida, he offered to lease the house in his absence, as an in-town residence for family & friends. The offer was accepted and he later purchased it outright.

With reports of big doings at Biltmore, Demens was encouraged to expand his thinking. Then when the chief architect for the Post Office Department began drawing plans for Asheville, he somehow used his influential connections to obtain the construction contract. Ground was broken on October 26, 1890, and he carried the project to successful conclusion, after which he continued to divide his time between Asheville & St. Petersburg, sometimes staying at the Belmont and visiting the fashionable new racetrack there.

Meanwhile, he was beginning to hear about intriguing possibilities for important development of the citrus business in Southern California. With attention to detail, he studied the situation in an area around Los Angeles and in 1895, he moved there and became a successful grower, purchasing a newspaper as well and using his talents to become a journalist. Except for visits, his Asheville days were over.

***

The Panic of 1893 restrained development of Montford and had a devastating effect on those who were caught in its financial undertow but had little effect along the line of the Florida East Coast Railway...or social life of the Rumboughs.

As a theatre buff, Martha had always been attracted to grand opera as well. If it wasn't too grand or too highbrow, music more for musicians than members of the multitude, and she became familiar with the stars. Before long, Teddy and their friends were brought into the audience.

"One night I was at a performance with a party at the Metropolitan and on coming out afterwards, we found a blizzard raging. There were no cabs and no street cars to be had. It was my first and last experience in the full blast of a fierce snowstorm, but we had a good time...after we were through it! Dr. Cheesborough was with us. He was a widower then. Dickie was still a girl. He walked in front of her and Teddy in front of me to shelter us. It was truly frightening.

"We bent forward, clutching on for balance, and made it down to Shanley's on Broadway where we got some hot food and hot toddy or something. It was February of 1899 and we were just staying at the Gilsey House that year. Fortunately, it was just a few doors south at 29th and after we had regained our composure temporarily, we made it back safely to the Pompeian Café there. That was a very nice hotel, and it never looked better than it did to us that night."

Many New Yorkers remembered the Great Blizzard of 1888 which struck in late February and continued into early March with gale driven drifts as high as 30 feet, the worst storm in city history.

***

The summer social season of Asheville had its counterpart in the winter social season of the Flagler System as it developed down the Gold Coast of the Sunshine State...and even out across deep water in both directions. Golf started at Linville in 1892, Pinehurst in 1895, Highlands in 1902.

From the beginning, the platform of the little passenger station at Biltmore became a social setting with carriages lining up to discharge or receive travelers & friends under the *porte cochere* there and nearby. Later, motor cars joined the parade and then finally displaced horse drawn vehicles in toto.

At the Depot, the crowd was mixed with everything from financiers & liveried chauffeurs to workmen & laborers, boarding separately for Columbia & Charleston, Aiken & Augusta, Knoxville & Chattanooga, Louisville & Nashville, Cincinnati & Chicago, Memphis & St. Louis, Richmond & Norfolk, Washington & New York, Atlanta & New Orleans.

For high society, coming of a new season often meant Tryon, Aiken, Charleston, Pawley's Island, Savannah, Sea Island & the Golden Isles. Jacksonville with its long Florida beaches, such as Ponte Vedra. And crossing St. John's River there was the start of a romantic new world for those who enjoyed the idea of sub-tropical resort life beneath swaying palm fronds, reached by plank roads and unpaved highways which were sometimes a mirage.

When Mr. Baker paid his initial visit there and saw the need for a capitalist of the first magnitude, he did not realize that one had already appeared the previous year. And although he moved in the Rockefeller shadow to some extent, Henry Morrison Flagler fit that description without question.

Henry Flagler was on his way to success, a man bringing about not just a new social order but an opportunity for economic development that would make its East Coast the new American Riviera.

***

Around Asheville, there was early interest and per size of city, perhaps more guests would be attracted to Flagler hotels in coming years than any other. From their connections in the hotel business & related railroading, the Rumboughs were familiar with both aspects of this growing empire.

In 1886, Flagler had organized the Florida East Coast Railway at Jacksonville where it connected with the Southern and other lines to form a north-south gateway. Becoming a parent vehicle for a dozen other companies now being set up, it was developing a first class line in a region of second & third class lines. Its charter gave this entrepreneur extraordinaire an exclusive ferry franchise across the St. John's River. Henry B. Plant was starting his system into the West Coast but this was Flagler territory.

While Martha was moving into her new home in 1892, he began building south from Daytona. Finding his judgment to be correct, he had acquired Hotel Ormond on the Halifax River there and was doubling its size. Meanwhile, the Rumboughs had been among early guests at Jacksonville and when the Ponce de Leon opened for the winter season on January 10, 1888, while the Bakers were making their first trip to Hot Springs, Colonel Rumbough had sent J.E. down as his emissary.

At first, these were more in the nature of business trips with dissemination of information about the Asheville area as primary objective. After a cold winter or two at Hopewell, however, they began regular migration south following the holidays. A week or ten days at first, then three weeks to a month. They stopped at Ponte Vedra and then went on to St. Augustine & Daytona. As in Philadelphia & New York, other members of the family came to visit.

James Edwin was the fourth of eight children. His eldest sister, Bessie, christened Kate but often called Tea Beck, married Frank, son of President Johnson. Mary Lee, called Tea, married Beverly Hill of Virginia. Martha became close to the younger sisters, Sarah Keys nicknamed Dickie and Anna Dandridge, named for family forebears in Lynchburg. Their married names created mild confusion.

***

Everybody turned out for Dickie's wedding to Billy Baker. His family stayed at the Battery Park and most of the others were lodged at the Swannanoa across the street from Trinity Church, where nuptials were held.

It was an important occasion. George F. Baker was co-founder of the First National Bank of New York, then on its way to becoming National City Bank, the most powerful investment factor in Wall Street. A triumvirate composed of J.P. Morgan, Bankers Trust, & National City. George Junior was his father's likely successor and Billy was his cousin. Some guests arrived by private railway car.

It was the last day of summer. September 20, 1899. And the church was packed. Three branches of Bakers, and Rumboughs galore. Surrounded by a good measure of leading families. Battles, Binghams, Blakes, Browns, Cheesboroughs, Colemans, Connallys, Coxes, Fletchers, Heywoods, Jordans, Kimberlys, Pattons, Pearsons, Rankins, Raouls, Rutledges, Sawyers, Westfeldts and others of equal prominence.

On the night before, the Battery Park was a scene of lavish entertainment at the formal wedding dinner. The chef outdid himself. And some of the groomsmen outdid themselves as well, including a few who got soused, looped, or smashed. Unfortunately, they "braced up" just a little again this evening, with the result that J.C. (Jack) Rumbough seated some guests behind the ribbon markers, causing minor confusion to the others and leaving a few front pews unoccupied while crowding ensued at the rear.

The church was decorated with palm brought in by baggage car from Palm Beach, dark green contrasting with gleaming white satin ribbons down the aisles. The Rumboughs' big Asheville coachman, Jason, sent to Martha for a wedding favor, so she fixed up a rosette for his high hat, arm ribbon & boutonniere, all white. He was delighted and received full notice with the rest of the party. With a deft touch, a German violinist played *Call Me Thine Own* and other solos.

William Corwin Baker was in good order. To preclude undue distraction from the wedding party, he and the "best man" had been registered at Kenilworth Inn as "Bugs & Nuts." An exceptionally handsome young man from a fine old Maryland family of the Eastern Shore, his friend J. Harding Wharton was a brother of Clifton Harding who had known Martha at Alexandria Bay, where his wife's family had a summer home. Of Billy's two uncles, one was the banker, the other a Presbyterian minister in Philadelphia. These two young men were poised & polished.

The only other hitch was that one of the bridesmaids, Betty Forbes, was detained in Texas by floods while she was on her way from California. Martha took her place, fortunately fitting into her silk mull gown, cream white with yellow crushed velvet belt & choker, marabou ornament *en coiffure*. All gowns were made & given by the bride and the maids wore corsages of roses & lilies. Martha thought Anna, the maid of honor, looked simply marvelous.

Music stopped and traditional *Lohengrin* pealed forth from the organ. Colonel Rumbough entered, bride on his arm wearing Martha's orange blossoms from Florida. Gown & long train were of white satin with front panel, collar of Brussels rose point lace. Cupids adorned the collar that came over the shoulders, train began at the shoulders, and a tulle veil completed her costume. Her bouquet was composed of lilies & roses, shower style. After the liturgical ceremony, Mendelssohn was played as recessional.

Reception & supper followed at *Hopewell*. Musicians from the Mountain Park hotel orchestra were on hand to provide a fitting mood. A table for 14 was set. Everything looked fine but "we had decorated the house ourselves," Martha recalled, "and our feet were nearly killing us. I got some powders from the Montford drug store to put in our slippers." Bridesmaids had been given the marabou aigrettes and groomsmen dragon & pearl stickpins, so when Martha somehow ended up with a stickpin, she suspected something amiss in the latter department.

She must have looked a bit askance because John J. Seibels came up to her in the dining room and asked if he could do anything to help. "Yes, make me a good cocktail," she replied. He apparently took this to mean a strong one. When he returned, they each had one for the spirit of the occasion. Not too long afterward, the half spring chicken course was served at dinner. "I went to cut mine and it slipped off my plate and into the napkin on my lap. So I just went on calmly cutting the piece of toast upon which it had been served," she remarked with a cheerful smile.

Marie Hill, then about 18, wondered "what I had done with the chicken. I ignored that but tucked the edges of my napkin around it and set it aside to rest until we were finished. I realized that I must be very careful because that drink had nearly sizzled my wits." When she learned during the rest of the meal that her brother-in-law had caused some zigzags in church seating, she realized that he might have been a source for that as well. She resolved that such matters should be under control of a responsible older man. And no cocktails.

Recovering her composure, she was pleased to see the rest of the evening go off in fine fashion. Champagne punch did not take its toll apparently, the general mood was mellow. Newlyweds were given a rousing sendoff. One old satin slipper of hers did land atop family brougham, however, and rode all the way to the station.

The couple went as far as Chateau Frontenac in Quebec before settling down in New York at the Marie Antoinette. After that, they found an apartment on Irving Place near Gramercy Park. From time to time, they stayed at the Baker house in Plainfield, New Jersey. Cigars later resulted in cancer of the tongue for her father-in-law but his widow survived to finish a beautiful house at East Hampton on Long Island.

In all these families of the times, old proverbs of Scotland were in evidence. "Many a mickle makes a muckle" was particularly apropos for the affluent. Another was "it's a strange road that has no turning." As their children were born, it seemed smooth sailing for this handsome young couple.

Then the road turned, taking Billy Baker back to Asheville and down the river to the little frame railway station at Hot Springs. In 1905, he would succumb to diabetes there.

Endnotes

1. The tsar was *absolut* Autocrat of All the Russias, of which there were a hundred, fifty in European Russia, the other fifty in Central Asia, Siberia, the Caucasus, Poland, and the Grand Duchy of Finland.

2. About 1880, a wave of anti-semitism sweeping across Central Europe resulted in a legal and extra-legal persecution. Jews were confined by law to the Pale of Settlement, a belt extending from the Baltic to the Black Sea north of the Balkans. Any reckless enough to go *beyond the pale*, would be subject to extreme measures. Ethnic and racial strife was rampant.

3. As 1889 progressed, it became clear that capitalization was inadequate to maintain the operation and meet payrolls on a timely basis and the company went into receivership. Insects, disease, and heavy rains contributed to its situation and he was forced to liquidate his interest.

4. The road ran from Sanford, where he had established a mill during his previous experience there, and Sebring, along with several lesser points.

5. General Williams built the first hotel and named it the Detroit.

6. The name was pronounced as in *demo*crat.

7. Name changes became more common because of difficulty with spelling, particularly in some Central European languages. Thus Chalgoxcolzyk became Charles and so on, notably in New York and environs.

8. In April of 1885, the 36th annual meeting of the American Medical Society was held in New Orleans. A paper was read posing the question: Where should a health city be built? It recommended "a large subpeninsular, Point Pinellas, waiting the hand of improvement." This was the site of St. Petersburg.

9. The Orange Belt was changed to Tampa & Gulf Coast before being acquired by the Plant System, which later became the Atlantic Coast Line.

10. A number of day coach passengers, and later some motorists as well, made stopovers in Jacksonville at the glamorous Ponce de Leon Hotel, that city being a convenient junction point with Southern Railway and other lines.

✻✻✻

1. After residents left for Montford or Grove Park, it became known as Factory Hill and then when it sank into poverty and the city's worst white slum, it was often called Chicken Hill for chickens clucking around amid barefoot urchins and old rubber tires hanging from tree limbs.

2. Whether features of the house helped sell products of Demens Woodworking Company is unknown.

3. After operating another planing mill for three years, he sold the Asheville operation.

4. On November 13, 1871, the elder Rumbough had purchased 638 acres around confluence of the two rivers. Parts of this land were later purchased by Mr. Carrier, Mr. Vanderbilt, Mr. Breese, and the Gazzam (Kissam) interests.

5. The house had ten fireplaces and tile work on them and other things was performed by S.I. Bean Tile & Marble Company, the city's oldest, with shops just below the hill.

6. Battery Park Place became known as Government Street. Actually a stub end of West College, the name west of North Main. Still later "west" was dropped and the street became College from end to end.

7. The big freeze of 1894-5 proved devastating to thousands of people in Florida but helped St. Petersburg because temperatures were moderated there. However, it may have had some influence on the decision by Mr. Demens to go to California.

8. After retirement in California, he became a foreign correspondent, reporting wartime political activity for New York newspapers.

9. The property became known as the Demens-Rumbough house and sometimes certain guests at Hot Springs stayed there as a sort of adjunct to Mountain Park. It was sold in 1919 and during the Twenties the new owner created the first art museum in the city there.

SIX

THE FLORIDA CONNECTION

On August 24, 1901, 71-year-old Henry Flagler and a 34-year-old spinster were married in her North Carolina farm home. The bride was Mary Lily Kenan of Kenansville, near Wilmington.

The Kenan family had many social connections with Asheville, particularly through the Binghams, and with the state in certain areas. Along with the Morehead family, it became principal benefactor of the state university and these relationships would have profound implications there...it became one of 21 members of the American Association of Colleges & Universities...and for the future of the Flagler empire as well.

By now, it appeared that Flagler's second wife was losing her mind. She had been suffering bizarre hallucinations for some time, telling people a lady of social prominence was the illegitimate daughter of European nobility and so on, but matters had grown worse. Now believing herself to be the czarina, she attempted to send jewelry to the czar. It was intercepted by the authorities.

Her name was Alice, his yacht was named for her, and he finally had to take matters in hand and have her committed before serious harm came of the situation. In obtaining a divorce, impossible under Florida & New York laws, he had made certain efforts to have Florida law changed with respect to separation, insanity, & adultery. While this caused something of a political commotion in certain circles and with some sections of the public, his arrangements proved successful. Divorce proceedings were finally completed in his favor.

***

Early in 1908, as soon as the holidays were over, Martha's husband, whom she called Teddy, boarded the train at Mountain Park for a trip to Charleston to see friends. After a few days, he took one of the through sleepers for Palm Beach to make sure accommodations were in full readiness for the family.

For several reasons, he had wanted to rent one of the private cottages there on what was known as *Breakers Row* but high & mighty of New York had always beaten him to it. The other Rockefeller partners, for example, and others who became tenants until their own houses were built.

As our era moved forward, connection between Florida and the mountains grew ever stronger because of the thousands who spent summer seasons in the Southern Highlands around Asheville, winter seasons in the Sunshine State, often with trips abroad or to New York in between. In Flagler's Florida, the Philadelphians enjoyed the most prominent social status, because of established cultural patterns and wealth. Boston society was based to some extent on family, Cabots & Lowells on Beacon Hill and all that, and certainly culture, but was entrenched too far north in New England to have any real impact.

Only a few decades out of Reconstruction, Southern society remained primarily insular. Traditional family life carried more weight and vacation haunts were patterned after low key life at mountain retreats and their seashore counterparts, New Orleans & Highlands, for example, Atlanta & Cashiers, or Savannah & the Battery Park, rather than rubbing elbows with Pittsburgh millionaires.

In the extremes, Charleston society was based on family, New York on money, and everything else in between. Land held greater significance in the South, industry & machinery in the North. Agricultural crops & commodities in the South, foreign imports in the North. And the ultimate in market commercialism was New York City, home of opportunity in the great melting pot. Always exceptions, to be sure.

While Southern and mountain resorts came increasingly into the picture at Palm Beach, the New York element, once dominant out of sheer size & hard cash, fell to bottom rungs of the ladder. Acceptability lessened by a common perception of loud mouths & aggressive behavior, cultural moorings cut adrift, its members began drifting southward toward Miami and the promise of profitable new development.

Many who replaced them were Southerners and a decade later there would be an expansion felt from the Gold Coast to Asheville, as we shall see in the pages ahead.

***

Perhaps influenced by Presbyterian experiences, Martha sought "moderation in all things," looking askance at the pretentious & ostentatious, particularly that of the more obnoxious New Yorkers and self-satisfied "robber barons" of profitable, smoke filled area around an emerging Golden Triangle in southwest Pennsylvania.

She enjoyed card games and became adept at poker. While in Daiquiri, Oriente, Cuba, she played cards but never at Monte Carlo or Bradley's Beach Club at Palm Beach. After 1909, she quit all gambling. "I think an old woman too fond of games or cards is a pitiful sight," she declared. "Even excessive bridge can give one a curiously hard look, unbecoming when she ought to be benign and gracious."

She was an indefatigable traveler. At one time or another, she and Teddy saw all the sights of Europe, visiting virtually every country from the Baltic and North Sea to Suez & the Mediterranean, from one end to the other. In New York, they visited or stayed at the Damm, Bartholdi, Waldorf, Chelsea, Hoffman House, Holland House, the Marie Antoinette, and others. They went to Brooklyn for dinner in the venerable and historic old restaurants. Luchow's down on 14th for traditional heavy German cuisine. To Martin's at Fifth & Tenth, where Harry Thaw shot Stanford White. Delmonico's at 26th.

When famous players came to Asheville, Martha & friends would join a throng of playgoers in evening clothes for dinner at the Battery Park, there at the other end of the street, before taking their places in the orchestra section to await dimming footlights & rising curtain. Among them was Duncan Cameron Waddell, a founder of the city's leading insurance business.

Known as "Cam" to his friends, D.C. Waddell accompanied the family on some trips to New York & Florida. Active in the Baker wedding, he served as captain of ushers and presented the couple with a handsome silver gift, selected by Martha at Bailey, Banks & Biddle to facilitate his request. In later years, he acquired *Chicora,* one of the Waccamaw River plantations, from the Alston family, and a number of Ashevillians were entertained there in leisurely fashion. He was a cousin of Charles, the city's foremost professional engineer.

In 1909-10, the Rumboughs took *Nautilus*, another of the cottages on *Breakers Row*. It was usually occupied by the Flaglers when they stayed late in season. They had no books to fill the cases and so she made some pretty sea green curtains to cover them, bought some nice vases for mantels, and later brought them to Asheville where they were put to good use. As elsewhere, they had a living room and five large bedrooms with plenty of room on the top floor for the help.

"Dickie and her children were with me that season. They went to parties and had many little friends. She especially enjoyed teas in Coconut Grove. When she was a girl, Teddy bought her a wonderful Kentucky horse. She rode it in fox hunts of the Swannanoa Hunt Club. Always in at the kill, usually getting 'the brush.' She still loved to ride and looked just fine on horseback. Colonel Brown was one among several older gentlemen who would devote themselves to her needs and pleasure. They were an amiable lot. He had been a member of the Rough Riders in Cuba but just what they did seems a mystery.

"She also captivated a young man's fancy. His name was Hamilton Hewitt of Lanark in Scotland. After telling her discreetly earlier that he was looking for an American wife, he earnestly proposed. She told him she had no money and he said that was unnecessary, he wanted a real wife. His father was a Scottish laird with an interesting background. She asked why he did not marry in England and he replied that the English girls only married that they might have a lover. He wanted more and was willing to adopt Billy...

"They seemed well suited to each other, it seemed to me, and I sometimes wondered afterward whether she should have said yes and accepted his offer. Well, no one knows where our paths in life will lead, and there are many decisions that each of us has to make as we go along. For better or worse...

"She had a lavender gown trimmed with fine lace for afternoons," Martha recalled. "When she wore it with a large matching scarf & hat, with her beautiful dark hair and almost French style... and fascinating ways...it's no wonder so many men admired her. She made a great impression on Lawrence Waterbury of New York who was a sort of satellite of Payne Whitney. But she had quite a crush on Reginald C. Vanderbilt. At teas, his wife would almost glare at us when we passed by. I told her she should stop flirting, but soon the season was over and we saw the last of him."

***

About this time, an invitation came from Mrs. Flagler for an afternoon musicale. They were excited, of course. "I wore a broad striped grey chiffon velvet gown trimmed with embroidered bands of color. It had a short train and elbow sleeves. I also had a wonderful matching hat, tucked and pleated, with four French blue ostrich feathers laid over the crown. It was March, much too warm for gloves, and so we did not wear them.

"A newly imported soprano *diva* sang. The music room was all gold and yellow with the full tone pipe organ opening into it. There was a lovely gilded cornice, a gilt screen and chairs. Afterwards, we walked through the patio, staring at the marble centerpiece. It consisted of three satyrs gazing up at an exquisite little female figure in the middle of a large flat bowl, their heads just above the brim and grinning in fearfully satanic fashion.

"We came to the door of the banquet hall and entered, finding chairs all along the sides of this beautiful room. We were served salad and sandwiches on marvelous china plates, with heavy forks. Heaviest silver I have ever seen. The food was excellent! Then we walked through the drawing room and were greeted by Mr. and Mrs. Flagler. We paid our compliments and ambled along to our wheelchairs for a slow ride around the grounds. It was enjoyable and we were happy to be there but I would not want to make a steady diet of that. In general, I dislike very large parties, except dances and balls which I do like...

"Dr. Owen Kenan was there, Mary Lily's cousin, and he greeted us warmly. I like him very much, as I said. He had well shaped features, very neat, with good strong white teeth and eyes of a beautiful shade of blue, with a sort of challenging look. A wonderful speaking voice. He had an admirable swinging walk, he was a good partner on the dance floor, and he was the most graceful swimmer and diver I have ever seen. As one of the 'rocking chair fleet,' I was certainly part of an appreciative gallery!"

Martha and Dr. Owen Howard Hill Kenan shared with others a feeling about life at The Breakers. It was good. Indeed it was difficult to imagine a more pleasant place to be.

***

For the following season, they had a large room on the ground floor of the hotel, facing north on the open, ocean side of the square. They stayed from December until the actual closing in April. It was highly satisfactory, with one or two exceptions from the general pattern of things.

Here they encountered the McLeans, social arbiters of the capital scene in Washington, and protagonists in a drama which led from the famous Hope Diamond to the Reynolds family in Asheville, a saga which generated sensational headlines in the metropolitan press and sent ripples through Asheville society.

The McLeans created a problem, as described by Martha, "Well, you see, they had ten rooms engaged there, all on the ground floor. It was almost intimidating. Much to everyone's surprise and discontent, management allowed them to keep two refrigerators out in the hall. Conditions at the north entrance doorway were also somewhat annoying...

"They had a couple of settees there for their detectives to lounge on. Sometimes others would talk to them. These men were supposed to be on guard, especially at night, so we had to make a detour to avoid them. Our close friends then were Col. and Mrs. A.M. Shook of Nashville in Nos. 12 & 14. They had two expensive rooms and baths, yet they had to put up with such doings. Some of the regular guests on that passage were furious.

"As the weather grew warmer, those detectives soiled the walls with oiled hair and perspiring heads. It just wasn't right. Afterwards, the McLeans occupied one of the far end cottages, which is what they should have done all along. Interesting things happen at resort hotels, and some details don't come to light until much later.

"Their son was a cute little boy. He had been a seven-month baby, prematurely born, his small life preserved in an infant incubator. Something unusual for those days. About three years old now and his head was rather large for his body. They dressed him in hand-made French dresses, but he wore a Jack Tar's hat. A private detective looked out for him, I believe. Well, somebody should have taken care of him, but I'm not familiar with all the details of his family life...

"We didn't know about all the bizarre things that were starting to go on then either, but Ned McLean, Edward B. McLean, was an overly large, sporty looking type of man and wild drinking parties were a topic of conversation..."

***

Returning, they stayed at the *Villa Marguerita* in Charleston, one of the old houses near The Battery. Still a bachelor in the days before he married Mary Lee Rumbough, Sydney Izlar showed them around at a leisurely pace.

Martha already had a passing familiarity with the city, having visited at the time of the exotic South Carolina Inter-State & West Indian Exposition, which lasted from December 1, 1901, to June 2, 1902. It covered an area of about 250 acres, buildings in the Spanish Renaissance style, coated in a dull white tint that gave it the name Ivory City.

They visited homes of his friends, including the Draytons, owners of Magnolia Gardens. Took boat rides to historic forts & gardens, walked old cobblestone streets, and fell under the spell of the city's charms. "Our little suite had been the dining room originally," said Martha, "and I well remember the distinctive heavy walnut furnishings and languid atmosphere.

"We enjoyed it there, so comfortable and relaxed, happy in that soft, genuine environment. Dickie and I were very congenial. She liked people and we had good times together. After we came home, we took piano and violin lessons together, and were just getting to be pretty good, I thought, but Teddy and Cam Waddell teased us so much about it that we finally gave it up."

***

The next season, her mother took *Reef*, between *Surf* & *Nautilus*, and brought her own servants down. It had been occupied for a number of years by Joseph Jefferson, the veteran actor Martha had admired so much in Philadelphia & New York. A good friend of Mr. Flagler. The arrangement was familiar, basically same as the other houses. The MacVeaghs had *Seaside* this year and the Leonard D. Ahls of Boston had taken a five-year lease on *Nautilus*. Mother & daughter immediately started taking long walks every afternoon, alone or with friends. No automobiles were allowed, only bicycle chairs. "Afro-mobiles" someone dubbed them.

On January 22, 1912, the first train to Key West left Miami, just in time for the six-week height or peak of season. Teddy and several male acquaintances got up a group for the inaugural trip with all the dignitaries aboard. Some felt there was a risk of disaster and declined. Martha had an adventurous spirit, made more so by the fact that she had already ridden the train to Long Key in 1907 when the line had reached that point, and she joined others of like mind. They went down the day before and stayed at the Royal Palm.

Running smoothly some 166 miles from Miami station, the trip appears to have been uneventful, no problems reported, and upon arrival at Key West, there was a mild celebration, anticipation of a decade culminating with prospects for a new era of crowds, commerce & communication with the mainland. Some wondered what the mighty Flagler could do to top this.

Before long, premium varnish such as the *Havana Special* appeared, direct from Penn Station. The *Florida & West Indian Limited* ran a distance of 1,475 miles to Knights Way, a through Pullman car from Boston included in the long train consist, and soon advertisements appeared proclaiming "The Longest Sleeping Car Line in the United States East of the Mississippi River." There were connections with the *Carolina Special*, *Crescent Limited* and mainline trains, not to mention *New York & Florida Limited*, *New York & Florida Special*, *Chicago & Florida Special*, *Southern Palm Limited*, *Florida Limited*, *East Coast Limited*, *Seaboard Air Line Limited*, *Atlantic Coast Line Limited*, and others. No whistle stops on these schedules.

During daylight hours, there was a train leaving Miami every hour. For pale urban dwellers and the affluent anguished, it was like going abroad, without getting seasick on a long ocean voyage. The railroad over the sea. The railway across the ocean. The ocean railway. Believe it or not.

***

After learning about her spouse's double life, Mary Lily divorced him but remained single as long as he was alive. Then in late April of 1920, she became engaged to Frank Chalmers of Front Royal, Virginia, an old friend of the family. Martha was her matron of honor for the wedding at St. Michael's Church in Charleston, during the April garden festival. Shortly before Christmas of that year, she suffered a stroke. She left twenty thousand dollars to Martha.

***

A handsome young man had come to Asheville to teach for Colonel Bingham. He and Martha had met at social functions at the school and the hotel and her home. He was a fine gentleman, educated at the best schools, and they became fond of each other. His name was DeBerniere Hooper Whitaker.

He had a friend. His name was Charles Edward Merrill, known to personal friends as Eddie. He was a likable fellow with a ready smile, full of drive & energy. He came from Green Cove Springs, a tiny town near Jacksonville, where his father, a country doctor, had a drug store.

From earliest recognition, young Merrill had grown up in the shadow of Mr. Flagler. He knew the story well and that chain of business had inspired him to aspire for success on a higher plane. He admired the concept of a chain. Hotels, islands, railways, stores, offices, whatever. And he was a born salesman. At 13, he had a newspaper route. On his way to a church picnic, he passed the railroad station, where he saw a bundle of newspapers, just dumped there from a passing train. Its banner headlines announced a smashing American naval victory at Santiago Bay.

Young Charles immediately invested his picnic money. Hastily drafting a couple of friends for pack carriers, he bought all the papers they could carry, at a nickel, and took them to the park where eager picnickers stood in line for the privilege of paying a quarter each. He became a strong believer in capitalism & free enterprise.

In Asheville, he showed little interest in becoming a cadet, scholar, or teacher, but did enjoy sports & social events. Found the flow of visitors between beach & mountain hotels of interest. Tried his hand at golf. Teddy liked him and invited him to play the small course at *Hopewell*.

A thoughtful romantic, DeBerniere was a subject of feminine interest. He was familiar with the literature of poets and considerate of the interests of others. His friend was more of the here & now, alert to new opportunities, ready to act on an upcoming schedule of the day. He wanted to get on with his life.

***

Among such interests was a grocery business back in Jacksonville known as Winn & Lovett. Win and love it. A promising new business that young Merrill believed could outsmart mighty old A&P, the venerable Great Atlantic & Pacific Tea Company. The five hard working Davis brothers became its new owners, a quintet that always answered their own telephones, while some other executives got lost in a maze of bureaucracy. The business became Winn-Dixie Stores and Merrill became its underwriter. Then he played the same role for Safeway Stores and it was a race to see which would rise to the top. Safeway became the largest chain in the country.

Along the way, he got the ocean boulevard mansion he always wanted in Palm Beach, along with one in Southampton. And remembering those cool summers in fashionable Asheville, rented one of the original fine homes in Biltmore Forest for a summer house…a Mediterranean style place in which to cool off beneath Dr. Schenck's towering white pines.

There he was so quiet, nobody ever knew he was around. But in time, after a string of mergers, including Fenner & Beane of New Orleans, they all knew Merrill Lynch, Pierce, Fenner & Beane. We the People. The Thundering Herd.

***

Over a period of six decades, Martha had been to the mountain lakes and seaside beaches, from Martha's Vineyard to Cape May to Old Point Comfort. Ridden the sleepers on a number of crack trains, from Kennebunkport to Key West. Followed the golden chain with Henry Flagler all the way. Knew all his hotels from flagship to fledgling.

She had been to Belfast, to Holyrood and the Royal Mile. The Outer Hebrides. Across the Continent. Ports of intrigue around the Mediterranean, ports of call in the Caribe. Amsterdam to Algiers, Calais to Cairo, Copenhagen to Constantinople, she had been there. Bermuda to the Bahamas. An eye for adventure.

After the Cuba years, they had found the sub-tropical ambiance of Charleston an agreeable substitute for Barbados & the British West Indies. Visited *Chicora* and plantations of Waccamaw & Santee. During the war, they found a large & comfortable house of a friend in St. Petersburg, headquarters of the Plant railroad empire.

Soon halcyon days would be over. Bookings canceled. Plans scaled down or discarded. The city of Asheville would have to retrench. A few, like Cornelia Vanderbilt, would leave the sinking ship for a floating one to take up residence in England or Paris or Switzerland.

Getting a room at an exclusive hotel would be no problem then. Mainly what you would need might be travelers cheques, or letter of credit from a substantial bank. Like Bankers Trust. Or Wachovia. Or private investment bank like Brown Bros., Harriman. A perfect time to own government bonds. Federal government, that is. After all, Treasury sound as a dollar. Maybe some shares in Coca-Cola or Reynolds Tobacco B.

Actually, things were tapering off anyway. The social register and the hotel register were no longer synchronized. In the mid-Twenties, they gave up the East Coast…prices had gone sky high by any rational yardstick…and went back to St. Petersburg & the Plant System each year from 1925 until the end of the decade. Ship trips only a romantic memory from the past.

Well, look at it this way. A lot of fellow travelers got off the train at the little station in Biltmore with a sigh of relief. Said things never looked so green & clean, so quiet & peaceful, tranquil & serene. They wouldn't take anything for their fascinating travels, but now they were at home in the quiet Land of the Sky.

SEVEN

AN UNDERGROUND RAILWAY

From that second railroad line between Charleston & Cincinnati, there was some progress to report. By November of 1890, four years after the first had connected with opening of the Battery Park, about 200 miles had been completed between Marion, North Carolina, & Camden, South Carolina. And Asheville stood to benefit.

While the historic route through Spartanburg & Flat Rock had been conceived in the Broad Street offices of Charleston, this primitive passageway through the clouds had started back at the beginning of the era with a romantic ride on a moonbeam. A vision of going to *Cloudland* in comfort by means of a railway line from Asheville to Roan Mountain. With the lure of Mt. Mitchell, the high peak, hotels & inns of the Asheville area had a stream of visitors interested in going to the *northern mountains.*

By now, thousands were arriving and with more to come, it was agreed that the various parties should work together and provide equipment to meet them at the station, and that a system must be developed to carry them on a scenic journey, at least those so inclined. Excursion cars were placed in service and more were on order. By early 1903, this had turned into big business. Then on November 23, Sunset Park Railway announced plans for a cable car system, inspired by one at Lookout Mountain, Chattanooga.

The Sunset company disclosed that it would provide service to recreational facilities atop the mountain. With equipment "of absolute safety" custom designed for this specific route with "cars operating at a speed of about 600 feet per minute...running straight up the mountainside on a line about 2,500 feet in length." They would be "of the 15-bench type with safety gripping devices and each will seat 75 persons...Every row of passengers will look over the heads of the row beneath...so that there will be an uninterrupted view of the scenery."

In all, there were 20 scenic carriage drives out from the city but on Sunset, visitors had easy views of Windy Gap, Bull Knob, Craven's Gap, Richland Knob, Hamburg Mountain, Elk Mountain, Piney Ridge. The French Broad. Bald Mountain, Beaver Dam Valley. Kenilworth Inn & Biltmore House. This was fine for those who wished to remain in the city but for those who *really* wanted to get into the mountains, a lot more was needed. And logging interests lent additional support, including friends of Mr. Pack.

The closest & best destination was Mitchell County, where Mitchell was highest & Roan the most beautiful. Only yards away, the Asheville & Craggy Mountain was the answer. It had been built with the objective of taking passengers to Craggy Gardens. Now rebuilt & electrified by Mr. Howland, it could be extended from the Craggies to the town of Black Mountain. The Roan would involve an extension to Spruce Pine & Bakersville, gateway to Roan. (Actually, Toecane station, at the confluence of Toe & Cane rivers.)

Meanwhile, the second road had finally reached Kingville southeast of the capital. Work was halted by winter weather but when it cleared, it would be resumed down toward Summerville. At the other end, it was 25 miles up into Kentucky at Whitehouse. The easy parts. In the center, some 25 miles was complete between Johnson City & Chestoa, Tennessee, and another 25 ended at Caney in the middle of the cane fields of Mitchell County.

In essence, the broad general plan would bring Asheville into the 20th century with a competitive system as envisioned by General Wilder at the outset, when he met with Colonel Coxe and others at the Battery Park. The route between Marion & Johnson City would contain a major loop through the city, starting with Spruce Pine (at Huntdale) and running through Burnsville & Weaverville to a new depot along the river at the end of North Main. From there, it would continue through Chimney Rock & Rutherfordton to Charlotte, via Shelby & Gastonia. An alternative route to major connections & destinations.

Then the bottom fell out. The sun never set on the British Empire, or on railway tracks the British had financed. So General Wilder had gone to London for financial support from John Bull. And come back with a deep line of credit. With funding no longer a worry, work progressed. Suddenly, Baring Bros. of Flat Rock fame failed and as ripples went out in ever widening circles, the Panic of '93 came on like a windstorm.

Where the Montford development project slowed down, the Wilder interests came to a halt, along with construction. At the south end of the Tennessee Division, tracks ended at Erwin, facing the great escarpment or wall of mountain separating the Volunteer State from the Old North State. The road to Asheville, or anywhere else, was blocked. By contractual agreement, the roadbed had been extended *around* the mountain barrier and down the river three miles to the state line. There it ended. A foreclosure sale followed.

Finally, a strong man entered the scene from southwestern Virginia. A substantial investor in the coalfields, George L. Carter had grown impatient and late in 1901, he and his associates met at his office in Bristol to form a plan. His Virginia Iron, Coal & Coke Corporation and other enterprises had proven so successful that some thought he was a genius. During the following June, he and silent partners consummated a pending transaction and acquired right-of-way.

***

Whether or not George Carter was a genius, he was certainly smart enough to recognize inadequate capital when he saw it. Early the following year, he formed a new company, the South & Western, sold the V.I.C.&C.C. and moved to Bristol to be closer to the scene. A city where the center of State Street, the main street, divided Virginia from Tennessee.

With proceeds of sale, capital was ample and from new offices in Johnson City, he directed plans to end the impasse. As soon as winter weather was over, new crews were riding their work cars down the Nolichucky to the remote place where the line ended, picking up where others left off. These were tough men, but recruited from native families for the most part and generally amicable. Early next year, the line was in Spruce Pine where mineral shipments, still hauled by wagon, could provide revenues.

It was a colorful little road but one that fell far short of what John C. Calhoun and the Charlestonians had in mind. Or George L. Carter and the Virginians for that matter. The awesome route ahead was beyond his means but there were compelling reasons to go forward. In May of the previous year, as his men were inching forward from isolated Caney, the Panama Canal Company, a French corporation, had been transferred to the United States. A difficult project on a much larger scale. If successful, cargo shipments from Charleston could go through the isthmus to the Pacific and reach untold world destinations.

After giving the matter much study and thought, Mr. Carter decided to go to Wall Street. Among those with whom he came in contact was Thomas Fortune Ryan, a major player in the world of high finance. It so happened that Mr. Ryan was a native of Nelson County, Virginia, near Massie's Mill, and knew the coal country. Having amassed a great fortune consolidating street railways & lighting systems in New York, Chicago, and other cities, he was then in the process of acquiring a controlling interest in the Equitable Life Assurance Society. Born with a quick mind for money, he had become a member of the New York Stock Exchange when he was only 23.

Carter also aroused the interest & curiosity of Norman B. Ream of Chicago, who acted as broker for Philip Danforth Armour when he cornered the pork market. W.M. Ritter of Columbus, Ohio, who had been associated with Mr. Pack before he came to Asheville, and who had become one of the largest lumber dealers in the world. And James A. Blair & John B. Dennis of Blair & Co., a leading private investment banking firm. In Dennis, Carter and his associates found a grand financial wizard.

The world had heard of J.P. Morgan, their contemporary, but few outside The Street knew anything about this man who shunned the limelight like the plague. Under his brilliant direction, Blair had become, at one time, the largest municipal bond house and a corporate underwriter of first rank. He was involved with high level industrial management as well. Some 50 or 60 corporations had been organized or reorganized by him and the roster of names read like a who's who of American business on a grand scale. Along the way, he had become associated with John D. Rockefeller and other oil magnates.

At the Hamilton Hotel in Bristol, an elaborate luncheon was arranged for major investors in the area, and a private railway car to bring in the big time operators. At the railroad's old fashioned offices afterward, Dennis learned the odyssey of this project. It appealed to him in a strange sort of way, but that did not influence his financial judgment. When he studied the books more carefully later, he liked what he saw.

The mastermind of Blair decided to size up the lay of the land for himself. With an assistant, he rode over to Burnsville in a horse drawn vehicle and spent the night at Wray's Inn there on the square. The next day, he came on down through Weaverville into Asheville and observed the situation, talking with Colonel Coxe, railroad men and others. He went down to Spartanburg, back up to Marion & Spruce Pine. From Johnson City, he looked over what was once the Lost State of Franklin, before returning to New York.

What he had seen was enough to turn one's head. At a point about three miles south of Erwin and three miles north of the state line, the roadbed entered a remarkable gorge extending a dozen miles through magnificent wilderness. Inhabited by all kinds of wild game, uninhabited by man. This region was so remote & isolated that names did not even appear in gazetteer, atlas, or encyclopedia. A wayfaring stranger could imagine himself back in days of the adventurous early botanists during their exploratory travels.

Headwaters began with a large spring at the crest of the Blue Ridge. One section flowed down the eastern slope into headwaters of the Linville River as it began its course across the entire state of North Carolina. The other flowed down the western slope to form the Estatoe River, commonly known as the Toe, which flowed by the birthplace & boyhood home of Davey Crockett, continuing into Tennessee where it became the Nolichucky. A deep silence, interrupted only by nature.

Passing along, one could see practically every species of bird indigenous to this part of the country. Fox & raccoon. Herds of deer scampering across the river and into the woods. Bald eagles soaring high above, from nests in lofty gorge bluffs too rugged for man or beast to scale. A big black bear could often be found sitting on a rock, fishing in the middle of the river. All around were some of the most turbulent waters in eastern America, white foam forming a dramatic part of one of the wonders in nature.

In many places, deep banks of *rhododendron maxima* dominated heavy masses of dark growth, standing in the shadow of soaring trees, adding their natural beauty to this impressive scene. Here forces of evolution had carved a winding but wonderful path upon which man could build from natural materials without destroying its integrity.

***

In Asheville, few understood what was going on but there was a growing sense that it was more than a mysterious legend, that something was about to happen, and during coming months, a dozen companies were formed to connect with the projected flow of traffic. A potential network of lines was emerging on paper and City Hall was definitely interested. So was the Board of Trade.

***

Mr. Dennis made his decision in the affirmative. On January 26, 1905, a new S&W came into being under aegis of Blair & Co. Well capitalized by a consortium of investors ready to make railroad reality out of a delayed dream that started with construction of the first steam railway in the country some 75 years before.

In early March, crews arrived in bunk cars on the outskirts of Spruce Pine, prepared to overcome all obstacles. They began laying track and building some new roadbed north to Johnson City. The big challenge, however, was south toward Marion where complex geologic convolutions were immense. Engineers directed start of boring the first tunnel into solid rock. Work progressed steadily on what became known throughout the region as The Loop.

In truth, the place was taking on the air of a mining town in the Wild West. Some Negroes were brought in as manual labor. Gradually, a mixture of foreign elements descended on the scene, many recruited straight off the boat by confidence men at pier, dock & wharf in New York. At the outset of this pre-war decade of imperial supremacy, every extreme of ethnic characteristic came to the fore, a foreshadow of world conflict in microcosm. Work was one thing, off hours something else.

Section Two

In the quiet Toe River Valley, signs of strife were not long in making their appearance...

A handful of French saw the food as an insult to the human race and became cynical and anti-social. Shrugging their shoulders and gesticulating. Germans showed intolerance for stupidity & inefficiency, muttering in disgust with guttural growls about putting menacing elements in their place, by force if necessary. *Sicilianos* or *Napolitanos* were ready to solve problems with *stiletto*, running index fingers across the throat. Russians harbored ominous mistrust of bureaucratic authority.

There were minor incidents. Here & there a few brief fistfights. Sporadic gunfire in the dead of night. On a siding, somebody stuck a stick of dynamite under a small hand car one day, blowing it clear off the right-of-way. A team of Germans took creosoted crossties and used them as battering rams for practice. Russians saw explosives as potential bombs. Italians made obscene or threatening gestures, followed by incomprehensible *staccato* strings of vowels. And blacks tended to visualize a potential lynching party.

Native mountaineers spat contemptuously on the ground, squinted laconically into the distance, and practiced expert marksmanship. Prone to consider preoccupation with fancy food as effete in general, they wondered how long the situation was going to last. If open warfare broke out, they were ready to call for reinforcements to wipe out the camps altogether. Walking narrow streets & sidewalks of the town with Anglo-Saxon attitudes, some lanky characters had guns hanging from heavy leather belts.

Aloof from the others, "locals" heard numerous reports of wrongdoing. Among the worst elements, rum & cocaine running, thieving & carousing, were prevalent among some who had arrived at the melting pot in steerage not long before. There was fear in the community. And native workers held a grudge against Yankee recruiters & bounty hunters for bringing low grade foreigners into such a remote & incompatible situation. The high sheriff came to camp headquarters and issued grim warnings, made some arrests out along the line, but generally deputies were understandably reluctant or afraid to enter housing areas except in armed groups, backed up by silent sharpshooters.

Cool, dark shadows fell early in mountain fastnesses & recesses. The occasional sound of a rare *balalaika* or lively accordion could be heard faintly in the stillness of night air. Bursts of loud laughter. As wild sounds emanated from crude streets and nearby woods, mountaineers took down old rifles from the wall near stone chimneys and stood or sat on cabin porches. They would talk in low tones and stare into the evening darkness by the light of hurricane lamps or filtering rays & shafts of pale moonlight.

Then one night the Italians grew impatient with the food and lack of pasta & wine and other ingredients of their accustomed diet. An unsympathetic camp cook was attacked and in the ensuing brawl lay dead on the floor. Several men were injured, two taken to a primitive infirmary in critical condition, and one died of stab wounds shortly thereafter.

A rumor started that some "wops" had insulted a young girl and assaulted her. The report was not confirmed but small posses were organized to strike back, an effort delayed when members were unable to locate their targets. Another girl was reported to have entered the camps in order to show contempt for critical friends & relatives. It was confirmed that she had gone there but there were no witnesses to her behavior. Nevertheless, she was taken to a clearing in the woods, stripped to the waist, and threatened with a whipping. Wide eyed & trembling, she returned home with her head shaven. Tears running down her cheeks. There were no further such incidents.

Lives were lost at an alarming rate. The upper part of a bank caved in one day and buried seven men working at the base of a 30-foot cut. Several others narrowly escaped suffocation. On the same day, a careless worker was using a sharp stone to break open heavy wooden dynamite boxes. Some 15 cases containing a hundred pounds each were stored in Bridle Path Tunnel. Suddenly, the whole mountain was rocked by a thunderous blast & repercussions. After the air cleared, the injured were carted off, three bodies were recovered, and another six had been blown to bits along sides of tunnel walls.

Other similar episodes occurred on a smaller scale. Minor accidents were commonplace. Bodies were buried along the right-of-way, sometimes where they fell, shallow graves dug by pick & shovel squad. Sermons were preached on the subject at every church in the valley, and Bibles were read to discern the significance of ongoing violence & tragedy. There were calls for a temporary end to construction.

One evening after supper, a riot broke out at Camp #6. A socialist agitator called Jimmy Mazone...Giacomo Manzonetti...had come down to lead a revolt. Unarmed, but his violent, fiery Italian rhetoric from the red brigades was inflammatory and soon it was every man for himself. Grudges ignited into a venting of grievances. When it was over, many were injured, a dozen seriously, others lay dazed & bleeding, five were dead. The next day, bodies were "buried under the chestnut tree by Honeycutt Tunnel, all being in a row." A period of solemn silence followed.

Capt. Felix Kidd was brought in by the company from *Bloody Harlan*, Harlan County, Kentucky, as gang foreman to maintain law & order. Fear spread because of his reputation but soon he was engaged in a duel with Jim Anderson, a cold blooded, reckless section boss. In the confrontation, others fired shots and both men were killed. At the subsequent trial in Bakersville, it was difficult to determine who fired each shot.

***

Despite these and many other problems, much hard work went into continuous construction and three years after it began, tunnels were complete and the line was approaching Marion. On March 9, 1908, the company changed its name to Carolina, Clinchfield & Ohio. No man had ever seen the likes of this railroad before.

The Loop was an unheard of thing, even for those who had worked the mountain from Old Fort to Ridgecrest. Unique. It wound around like a serpent for nearly twenty miles through a series of seven stages. In one of these, elevation changed 300 feet through nine tunnels of a seven-mile stretch. At one point, you could see through three of them in sequence.

At another, the direct line to a corresponding point on the upper grade was some 300 feet while the rail distance between the two was over two miles. On a clear fall day, one could stand at a certain vantage point and observe 14 different views of a train passing there. South of Forest City, it was a different story but north from there it was hard to find an ordinary stretch, what with viaducts, trestles, bridges, cuts, fills and other man-made works, and tunnels, of course, and all kinds of curves. *Some 42% of main was on the curve.*

When completed, there were 55 on-line tunnels, longest of which was one & three quarters miles in length. Sandy Ridge between Trammel & Dante, some 7,854 feet long. Copper Creek Viaduct was 185 feet high and 1,160 feet long. Clinch Mountain Tunnel 4,200 feet long. Where the line made a junction with the Southern at Mountain Home, *Soldiers Home Cut* at a corner of the veterans grounds was 85 feet deep and a mile long from grade ends.

Even at the crest of the Blue Ridge, Summit Tunnel ran more than half a mile. From Spruce Pine, two miles west of Altapass, a railway station at the crest, to Marion there were 20 tunnels in The Loop alone. Some called it an underground railway.

At 12:01 a.m., on Monday, September 7, passenger time table No. 1 for the South & Western Railway, still operating under that name, went into effect through the Spruce Pine Mineral District from Johnson City to Marion. Before long, it would become one of the most popular excursion routes in the country.

***

Like Chickamauga, the saga of the Clinchfield became a mountain legend that lingered long in memory and it was fitting that a leader in one became a leader in the other. It was a bridge line, a 277-mile connector, and it certainly had connections, some twenty in all.

The primary coal carriers were known as *Pocahontas Lines* and it connected with all, along with many other roads of the entire region. It ran more in the cold & dark than any other Class A Railroad in the nation. It was the costliest, took the longest to build, and was the most profitable. Like a conveyor belt for black gold.

Along the way, many a barefoot mountain boy, knapsack over his shoulder or school books in hand, stood amid cane & corn, as cool afternoon shadows lengthened across isolated coves & hills, watching cars roll by. Winding & twisting their way down into the flatlands, with hundreds of millions of tons of heavy cargo. And many a lad among them wondering where it was all coming from and where it was going.

Past Forest City, across Piedmont and Coastal Plain into Low Country. Onto quays & docks near ancient cobblestones of Charleston. And Savannah. Out into the Atlantic. Across to Europe or the colorful Caribbean. Through locks of the Big Ditch. Manzanillo & Colon. Gaillard Cut. Gatun Lake. Emperador & Paraiso. Miraflores & Bay of Panama. Tavernilla & Obispo.

Out of the mines and the pines, where the sun never shines, and into the ocean for great ports of an unknown world beyond.

Endnotes

1. A funicular railway is a cable line, ascending a hill, specif., one in which weight of an ascending car is partly or wholly counterbalanced by weight of a descending car.
2. The engineer was Milton H. Bransdon, who had designed the College Street incline in Providence, where Mr. Howland became familiar with his work. There were operations of the type in Pittsburgh & Cincinnati.
3. Many advanced methods & devices for mountain railways were developed in the Alps between 1880 and turn of the century.
4. In tourist lines, a cogwheel working in a central track was generally the sole means of propulsion up the inclines. Where ascent was steep, straight, &fairly short, a cable was employed.
5. On April 17, 1904, front page newspaper articles reported that "the city's long awaited second railroad is coming." Not long afterward, it was reported that the S&W was building an extension to Lincolnton "where it would connect with the Seaboard, to which it is believed to be connected." During the first decade of the century, a dozen companies were formed to make connections.
6. Learning the news, Julian A. Woodcock Sr. left Lincolnton and came to Asheville where he established Citizens Fuel Company to handle coal shipment & distribution, a prospering business inherited by his son.
7. On April 30, Theodore Roosevelt pressed a button in Washington opening the Louisiana Purchase Exposition in St. Louis, popularly known as The Fair.
8. On March 17, announcement was made that a bottling works would be established at 92 Patton Avenue, in the Coxe frontage, for production of beverages under franchise from the Coca-Cola Company of Atlanta.
9. Someone had the "wild idea" of replacing ballast with ice as substitute, thereby making a double profit. Packed in straw or hay, the ice scheme worked and the Dennis family with its ice house did very well.

DAVID COLEMAN BAILEY

***

1. Early in his career, Blair reorganized the financial structure of the State of Tennessee, under his personal direction.
2. Friendly and sociable at golf, sailing, or parties, and as host at private dinners on his estate at Oyster Bay, L.I., Dennis declined to engage in politics, run for public office, or attend public functions if he could avoid it. He never made a speech in his life.
3. Carter had purchased 350,000 acres of coal lands in Virginia. Before liquidation, Carter Coal & Iron Co. had about 700 coke ovens in operation.
4. A secondary operating office was established at Erwin, on the edge of the Iron Mountain range separating the Asheville Plateau from Upper East Tennessee.
5. Passenger service commenced at Spruce Pine on July 1, 1903, and was augmented on August 28, 1905.
6. The first carload of kaolin (china clay) from the district was shipped out of Penland station by Col. I.H. Bailey early in 1905.
7. By the first day of spring, the baggage room section was finished and in use. By the end of May, last sections of the old station had been demolished.
8. The disease had been introduced from Havana or Colon and got out of control, with thousands of cases and hundreds of deaths. Incidence was centered among fruit suppliers and vendors in the Italian districts.
9. Accommodations on all lines leading to Asheville were booked to capacity.
10. The modern depot was of the style recently introduced in Savannah. Workmen continued applying finishing touches to the rotunda dome from Memorial Day to Labor Day. Offices were located in the balcony, which ran all the way around the four walls. The new Atlanta terminal was also being opened at this time, with special excursions between the two cities.

***

1. Promoted by the Wilder interests as part of broader participation in the great Civil War battlefields, it opened in 1887 and was so successful that a competing cog railway was begun the following year.
2. A steam operation was conducted by Asheville & Craggy Mountain, incorporated by Walter B. Gwyn in 1889. When Howland acquired it, this was the beginning of the Loop Line and other ventures, including Asheville Rapid Transit Company.
3. The original Wilder plan produced the East Tennessee & Western North Carolina but it only ran 30 miles, plus the extension to Crabtree.
4. Queen for Cincinnati, Crescent for New Orleans.
5. Air was circulated by large central fans, with central roof exhaust.
6. It operated via Hendersonville, where cars from the south were attached, and Brevard.
7. In 1902, financing for the resort was accomplished and construction of Toxaway Inn started. Right on the lake shore, it was opened on the Fourth of July the following year.
8. In reverse order from normal, dam & lake were built after the inn was opened. It was the first artificial lake in the Appalachians.
9. On May 10, 1903, stockholders met at Sapphire Inn to decide their course. It was agreed to go forward without delay.
10. In addition to Pullmans, typical consists included two baggage cars, a coach or two for employees, and a diner and club car.
11. See *Treasures of Toxaway*, Jan C. Plemmons, Jacksonville, 1984.
12. In the great flood of 1916, which originated in nearby Rosman, the dam broke and the social phenomenon of princes and Pullmans was washed away with the times.

***

1. An electrified line was built from the Square in Asheville to Lake Louise, near Main Street in Weaverville. A competitor obtained approval for a line along Water, Hiawassee & Flint but the route was very steep and financing arrangements made too slowly.
2. Charles E. Hellier stepped in as high bidder and reorganized as Ohio River & Charleston. Crews entered the gorge and did some sporadic, superficial work for 20 miles but because of Wilder's previous difficulties, adequate financing was unavailable and the company began selling off large sections of line to raise cash, particularly between Whitehouse & Ashland and between Marion & Camden. Construction was limited. Some said it was a sorry sight or sad situation.
3. The Lost State of Franklin had similar configuration with Upper East Tennessee, including Erwin, Elizabethton, Johnson City, Kingsport, & Bristol. Washington, Sullivan, Greene, part of Carter counties. John Sevier was governor, Jonesboro oldest town in the state, the capital. Confused with Tennessee, it eventually returned to North Carolina, which had ignored it, but then became part of Tennessee, when western counties were separated to form a new state.
4. One of the most spectacular was Blue Ridge Tunnel near the crest.

5. By executive orders, every tunnel was cut high enough for the tallest mountain man to stand on top of a box car as the train passed through, a clearance of seven feet.
6. The first passenger train arrived at Marion station from Altapass over The Loop on September 7, 1908.
7. At Confusion Bridge, a long freight consist could be seen moving in three directions, north on one side of the river, in the opposite direction on the other, and at an angle in between.
8. At Miller Yard, there was a junction with the Interstate, which operated entirely within the state of Virginia, over 35 miles of track to Andover. The company owned so many coal cars (more than four thousand) that had they all been returned, the main track would have been inadequate to contain them.
9. From headquarters at Erwin, it was 137 miles to Spartanburg, 140 to Elkhorn. Holston Land Company laid out a town for employees.
10. Clinchfield Navigation Co. operated ships to Cuba & the West Indies. It later became unprofitable and after losing its last vessel at sea, went out of business.

***

1. Sometimes termed Mayland for Mitchell, Avery & Yancey, this area was centered around Spruce Pine.
2. A native of Gardiner, Maine, Dennis typified the New England Yankee of fictional fame. An associate said of him that it took only a matter of minutes for a balance sheet to disclose its secrets, not only in an accounting sense but also in terms of possibilities.
3. Companies included household names such as U.S. Rubber, Otis Elevator, Borden, Swift, National Biscuit. Major steel companies. And George Eastman, founder of Eastman Kodak.
4. After the line from Asheville to Weaverville became reality, the possibility for other such lines was explored for Hendersonville and for Canton, where the Champion Paper plant was opened in 1905. Chimney Rock was also considered as a destination for tourists.
5. The old Southern Railway station for Sulphur Springs became a station for the Asheville School.
6. A veteran journalist & first rate news correspondent, Ashton Chapman of Spruce Pine later wrote that "these construction years were the most turbulent this area has ever known. With such an admixture of racial background and temperaments, some laborers crowded into tarpaper shacks lining rocky, sometimes muddy camp streets, anything could happen and often did. Fights and murder were natural results."
7. Immigrants arriving without proper papers had documents stamped W.O.P. for *without passport* and many were sent home. Previous arrivals started calling them WOPs and those remaining were viewed with suspicion. Some derisively shouted "call the cops and stop the wops."
8. A half million cubic yards of earth had been removed at this crucial point alone, to ensure adequate, safe transfer of cargo & passengers.
9. In the course of her activities, Mrs. Dennis founded the French Broad River Garden Club of Asheville and became its first president.
10. The line ran to Elkhorn City, Kentucky. It connected with the C&O there, and at Dante. The N&W at St. Paul, the Interstate at Miller, trackage rights to the Virginian. The L&N at St. Paul, the Frisco at Frisco. The Southern at Johnson City & Bristol, at Clinchcross in Marion, & at Spartanburg. ET&WNC at Johnson City, Black Mountain Railroad at Kona, Seaboard Air Line Railroad at Bostic and at Spartanburg, as well as other South Carolina railroads there at the southern end of the line.

Visionary Project

At the start of our progressive era, the dream of a canal across the Isthmus of Panama was beginning to take form as crews commenced the task of ground survey for a ship channel from ocean to ocean Under auspices of Ferdinand de Lesseps, an international congress of 135 delegates was held at Paris in May of 1879. After two weeks of discussions, it was decided that a sea level route without locks would connect the cities of Col6n & Panama...and thus the Atlantic with the Pacific.

For purposes of construction, a company was organized, Compagnie Universelle du Canal Inter-oceanique de Panama. The scheme was estimated to take eight years and it fired the fervor of patriotism in the gallant Gallic spirit. In point of fact, the 35-year construction period of the canal (1880-1914) matched from beginning to end the 35-year construction period of the railroad (1882-

1916) and a dream of the latter was motivated psychologically by plans & progress of the former, although few were aware of it.

The Great Ditch was one of the Seven Wonders of the Modern World. It would be a great boon to commerce in general and to world supply of bulk commodities in particular. And it would be another wonder if the high level centerpiece of the visionary railway could be completed in time for opening of the 50-mile waterway which could affect its viability. Out of fanciful dreams come workings of practical miracles in reality.

EIGHT

THE MEDICAL PIONEERS

The era of fashionable Asheville coincided with rise of the city as national center for study and treatment of pulmonary tuberculosis, most dreaded disease in the world and leading cause of death in this country. Known by many as consumption because victims often seemed consumed by it, wasting away. Sometimes called White Plague, it spread readily in crowded, rapidly growing cities.

The first sanitaria for this purpose were established here after various studies indicated that this was the best combination of altitude, atmosphere, & climate. It was suggested that by inhaling sun & moon & stars, and enjoying good clean, pure, cool, mountain air & water, many patients began to regain strength, enabling them to recover from a demoralizing scourge. Combined with rest, in short, it was generally believed conducive to healing of pulmonary lesions. A bright ray of hope in a dismal scene.

In the days before American specialization, treatment was pioneered by the Germans and much early work in the field of psychiatry was carried out by them as well, along with the masterminds of Vienna. With arrival of the railroad, sufferers began coming in numbers and many residents were concerned for safety and for possible negative effects on economic development. From time to time, some measures were taken to keep new facilities from being established inside city limits, which were expanding.

While treatment was being commenced in the city, Dr. Karl von Ruck was practicing medicine in Ohio. From student days at Stuttgart, he had been drawn by the mystery of this malady and in 1882, was present when Robert Koch made his revolutionary announcement at a meeting in Berlin. The world's foremost bacteriologist had succeeded in isolating the *tubercle bacillus.* A native of Klausthal, Hannover, Koch was a fellow Prussian. The Prussian school did not suffer fools gladly. Von Ruck saw him as a kindred soul and started following in his footsteps. He also began studying climatology and seeking out the best geographical locations from that standpoint.

In 1885, Dr. Battle came to observe construction at the Battery Park. Learning of a common interest, these two opposites in personality began corresponding. In the following year, Battle invited him down for opening of the hotel. Von Ruck went to Cincinnati and boarded the train. He was greeted and treated warmly and upon returning home, made arrangements to close his practice and move his residence. Making his new home at the Swannanoa Hotel, he established himself as agent-in-charge of a new station for the Weather Bureau.

After construction was started on the Asheville & Craggy Railroad, he found a site near the right-of-way. Situated on the lower slopes of Sunset, it offered good exposure to sunlight & fresh air. He opened a small sanitarium there for treatment of patients who had contracted tuberculosis. He became convinced that he had done the right thing.

East of Charlotte Street, he became interested in land owned by Charles E. Porter of Georgetown, South Carolina, an Episcopal clergyman and rector of the church there. He called the site *Winyah* after Winyah Bay at Georgetown. Porter did not want to sell any land but offered to build a sanitarium according to Von Ruck's specifications and lease it to him. The facility was opened in September of 1888 and in time, became so popular with affluent patients that there was a substantial waiting list for admission.

In 1890, he received an exhilarating cablegram from Berlin. Koch had developed a long sought remedy, which was named *tuberculin.* Von Ruck booked passage on the first available steamer for Europe to visit his laboratory, study his methods. He returned sanguine. Things were happening but enthusiasm was dealt a blow when it became apparent that the vaccine was proving a failure. However, his attitude was only reinforced. He rededicated himself to immunology. Where others failed, he would succeed.

Eventually, Von Ruck decided that a second facility was needed, one catering to the well heeled. He made Mr. Carrier an offer and leased the Belmont from him for ten years. His plan called for eventual construction of attractive cottages around the grounds. He and a few others moved in. Then on Wednesday, August 24, 1892, all was quiet. Some 138 guests had retired for the night when a fire ignited about 11:30 o'clock in the engine room and laundry. The building was described as fireproof but before long it became nightmare.

The blaze was discovered by a group of male servants in an outlying dormitory building about fifty yards away. One fired a pistol several times to sound an alarm but by then, flames were shooting up the electric elevator shaft. There were no night watchmen, fire escapes or alarms. Roused from slumber by startled shrieks and piercing screams of women, loud shouts from men, guests threw on a few clothes and sought to flee. There was no panic but confused pandemonium was terrifying.

Guests on the second floor went out into the halls, seeking to escape down stairways but many were shut off by flames approaching rapidly from below. Dr. Von Ruck was sound asleep. His wife was seriously ill, asleep in an adjoining room with a nurse nearby. He went in and picked her up in his arms, carried her down the hall and was approaching the bottom of the stairs when flame spurted forth. He turned around, carried her back up and started down the hallway, when he collapsed from the unexpected exertion. Two servants picked her up and carried her to safety.

Revived by someone, he hurried outside and managed to shut off the gas tank in a shed on the grounds. His wife's sister, Abbie Moore, was one of the more seriously injured. Trapped on the porch outside her room on the second floor, she was forced to jump for safety, severely wrenched both ankles, and suffered other lesser bodily injuries. Many others encountered similar situations but because of wide halls and porches on all sides, there were no fatalities.

Some escapes, particularly on the third floor, were considered near miraculous as certain persons managed to find hidden escape ways and others ran through curtains of fire to find safety. A quick thinking night clerk escaped, taking the guest register with him. It included prominent names from Charleston to Atlanta to New Orleans, and elsewhere. Some were taken by carriage to the homes of physicians, others to the Battery Park, Glen Rock, Swannanoa and other leading hotels. Dr. Battle came out and helped get those in need to the hotel. Horrifying stories circulated across town. Long remembered. The night the Belmont burned.

***

Von Ruck was gratified that no one perished but it was a terrible blow nonetheless. He abandoned plans for expansion. Meanwhile, he had acquired 17 acres north of *Wychewood* in Ramoth, west of Beaver Dam Street, a site adjacent to the country club. Leasing additional acreage, he established a 150-acre dairy farm, poultry production, and extensive vegetable gardens to supply the sanitarium.

Son of Mrs. Von Ruck's sister, the former Grace Moore, and William W. Schoenheit, the business manager, Edward Schoenheit was born at *Winyah*. He enrolled in the School of Veterinary at the University of Tennessee with a view toward managing the property. Later he decided to become a doctor and received his degree in medicine from Jefferson Medical College, a leading institution. Eventually, he became clinical director.

Once things were off and running smoothly, V.R. began turning everything else over to others. In 1895, he founded the Von Ruck Institute and appointed as laboratory director Edwin Klebs, also German, one of the world's foremost bacteriologists. Dr. William L. Dunn came in as his assistant. This became Von Ruck's life work. He was interested in establishing facilities, not managing them. He wanted to find the cure for White Plague. If that could be achieved, soon there would be nothing to treat. Every day that passed counted.

Unable to proceed at Sulphur Springs, he began construction of another sanitarium at the farm. Work began early in 1899, making a small park in the process. There was a large central building and outlying cottages, 60 private rooms, all connected by pathways for walking, with an electric car line running through the grounds. *New Winyah* opened in January of 1900, a contemporary of the Manor at the turn of the century.

While the "new san" was under construction, Dr. Martin Luther Stevens of Ohio came to Asheville and became physician-in-charge of the old. When it was closed in 1902, he left to enter practice for himself and Von Ruck's only son, Silvio, became clinical director at the new. In 1905, Dunn became lab director. C.C. Orr came down as assistant. Scotch-Irish physicians found Karl Von Ruck austere and one by one, they would leave.

The tuberculosis fraternity was formidable, nationally recognized, and "the TB doctors of Asheville" became famous. Von Ruck had connections with Michigan and they began referring a number of their most promising graduates to Asheville. A true scholar, Dunn had graduated while under 21 years of age, a fact that made him ineligible for license to practice medicine. Some saw him as a prodigy, a person setting high standards.

Among these renowned men were Ambler from Western Reserve, Dunn from Michigan, Minor from Virginia, Ringer from Columbia, Stevens from Johns Hopkins, Cocke from Michigan and Cornell, Orr and Colby from Michigan. George Alexander, Paul Paquin, Karl Schaffle, Weir Mitchell, John W. Huston. Carl V. Reynolds of an old Asheville family. In presenting an honorary degree (1926) to Dr. Minor, of whom he said, "he ranks without superior," Dr. Archibald Henderson, the internationally famous historian and mathematician of Chapel Hill, paid tribute to this contingent.

Generally witty and charming, many became president of the state medical society and other leading state and national associations. In total, they studied at London, Vienna, Leipzig, Berlin & Paris, and delivered hundreds of professional papers there. Founding members of both country clubs and board members of churches, particularly First Presbyterian & Trinity Episcopal. Active in civic & cultural affairs, especially musical societies, literary & scholarly associations, and good samaritan organizations.

Chase P. Ambler was the first chief of staff. He reorganized Merriwether Hospital. A great outdoorsman, he led the campaign for establishment of the Great Smoky Mountains National Park, having suggested the proposition in 1899 while *New Winyah* was under construction. Charles L. Minor spent two years in hospitals of Vienna, where he received the most advanced training, and the Italian government cited Dunn for outstanding service in hospital liaison during the war. The two men had different personalities but were brilliant scholars, close friends & associates.

Arriving later, Dr. Paul H. Ringer came from a highly educated family in New York, his father a professor of foreign languages, his mother an accomplished musician. He came to Asheville from Presbyterian Hospital in New York. Attending Episcopal High, C. Hartwell Cocke of Mississippi was the school's top scholar every year he was there. A Davidson graduate from Charlotte, Orr spent a year in chemistry & bacteriology in Von Ruck's laboratories.

Charles D.C. Colby was a medical school classmate of Dunn. His home at *Sun-Up* on Forest Hill, overlooking the city, became a landmark. Dr. Stevens organized Strawberry Hill. Son of Chase, Arthur C. Ambler engaged in tuberculosis specialty before becoming the city's first specialist in anesthesiology. And dedicated Samuel L. Crow had the greatest longevity.

In 1904, as Dr. Grove was starting his little park, Von Ruck bought from Dr. Reed 20 acres adjacent to Albemarle Park on the south side. Two houses were included. The Charlotte Street line was extended from Chestnut to the Manor Gate House, and he established new residence, adjacent to the now defunct old sanitarium.

***

In that same year, Dr. Robert S. Carroll also closed his medical practice in Ohio, to go on a national search for the ideal location at which to establish a sanitarium for treatment of nervous disorders. He wanted it to be convenient by rail from various locations. He knew Von Ruck and had learned about Asheville from him. While this was no Main Line, it met minimum requirements.

One of the founders of modern psychiatry, Dr. Carroll went to Cincinnati to board the *Carolina Special*. Arriving at the brand new Depot, he took the *Battery Park Special* to the hotel, where he had an appointment with the ubiquitous S. Westray Battle at his offices on the hill. In that cordial atmosphere, he told an interested Dr. Battle some details of his specific thinking. His host donned his cape to walk him down Patton and show him the town. He then put him aboard an electric car to The Manor.

There he met with Von Ruck and his chief of staff, along with Mr. Raoul, who showed him around a bit. After lunch, the others bid their host farewell and sauntered south along a pathway through the grounds to a private street. Von Ruck gave the visitor a tour and then explained the situation at the other property. Together the two men rode the East Street car to the site.

Carroll found it attractive. His host suggested that a similar situation would be appropriate for a psychiatric hospital. If not nearby, then perhaps in Chunn's Cove. They shared similar ideas about therapeutic environments. Back at the hotel, Dr. Battle listened with interest but said he thought the downtown area might be preferable because of convenience for patients. He suggested keeping an open mind.

The following day, Carroll looked at earlier sanitarium sites downtown before boarding the cars again, with an assistant supplied by Battle. This time he rode to the ends of the same line. Up Lookout and then past the fantastic Russian (Demens) house to Park, above the river, another interesting possibility. Paying two cents for a transfer, he went out Montford to Santee where he admired *Hopewell* and *Klondyke*. On March 28, 1904, he purchased a lot on Haywood across from the Auditorium.

Once home, he mulled things over and decided that it was too important a decision to stop there. He continued his tour of inspection. After visiting some sixty sites over a period of four spring & summer months, he was satisfied that Asheville was the right choice, for reasons advanced by Ashevillians and others. He returned to the city and Battery Park. Dr. Battle said he wanted to show him something. Off again down the hotel pathways they went. Stopping at the foot, they looked across the street at a 20-room office building called the *Halthenon.* Nos. 29-31 Haywood. It was well built, available for lease. Centrally located, convenient to everything. Post office across the way.

Back at his office, congenial Dr. Battle explained the situation. The Coxe interests had opened the first in a row of commercial buildings the year before, along Government Street at the base of the hill properties. Within a year, he and his colleagues would be moving into the Medical Building going up in the center of the block. And the center of things.

Battle was a master salesman but the product was easy and the prospect was sold. Battery Park Bank and the new Wachovia nearby were willing to finance the proposition and on August 22, doors of the sanitarium were opened. Private mental hospitals had already been established in large metropolitan centers, where need was intense, but this was the South's first. Dr. Carroll was a happy fellow.

The man who thus realized his dream was yet another recruit from ranks of the Scotch-Irish. Son of a Presbyterian minister who was the great grandson of Charles Carroll of Maryland, signer of the Declaration of Independence, he was educated at a number of leading colleges & universities. And he had also studied hydrotherapy and other forms of treatment at Battle Creek. "Man is mentally, morally, and physically so attuned," he once said, "that when disordered, his perfect restoration demands intelligent readjustment to each element."

As a physician, he had become increasingly concerned with a growing number of cases that did not lend themselves to conventional treatment. From this, he developed a lasting interest in general physical & mental health, employing new approaches to dietary nutrition & scheduled exercise, along with rest and changes in attitudinal interests. He had some unusual ideas, notions that seemed strange to some. Fresh fruits & vegetables served regularly. Whole grain cereals and other natural foods.

The objective was "brain health." Nicotine, caffeine, alcohol & narcotics prohibited. Raw or steamed food substituted for fried. Exercise with proper consideration for physical condition of each patient. And he consistently encouraged, even demanded, constructive habits with a view toward individual relationships to the world at large.

From the start, the operation was successful but there was a problem. No available supply of registered nurses trained in this specialized practice. As soon as things were running smoothly, he established a school of nursing. Opened the very next year, it gained national recognition and came at a time when graduates could find employment in many places.

The scene at *Hopewell* and the land on which it stood still appealed to him and early the following year, he moved into a house in that socially active neighborhood. It was not far from *Winyah*, to the east across North Main. He acquired an eight-acre tract with a frame house, adjoining the Rumbough property. For three years, he used both places, the downtown location handling most office work, and then in 1909 he closed it and began expanding at Montford. In 1912, he named it Highland Hospital.

Carroll had been able to obtain some food supply from the Winyah farms but here at the new location he had an opportunity to develop his own. Over time, the hospital grew to ten buildings on 80 acres, including miles of walking trails & paths threaded through the grounds of Highland Park and 400 acres of farm land running from Beaverdam Valley up the side of Elk Mountain.

In the professional realm, he had formed a close relationship with Dr. Adolph Meyer, then dean of American psychiatry. At Johns Hopkins, Meyer sent patients to Highland and vice versa. They compared notes regularly. Later he established a connection with Duke University and by then patients had been admitted from many countries. Dr. Carroll himself was an experienced world traveler, an eminent scholar as well as practitioner, and his papers were read at gatherings of learned societies around the world.

His wife, Grace Stewart Carroll, was an internationally recognized musician, a former director of the Bush Conservatory in Chicago, where they met. Her piano recitals and other concerts at their beautiful home on the grounds became gathering places for teas and similar formal social functions on a regular basis, with guests from across the city and beyond. A fine second residence was used for the same purpose.

As our era and the tuberculosis era both came to a close in 1930, Manfred Sakel in Vienna discovered the insulin treatment, later used at Highland, one of the first medical facilities in this country to do so. And in the decades to come, its close relationship with Duke would keep it in the forefront of modern medicine as applied to this challenging field.

Along the way, the practice that he had entered for a select few had grown to the point that when he retired, psychoneurotic patients numbered in the millions...one of every 14 persons would spend some part of life in a public mental hospital. More mental patients occupied hospital beds than all other sick people combined.

***

Back where *Old Winyah* once flourished, our eminent wagnerian scientist was creating a new center of activity. Starting in 1912, Dr. Von Ruck employed an imaginative architectural design to connect two houses in an ingenious manner. The street became known as Von Ruck Terrace, which connected from Baird Street.

The house at the north end was a lavish structure with rounded projecting bays and a finial topped octagonal bay. On the south, he built a physicians residence hall with enclosed porches, later used by outpatients. It was finished in shingle and pebbledash with intricate, parqueted hardwood floors.

In 1915, he connected the two with a grand two-story music room comprising twin elliptical conservatories with Victorian, crafted mahogany woodwork to house a 67-rank Aeolian organ with 4,800 handmade wooden pipes rising two stories behind a curved mahogany screen. Mrs. Von

Ruck was a successful hostess and entertained at pleasant musicales. A singer, she gave recitals at the conservatory and arranged for concerts there, bringing in first class groups for chamber music.

Meanwhile, various facilities related to "TB" could be found all over the place, side streets, suburbs, hillsides, and the ubiquitous sleeping porches common to all. Bed capacity ranged from five to fifty, or even five hundred. There was Roye Cottage. Hillcrest & Hillcroft. Abernathy. Wellington. Edgewood, Elmhurst. Oakland, Onteora, Ottari. Strawberry Hill, Violet Hill & Zephyr Hill. Sunset Heights. Greystone Lodge. St. Joseph Sanitarium, later converted to a hospital. Overlooking the city from Sunset was Fairview Cottage, a large sanitarium with four central buildings and 27 cottages, providing capacity of five hundred.

At Fairview, Mrs. Perkins was manager with a staff of 50 to 60 nurses and attendants. Many patients were housed in what were known as "shacks." A collection of two-bed to four-bed buildings, open on the sides above window level, except for rolled down curtains. Outfitted in spartan fashion with plain beds, stove, & enclosed bathroom. Mrs. Perkins was highly regarded because she took good care of patients, regardless of means. Wholesome food was prepared in a large central building.

***

Von Ruck finally succeeded in developing a vaccine but was upstaged by development of the Calmet-Genghou vaccine, which became widely recognized. Silvio went to Boston to conduct experimental testing at a public orphanage. While so engaged, he contracted influenza during the great epidemic and within 48 hours died in New York as a result. His wife and young daughter, Silvia, contracted the disease from him and while returning home aboard the *Asheville Special*, the child died in a sleeping car berth during the night.

The senior Von Ruck became obsessed with things to the point where he began making unsubstantiated claims that his vaccine not only provided immunity but also strengthened the human body by increasing resistance to disease. In Washington, a senator was impressed to the point that he introduced a bill to require "doughboys" to be inoculated as part of the army induction process.

This proposed legislation created controversy and a congressional commission was established to investigate the situation. It rendered findings that there was no basis in fact for such claims. This made it appear that Von Ruck was a quack or inclined in that direction. Embittered, he launched another crusade, this time for the purpose of demonstrating that his critics were misguided. In 1921, two things happened. The French vaccine was accepted and his wife died.

His son had died away from home, his only grandchild on the train, his daughter off in music school, and now his wife. Was he compulsive or obsessed? Or doomed. The great organ in his quiet mansion was like ominous background. Lonely, he started brooding...A great life ambition had resulted in affront to his character & reputation. Colleagues & associates seemed to see him as a martinet and left to found their own institutions. Even Dr. Ambler was building a 50-bed sanitarium of his own. Von Ruck was a broken man. He succumbed to nephritis the following year.

As principal heir, Schoenheit received the sanitarium. In 1924, he married Elizabeth Kimberly of the family that owned the Kimberly lands and they made the Von Ruck residence their home. When the financial collapse came on, he closed the operation before going to Vienna to study cardiology.

During the Twenties, private institutions for tubercular patients went into a slow decline, brought on by lessening confidence in theory of therapeutic efficacy & potency and by rise of state supported facilities where charges were modest, minimal or nominal. *Winyah* went out with the tide. One by one, the others closed as well. The great consumption cycle was over.

***

Many famous persons came to the city because of TB. One was Herbert Hoover Junior while his father was in the White House. He had an incipient case and Mr. Seely offered to make arrangements, which were worked out with Dr. Joel T. Boone, the White House physician and personal friend of the younger Hoover. They settled on *Blue Brier Cottage.*

This attractive white frame house with lots of windows was located on Sunset behind the Inn about a quarter mile below *Overlook.* Built in 1906-7 by Mr. Randolph, it had a fine view of the city and beyond. Mr. Bryan owned it when construction began on his house on Evelyn. It was later acquired by Henri Berger, a prominent social figure of Paris & Monaco, with whom a lease was arranged.

A crew of 30 men set to work refurbishing house & grounds there on the old toll road and Hoover's wife, a popular socialite, came down with the advance party to supervise arrangements. The patient arrived in early November of 1930 from Camp Rapidan in Virginia, the Presidential retreat. His stay there was successful.

Endnotes

1. In 1871, Dr. H.P. Gatchell came to the city from the faculty of Hahnemann Medical College. His brother, also a physician, joined him in opening *The Villa* near the Turnpike at Forest Hill, a village between Pack Square & the Swannanoa River. It was the first tuberculosis sanitarium in the country. The science in which they were engaged was called *phthisiology.*
2. Arriving from Baltimore in 1876, Dr. J.W. Gleitzmann converted the Carolina House on North Main to Mountain Sanitarium for Pulmonary Diseases. It was located on the west side about a hundred feet from Woodfin Street. Wide porches or verandahs set the pattern for those to come. Born & educated in Germany, he was a forceful advocate for the cause.
3. At some point, the Gatchell brothers found they were too far out and moved downtown to the northeast corner of Haywood & College, where operations were continued for several years. Gleitzmann came in to continue their work.
4. As early as the late 1870s, Dr. Stanford E. Chille of Louisiana had been impressed by the fact that the disease had not been found in local residents. Professor of physiology & pathological anatomy at the state university, he visited Gleitzmann and prepared a paper extolling his work. It was presented before the New Orleans Medical & Surgical Society. Papers were delivered to similar groups around the country, widely published by Gleitzmann and others. Included in atmosphere, temperature, humidity & barometric pressure were considered.
5. Gleitzmann acquired an adjoining building but in 1880, when he attempted to expand his operation, he was hampered. With arrival of the railroad that fall, residents became concerned and opposed acquisition of property for the purpose. He attempted to acquire the Woodfin house. Some thought conflict of temperaments between prototypes of vigorous, assertive Teutonic and predominant, laconic Scotch-Irish contributed to a consensus. Unable to expand facilities, Gleitzmann finally gave up and left town in 1883.
6. Recalling the era later, Dr. Gaillard S. Tennant observed that these events marked the beginning for a steady stream of travel related to tuberculosis.
7. Coupled with introduction of immunotherapy by Jenner and Pasteur, Koch's discovery was a milestone in the history of phthisiology. Originally, bacteriology was a branch of pathology.
   8. This was the first extension of that line and it made use of A&C tracks.

***

1. According to *Webster's Unabridged,* 1924 edition, *sanatorium* was an establishment for treatment of the sick, especially one making much use of natural therapeutic agents or local conditions, or employing some specific treatment, or one that treats

specific diseases. It describes a *sanitarium* as a health station or resort, sometimes restricted to prophylactic treatments. In practice, terms were often used interchangeably.

2. He was an astute capitalist, "getting in on the ground floor" several times with successful ventures. An early investor in Spray Cotton Mills, he became a principal stockholder. When his 1,880 shares had a big increase in market value, he made a fortune.

3. Schoenheit's parents were both burned in the fire but recovered fully. An attractive & spirited young lady, Miss Grace Moore was the sister of Delia. She was married to William Schoenheit on the grounds of *Winyah*. Schoenheit had come there as a patient and successfully regained his health. He entered practice a year before Von Ruck's death.

4. A native of Koenigsberg, Klebs was known the world over for his successful research in diphtheria, anthrax, gunshot wounds, malaria & syphilis. He later became a member of the faculty at Rush Medical College. Dunn went to study at Liepzig, Berlin, Vienna & Paris.

5. Porter suspected that they were going to move first class clientele to the new "san" and use the existing facility for secondary patients, did not renew the lease, later demolished the central building and built houses instead.

6. His little book, *Asheville* (French Broad Press, 1900) describes the Asheville plateau as 30 miles wide with Blue Ridge southeast & northeast and Smokies west & northwest, the city on a bluff about 350 feet above the river valley with confluence of rivers a mile from the center of town.

7. He wrote that "the highest temperature recorded in the past 12 years was 91.3* but 90* has been reached frequently. Bed-covers are needed, at least after midnight. On average, total annual rainfall has been 40 inches, a figure lower than for the surrounding mountains." He and others reported mean annual temperature of 55*.

8. Among the city's assets, he cited very low mortality, malaria unknown, phthisis among natives rare. Carriage hire & riding horses available at very reasonable rates. Popular baseball games. An excellent School of Music & Languages, directed by Prof. F. Dunkley. And direct railway connections, including New Orleans and all significant points in between.

***

1. There was concern over possible transmission of disease in the central district. In 1900, an injunction was issued by the court to block construction of Mission Hospital and three nuns known as Sisters of Mercy, from Belmont Abbey, converted the old Asheville Female College at 40 North French Broad into St. Joseph's Retreat, which provided 18 beds. In 1905, it was moved to larger quarters on Starnes Avenue and in 1916, when South Main was changed to Biltmore Avenue, a new building was established there at Forest Hill as St. Joseph's Sanitarium, with 95 beds.

2. Spears Avenue was the city limit and the sanitarium was on the north side, making it outside the city until limits were extended. Farther out, Ottari Sanitarium was in operation from 1912 to 1930 on a splendid site above Kimberly Heights and Grace School.

3. After a decade of clinical trials, he published results in the *Journal of the American Medical Association.* (5-8-11) He published *Journal of Tuberculosis*, of which he was founder & editor. The first medical journal devoted solely to that disease.

4. Von Ruck created a large library with card files describing the entire world literature on this subject, most of which was in German. After his death, it was purchased by Army Medical Library, largest medical reference source in the country.

5. In 1905, Dunn established Edgewood and then added Sunnyside, operated by his parents. Miss Anne O'Connell, a retired nurse from Johns Hopkins, operated Edgewood Cottage in Porter's old summer home. For distinguished service, his alma mater awarded Dunn an honorary degree. Dr. Campbell conducted his funeral service on 5-25-28.

6. Some had contracted tuberculosis themselves. Some Asheville physicians also became specialists, notably J.M. Burroughs, L.B. McBrayer & John Hey Williams.

7. Ambler was referred to Von Ruck by his dean. He became founder of the American Forestry Association. As a result of his many activities on behalf of conservation, he was sometimes called father of Pisgah National Forest.

8. In 1914, Von Ruck presented a major report at an international conference in London. It was favorably received but outbreak of war resulted in cancellation of clinical trials for his vaccine and his work was forgotten.

9. Ringer married an Asheville girl, a member of the prominent Morrison family. He became associated with Minor in 1906. When Ambler Heights was opened, he became clinical director.

***

1. After being graduated from Denison University, he was educated at Chicago, Cleveland, St. Louis & New York. He came to the city from Marysville, Ohio, having practiced previously in Texas. He was familiar with work & writing of Sigmund Freud, whose most fertile years were those between 1895 & 1900.

2. Charles Carroll of Carrollton signed in that fashion to distinguish himself from Daniel Carroll, a signer of the Constitution. He survived by six years all other signers. His younger brother, John, became the first Roman Catholic bishop of the United States.

3. On the north, the *Halthenon* adjoined the new Y.M.C.A. building. Patients climbed the central Battery Park driveway as part

of daily exercise regimen. Referring to Asheville, he said, "Nature was prodigal in her bounty when she formed this natural park."

4. He believed that the primary offender was red meat which, when consumed by the sedentary, became a toxin producing drug, and he allowed only a small amount of sugar and only at the end of a meal.

5. During its first year, a helpless polio victim, nine months old, was brought in on a pillow by his parents and became the hospital's ward. After 12 years of daily hydrotherapy, he was released. At graduation from Asheville High School, he received a gold medal for four years of perfect attendance. He later married and fathered two children.

6. Gardens & orchards were made & tended by patients & staff. Some orders were combined with *Winyah* for outside sources of supply. The Rumboughs apparently thought highly of Dr. Carroll and his activities but were not altogether pleased with prospects for having a mental institution nearby and declined to sell him anything. Earlier, he had offered to purchase the house.

7. Carroll was a native of Cooperstown, Pa. The private park at the hospital included a baseball diamond, that sport being his choice for team play. He was a participant, his favorite position being that of pitcher. Some thought he was from Cooperstown, N.Y., that being national shrine for the game.

8. Early on, he realized that certain physical conditions could not be treated through established behavioral patterns alone, or even with attendant recovery from ordinary disease, and he developed some of the techniques involved with a new form of treatment becoming popularly known as shock therapy.

***

1. Buildings extended over 20 acres while the park covered 60 acres. Major structures included *Highland Hall*, a 40-room brick building; *Central Building*, the old with 65 rooms, the new with 100; and *Oak Lodge* with 60 rooms for men. Other structures included *Brushwood Bungalow, Corner Cottage, Highland Terrace, Hill House,* and *Barr Cottage*, a farmhouse with outbuildings. Many patients hiked to the farm, some camping out in the woods overnight. Various activities included cooking there. A favorite was gathering apples and baking pies.

2. The Carroll residence, Homewood, also located on the grounds, was a 30-room mansion. (Not to be confused with Hopewell.) The music hall there became widely known for social events.

3. Dr. Evelyn Ivey-Davis recalled seeing two persons walking from *Highland Hall* to *Central Building*. "One a nurse in starched white uniform with high collar and distinctive little organdy cap with black band above lacy ruffles. The other a tall man, straight as a ramrod, balding head fringed with white hair, frameless glasses and starched white suit, jacket of which resembled a navy officer's *dress white* without the brass buttons."

4. On November 21, 1918, ten days after the Armistice, he bought 210 acres on Elk Mountain from Frank M. Weaver and 159 adjoining on December 11. He purchased 32 additional acres from H.A. Dunham, the music store owner, on September 24, 1923. The latter adjoined the historic property of Roy Cagle, a neighbor of Dunham's in the music business.

5. Evelyn Ivey-Davis also remembered playing tennis with Zelda Fitzgerald. "She played with varying form but usually maintained precision. A charming companion, always interested in others, willing to share some anecdote about her travels and persons she had known."

6. One of these techniques involved injection of normal inactive horse serum in the spinal canal, an element in treatment of *dementia praecox*. On January 13, 1923, he gave the first in a series of such injections by lumbar puncture, with successful results.

7. He later purchased a handsome, pink granite mansion at No. 391 Midland Drive in Lake View Park. In use of stone masonry, the structure was reminiscent of his house on the hospital grounds. His library contained many rare & interesting materials that he was pleased to share with others, including Dr. Sondley.

8. On April 10, 1952, *Hopewell* was conveyed by Rumbough heirs to Duke University as an administration building, in exchange for the Beaverdam property, 450 acres along both sides of Elk Mountain Scenic Highway for about a mile. Differences in appraised value adjusted in cash to the Rumboughs. The hospital had been given to the School of Medicine.

***

1. Son of a German diplomat, Von Ruck was born in Constantinople when his father was stationed there in days before the Crimean War. He received his medical education at Tubingen. He wanted to do for plague what Jenner had done with smallpox.

2. He married Delia Moore of Ohio, the gracious & charming daughter of a Presbyterian minister. She provided a tempering influence on her baronial and sometimes aloof husband, a primary factor behind social contributions. Among other things their spacious greenhouse was much admired. His warmer side was seldom displayed in professional life. He sometimes seemed to feel that perhaps his strong personality might have led to misunderstanding of his attitude toward colleagues and on occasion went out of his way to speak well of his brethren and make clear that he thought highly of their work.

3. Outbuildings included servants quarters and a stable, later used as a residence by the head gardener.

4.   Winyah was originally an Indian name. Many called all Von Ruck properties that, thereby creating some confusion.

5.   A primary source of information about the tuberculosis era was a special article by Dr. Irby Stephens, on file at Pack Library

6.   The Schoenheits later moved to Biltmore Forest and a house with library overlooking the first hole of the golf course.

7.   In 1922, Ambler built 50-bed Ambler Heights on a beautiful knoll in Swannanoa Valley. It became a model for others. Proficient in woodworking, he built a house at 27 Hilltop, around the corner from Schoenheit. It was completed in January of 1929. The site was the highest lot in elevation there. A sitting room with an expanse of casement windows was used by certain of his patients at various times. He died there in 1932.

8.   Sunday *New York Times* (8-2-14) carried a big feature article with photographs of the house under a headline reading SECRETARY BRYAN'S RETREAT in the LAND of the SKY. A small cottage was built by the driveway for the Secret Service.

9.   The house at 241 Old Toll Road was transferred from Randolph to Grove to Bryan, back to Grove, and then to Berger.

NINE

RECUPERATION & RECOVERY

Away from military training camps, the city's war role in 1917 was continuation of what the area had been since 1817 when Flat Rock had been discovered, a place for restoration of health. City fathers wasted no time in addressing needs and the result was not one but two army general hospitals.

Following the Spanish-American War, the government had established magnificent Soldiers Home north across the mountain, outside Johnson City. Buildings architecturally detailed in classic style. Landscaped grounds including lawns, fields, lakes, great trees, & extensive shrubbery. Some civic leaders wanted to see a beautiful domicilliary for disabled veterans at Asheville but authorities felt the existing facility was adequate for needs of the mountain region.

Now a different opportunity arose. Plans for rebuilding Kenilworth Inn had not come to fruition but late in 1913, construction commenced. As constraints & restrictions resulting from war began to take effect, however, work slowed down. And then on April 6, 1917, the U.S. declared war on Germany and progress was reduced to fits & spurts. The Army began constructing temporary barracks & hospitals.

Here one would emerge in a modern, indeed brand new resort hotel designed for socially prominent visitors, the other on broad, rolling farmland nearby. The first was operated on a temporary basis; the second would become one of the leading institutions of its kind.

By now, the inn was nearing completion. And Dr. Battle was following things closely, his dramatic & courtly appearance attracting the usual admiring attention. Always prepared for battle, he discussed the situation with Drs. Cheesborough and Jordan, his colleagues, and several prominent lung specialists, including Von Ruck & Paul Ringer. They devised a plan of campaign to bring about use of this handsome edifice, with its spacious grounds, for military purposes. To them, it seemed only natural.

In essence, the idea was for them to bring to the attention of the Surgeon General those characteristics of the city and its environs that they had promoted all along. With their contacts at high levels, the medical leadership encountered no great difficulty in bringing about the desired result. Soon thereafter, certain members of the chief medical officer's staff went to Union Station in Washington and boarded a sleeping car of the *Asheville Special*. At Biltmore, a delegation from the medical fraternity was there to greet them.

Timing was fortuitous. The War Department was making a study of possible places for recuperation of military patients, and some of those possibilities posed problems. Looking up from the station platform, through the trees, officers of the Medical Corps beheld an imposing new stucco-on-tile Tudoresque structure. A clean new facility, built to house 500 guests with 250 bedrooms and other accommodations. All of this contained in five-story gabled wings organized around a central circulation & service tower that focused the façade with a large bay window, also five stories.

In their reconnoitre, the visitors were impressed by site & setting as well. From both a military and medical point of view, it seemed ideal. No construction required. No site acquisition & preparation, both of which could present unforeseen complication & delay. Ambulance drivers and other military or quasi-military personnel such as that of the Red Cross would have direct access to the passenger station & yards on the riverbanks below. And concrete paved streets & sidewalks led not only into the village but also directly to various medical facilities and supply sources of the city.

Back at the capital, these scouts reported favorable findings directly to the Surgeon General's office and soon the Quartermaster General was contacted with a view toward making necessary arrangements. Fine salesmanship by Battle & Associates, and the natural situation as well, led to conclusion that *de novo* facilities were also indicated.

Returning to Biltmore, the officers went back down the line, looking for a site on which to build. It was 3.75 miles to the next station. Azalea, home of the Cheesboroughs. There, stretching out to the north, they found beautiful rolling countryside. Complete with panoramic view and a river nearby as well. One short station stop away from the main hospital.

Again calling on the judge advocate and quartermaster corps, they went to work securing property. From Berkley Cain Brown, they acquired cow barns, meadows, cornfields, horse barns, & wheat fields, along with his homestead and some woods. In all, some 179 acres. It was the central or primary tract for what would eventually become a 337-acre proposition, one of the most beautiful pieces of land in the U.S. Army. A place to build one of the finest hospitals in the country.

On February 27 of the following year, the new commandant for Kenilworth Hospital arrived at Biltmore with his headquarters detachment. They stepped down from the train to a special new Army loading platform. On March 1, the Army took over General Hospital No. 12. Over the following weeks, medical personnel began reporting for duty, some from a Red Cross hospital on Long Island, and then on the 25th, two things happened on the same day.

In the morning, ground was broken at Azalea and in the afternoon, work crews completed their job at Kenilworth, with exception of minor finishing touches by sub-contractors. The first hospital operating on a temporary, wartime basis, the second on its way to becoming one of the leading institutions of its kind.

By now, nearly all of Asheville society was keenly aware of the situation and ready to participate. Both men and women volunteered to be responsible for the supporting activities at Kenilworth and both summer sojourners and permanent residents adopted the two projects as if they were their own. Every possible need was met, men even signing up as unskilled labor without pay for construction work.

At the 500-bed Kenilworth facility, final equipment was installed, and first patients admitted on May 18, about a week before the last details were completed. In due course, every bed was filled the station platform below becoming a sporadic hub of activity in the process.

***

Pioneering work by Asheville physicians was also a precursor to thoracic medicine later practiced in the community. The German tradition had also aroused concern for condition of patients subjected to poison gas in fields & trenches on the Western Front, all part of advancement in medical science of warfare.

Battle continued to impress upon others significance of the Asheville Plateau and the many studies that had been made, along with exhaustive research in which Von Ruck Institute was engaged. Professional papers on these and related subjects were being read at meetings of medical societies.

***

Meanwhile, quiet little Azalea Station was becoming a busy place. A spur line was constructed across road & river into the farm site. Difficulty imposed by elevation of terrain was overcome by construction of an inclined plane.

Some materials were brought to Azalea from the Biltmore freight station, facing the passenger station across the tracks. To provide additional local transportation for workers, prominent citizens of Asheville turned out with drivers and motor vehicles of every kind, sedans, broughams, cabriolets, limousines, touring cars, delivery wagons fitted out with seats, small panel trucks similarly equipped. A modified local version of the famous "taxicab army" that saved Paris. At its peak, a force of 1,509 men was engaged, with another two hundred or more persons involved in ancillary work. Morale was high.

The original idea of a large building to handle overflow from Kenilworth, Hot Springs and other facilities had become a formal plan for 49 frame buildings of cantonment type and even before ground was broken, that number had been increased to 64. Realization spread that the Army had found one of the prime locations anywhere in the country, particularly where climate, air & water were important considerations. Situated near North Fork, the site was ideal. The Quartermaster described it this way...

Water for the reservation is obtained...from the city main, which runs through the property. It comes directly from mountain streams, (with) a watershed on which there is no human habitation. Supply is far in excess of requirements for city and hospital combined...and further assurance of an ample supply in case of fire or accident to the main may be found in four great tanks, which together provide reserves of half a million gallons.

Work progressed rapidly and on September 4, the first patient was admitted. When the project was completed early the following April, there were 1200 patients and an Army garrison of approximately 800. Under command of Col. Henry W. Hoagland, it was now identified as General Hospital No. 19, consisting of 104 buildings. Recognizing its value, officials decided to make the most of it. Authorization for an additional 500 beds was obtained and by the first of June, the number of buildings had increased to 228, an astonishing cantonment scattered throughout the woods and even extending up near the top of ridgelines.

Meanwhile, the Army maintained a successful operation at Kenilworth until needs had declined substantially and on September 1, 1919, it withdrew. A total of 2,351 patients had been treated, most of them with after-effects of pneumonia while serving overseas.

***

Having fulfilled wartime purposes, Kenilworth was transferred back to its owners and on October 16, 1920, Azalea was transferred to the Public Health Service. Veterans continued to be accommodated, along with some others who had rendered public service to their country.

In recognition of its Cherokee land heritage, Azalea was then named *Oteen.* A place to restore health to the disabled. Because of its setting, diseases of the chest had been treated from the beginning. Now it was determined to specialize in cases of tuberculosis.

During the course of the following year, it became apparent that the original frame buildings were inadequate for that purpose and plans were begun for conversion to permanent structures. On May 1, 1922, the hospital was acquired by the Veterans Bureau and the plans taken over. From this, a master plan for utilization of the property was drawn and put into effect the next year.

Not by coincidence, the first director of the bureau, when it was established in 1921, was a friend of Dr. Battle. Early in 1924, construction of a handsome tile-and-stucco edifice was commenced, the first of a series. It was a good time to begin such a project, coinciding as it did with that splendid building era, and many handsome buildings that were erected there reflected the quality of architecture during the period. It would make Oteen one of the most beautiful hospitals of its kind in the country.

One by one, a new structure went up and when it was completed and in use, certain old frame structures were demolished. With grand views in several directions, 15 acres of lawn and 60 of fields, flower & vegetable gardens, and seemingly endless walking paths, it became a bird sanctuary as well as a sanctuary for those whose health had been impaired while serving in defense of their country. Patients came from nearly every state. The massive central administration building was completed in 1928. Thus the building boom in Asheville was reflected here beneath the Craggy Mountains, a collection of Georgian and Colonial Revival work. A dozen buildings with ancillary facilities, including half a dozen dignified residences along Riceville Road for ranking officials or staff.

In the spring of 1930, when the last of the old frame structures was demolished, it had gained a wide reputation for living up to its name. A telephone at the railway station made it easy to call for prompt transportation. Transient emergency cases were accepted and patients were not forced to sign papers of any kind. The veteran was given a set of rules & regulations to read and welcomed as a guest. Under this dedicated philosophy, it became the largest hospital of its kind in the land with one of the highest rates of recuperation.

***

When a classic little bank building was opened next to the railway passenger station in Biltmore, the wartime link was continued with opening of a branch near the entrance to the hospital. The name Biltmore-Oteen Bank was adopted. A post office was established next door to the branch bank on the hospital grounds. Horse drawn hospital wagons were no longer to be seen but an old road & bridge across the river to the hospital grounds, a mile north of the station, was still in use.

As late as 1911, tuberculosis was still the leading cause of death in all age groups but by 1930 it was beginning to yield to modern methods & technology, and the value of mountain air and screened porches for rest & therapy was being seriously questioned. Whether a certain kind of mountain environment & climate was salubrious & efficacious or not, many persons believed that it was and perhaps it is a bit presumptuous to render categorical judgments in matters of this kind.

By this time, the business community had belatedly come around to recognition of the value of the tuberculosis trade, at the very time that the era was coming to an end. Medical research was forging ahead with new classes of drugs and the T.B. business quietly faded away, much to the relief of many, including some of the city's relentless press agents who could not reconcile it with their commercial fairy tales.

The German Invasion

When Mr. Wilson signed a declaration of war, it brought Germans to Asheville well before American servicemen arrived at the hospitals. Within minutes, German and Austrian commercial ships in neutral American waters were seized. Seamen suddenly became enemy aliens but since they were not prisoners of war, their future was uncertain.

These men served on the more than 30 Hamburg-Amerika and North German Lloyd ships, including the palatial *Vaterland,* largest vessel afloat. Fleet Commodore Hans Ruser of that ship had commanded his country's superior flagships, including *Imperator* and *Bismarck.* Under his command, *Imperator* carried a crew of 1,100 and up to four thousand passengers.

During the first week in May, rumors began circulating in Hot Springs that the Germans were coming. The general manager of the Mountain Park came to *Hopewell* for conferences with the Rumboughs, their attorneys, and federal officials, after which they all boarded the *Montford Special* car for the Depot and Washington to negotiate a lease. Authorities accepted the idea of a ready-made solution to the problem.

The first aliens to arrive came off the train on June 8th, an advance unit of 18 men. Four days later, five officers and 53 crewmen followed. During succeeding weeks, hundreds more continued to arrive, remaining in railway cars on a siding until they could be marched down to the hotel, where officers were housed. Sailors were assigned to crewmen's barracks, temporary structures of the *cantonment* type built along the river near a steel truss bridge.

Each move took about an hour and curious townspeople turned out in number to watch the procedure. It was the start of a close relationship, gradually becoming a way of life based on mutual respect. Some wives obtained rooms or rented houses to be near their husbands, some children among them. The widely known qualities of Teutonic industriousness were evident immediately and the men built a community with many characteristics of an enclave or village in the old country.

German was spoken frequently in the streets and cultural aspects of the "invasion" were manifest. One of these was the German Imperial Band. The harbor of Tsingtao had been seized by Imperial Germany in 1897 and band members were caught there by Allied capture of the colony during early days of the war. Both soldiers and Red Cross workers had been held at Ellis Island. At a depot platform converted to a band shell here, they gave rousing concerts that proved stirring to the community.

In November, a new infirmary was finished, replacing one that had been maintained in Hampton Cottage. The men could forward any complaints they might have to the Swiss Embassy in Washington but there were few. Early the following year, additional aliens were taken into custody at Charleston and in Panama & the Philippines. On February 8th, 460 arrived in two special troop trains from San Francisco and a week later 163 more came in from New Jersey, having boarded the cars at Trenton, bringing the total to 2,185.

This was the high water mark of the internment camp. In May, a few were paroled and then some others were transferred elsewhere. Somewhere along the line, it seems there was a growing feeling, resulting from newspaper publicity, that enemy aliens should not be housed in luxury quarters. Reports of American casualties and German atrocities were mounting. Orders were prepared for transfer of all inmates to the nearest military war prison, that being at Ft. Oglethorpe, Georgia, a suburb of Chattanooga.

This would make way for conversion to a convalescent camp for soldiers, American soldiers, returning from the battlefield. An army post for those who needed it most.

Endnotes

1. Started in 1901, the facility at Mountain Home paralleled building of the Clinchfield, with which it connected. The first building was completed early in 1903 and by 1909 it was complete.
2. On June 18, 1914, the Archduke Ferdinand was assassinated at Sarajevo, thus precipitating war between the Central Powers and other allied European nations.
3. As commander of the American Expeditionary Force, General Pershing arrived at Paris on June 14 and on October 21 units of the 1st Division moved into the Toul sector, relieving French regiments holding the line.
4. The agreement called for completion of the Kenilworth company's building plans, which were nearly finished, minor changes to accommodate military medical operations, and return of property at the end of the term.
5. Elevation at the base of Kenilworth Inn was 2,250 feet above sea level. In latitude & longitude, the Square was situated at 35* 36' north, 82* 32' west. A benchmark at the post office showed 2,210'. Highest elevation in city was about 2,700'.
6. Writing a report of the station, a medical officer described Kenilworth as "situated in the center of a circular plateau, horizon of which is one continuous circle of mountain peaks. A view from top of the building is one vast panorama as far as the eye can see, surpassed by none and equaled only in Switzerland. Air dry, bracing, & invigorating, average mean temperature 35 degrees."
7. The first major contingent of patients arrived at Kenilworth by military medical train from Camp Lee near Richmond on June 22. It consisted of 150 soldiers suffering from emphysema.
8. Modified from a promotional gate house, entrance to hospital grounds from Biltmore Avenue was marked by a sentry post at Kenilworth Road. Following reversion to civilian use, it was again remodeled, its old street lamp posts a familiar sight to generations of Ashevillians.

***

1. Contract for Azalea was let on March 13, 1918, to Gude & Co. of Atlanta, A.J. Krebs general manager. This firm had built barracks for an internment camp at Hot Springs.
2. In order to ensure adherence to construction schedule, railway officials offered to operate a shuttle from Biltmore, if necessary.
3. Additional land was acquired, particularly the Folsom family tract.
4. Some supplies & materials were conveyed from the station by special fleet of vehicles with solid rubber tires.
5. The word *cantonment* comes from quartering troops in parts of an occupied city, dividing them into districts or cantons composed of individual lodgings or dwelling places, perhaps in or near a native quarter.
6. First Battle of the Marne began on September 5, 1914. Two days later, with Joffre in distress and the capital threatened an emergency was declared and city taxicab drivers came to the rescue. Two convoys of 600 cabs, mostly Renaults, raced into action, loaded with *poilu*. Actual military effect was questionable but it galvanized Gallic spirit. Wild rendering of *l Marseillaise* followed.
7. On behalf of his fellows, a workman wrote a poem. It may not have won any medals but did a fair job of expressing spirited sentiments then prevailing among those with loved ones in service or who were otherwise motivated by patriotic fervor.
8. Opening lines read: Calls the voice of fifteen hundred, As the men put out to sea, We are out here at Azalea, In the cause of liberty. 'Tho we can't dress up in khaki, And go fight the Devil Hun, Yet we're pulling for you, comrades, Every day 'til set of sun; And, by God, we'll labor for you, So that we prepare a place, For the soldiers that come shattered, But a smile upon the face. You will find Camp Nineteen ready, 'Mongst the hills of old N.C. And the very pines will welcome, You, the sons of Old Glory.

***

1. Many workers were older men, some elderly. In a sentimental mood, they contributed a generous portion of their pay to a fund that was sent to Washington to help returning boys in uniform.
2. The optimistic target date was six months and work was finished well ahead, being complete within five months except for installation of certain equipment & materials, delayed in delivery.
3. As soon as the first tract was acquired, the Red Cross went ahead and built (1917) a sturdy recreation building which became very popular. In 1919, the property was deeded to the Army and continued in permanent use.
4. There were 34 standard main wards, each with two 30x84 wings providing superb outdoor sleeping quarters. There were 19 other wards of various types to accommodate officers, nurses, barracks staff & so forth, plus administration building, operating pavilion, mess halls, and many other entities.
5. There were also several auxiliary buildings, including those of the Y.M.C.A. and Knights of Columbus. Others consisted of small living quarters, offices, utility structures and other service facilities.
6. Heat was furnished by a battery of 11 150-horsepower boilers with nine miles of steam lines & returns. There were also nine miles of electric pole lines and 3.5 miles of high tension transmission lines along railway tracks from the power company's Biltmore sub-station.

***

1. The army hospital magazine was called *The Oteen*. It was believed that the Cherokee called this particular area by that word, meaning a felicitous condition in which health & cheer were the chief aim, a place of recuperation for debilitated & infirm.
2. Colonel Hoagland remained commander from start to finish. He thought *Oteen* was a good name and suggested it to successors of the Veterans Administration. They received the recommendation favorably and the idea was promptly adopted.
3. A widely recognized feature was *heliotherapy* or treatment of disease by sunbaths. Made possible by climate, it was carried out during rest periods in spacious open air porches & decks.
4. Patients included veterans of the Civil War & Spanish-American War. Nurses were included, along with a few other government employees who had rendered public service of a qualifying nature, as well as some soldiers & sailors of Allied forces during wartime.
5. Dr. Herbert was interested in both projects but had volunteered for the British Army before America entered the war and was serving with the Royal Medical Corps as a field surgeon.
6. Most of the fewer than a hundred remaining patients at Kenilworth were transferred to Ft. McPherson.

***

1. During 1925, two large structures were placed in service for handling infirmary patients. The following year, provision was made for erection of a receiving pavilion to house clinical facilities, along with physicians quarters and a new kitchen.
2. In 1929, work was started on a model home for nurses and a mess hall containing three large dining rooms, both put into service the following April. Over the next two years, central heating plant and laundry were replaced, two additional buildings for patient care added, and the plan was complete with 37 buildings, 527 employees, and bed capacity of 852.
3. On July 21, 1930, President Hoover established the Veterans Administration by executive order, the purpose being to consolidate all government activities in behalf of veterans.
4. Patients were primarily those with diseases of the chest, including consumptive ailments and those brought on by chemical warfare. As additional personnel came in, the name Asheville brought this to mind in some quarters. "When someone said *Asheville*," a New Yorker later remarked, "I immediately thought *chronic coughing*. Consumption. T.B. But some thought about consequences of trench warfare. Mustard or chlorine gas."
5. The same solution proposed earlier to overcome gradient from Depot to Square downtown. Operated by a hoisting engine, the inclined plane snaked unbroken loads of material up a hill in a fraction of the time that would have been required for horses & mules or trucks, had there been roads for the purpose.
6. Fancy promotional brochures published by civic boosters boasted of two dozen TB specialists and a thousand beds for patients all over town, five here, fifty there. One title was *Health & Happiness in the Land of the Sky* and it was predicated on an assumption that consumption or any other malaise or scourge could be contained by positive sloganeering & fictional approach to problems through a romance of the mountains.
7. At Kenilworth, most of the fewer than a hundred remaining patients at Kenilworth were transferred to Ft. McPherson.

The German Invasion

1. Secretary of the Navy Josephus Daniels of Raleigh called these prizes of war "the fleet the Kaiser built for us." When Great Britain declared war earlier, these men took cover in American ports.

2. His grandson, Alfred Rumbough, a government official in Washington, first suggested Mountain Park for this purpose.

3. The Presbyterian school there was called Dorland Institute. Its guest register contained signatures of many prominent persons, including Mr. Vanderbilt. Relatives of John Quincy Adams. During the war, it was signed by prominent German scholars visiting their countrymen.

4. In November, Commodore Ruser was dismayed to learn that the *Vaterland* was being stripped of furniture, carpeting, & artwork, elegant rooms now recognizable only by their handsome wall paneling. Renamed *Leviathan*, it was ready to carry up to 17,000 doughboys, triple bunked in every corner.

5. In early days, Commodore Ruser came over to the Asheville Depot to meet arrivals and greet internees. Many saluted but as time went by, customs were relaxed.

6. A 19-year-old inmate was apprehended by camp guards near Sandy Bottom about 15 miles up river. Formerly a cabin boy, he had become alarmed about prospects for being held prisoner at a military base and escaped during the night. Found next day, Monday, June 17, he was confined to camp jail overnight, sent to Ft. Oglethorpe the following day.

7. Although the men arrived at Biltmore seriously ill, without money or clothing, the War Department insisted that they be guarded and sent 18 soldiers from Oglethorpe for the purpose.

8. A full account of the episode may be found in *The German Invasion of Western North Carolina*, Jacqueline Burgin Painter & Jonathan William Horstman. A pictorial history. (Biltmore Press, Asheville, 1992.)

PART FOUR

THE STREETS OF ALTAMONT

ONE

FOOTLIGHTS & FOOTNOTES

As the turn of the century approached, the opera house was going strong but competition emerged with talk of building a regular theater auditorium. Like hotels and livery stables, theaters were firetraps and there was some concern that the opera house might be dangerous. The man in the street did not use it and was not overly concerned.

The City had required owners to make renovations for purposes of safety and this had allayed fears to some extent but a problem remained. Fashionable merchants had space on either side of the entrance from the sidewalk and a staircase to the upper floors was hazardous in the event that fire should break out.

Even if the situation could be contained, however, demand exceeded seating and so a larger hall was needed. In later years, when the road company of *Ben Hur* came to Asheville, it involved horses on a moving platform, a good example of why more modern equipment was required. With organization of the Board of Trade, businessmen were ready to move forward.

Its first order of business was the auditorium question. On February 3, 1898, a special committee met at City Hall to determine a proper course. On the 19th, it met again to consider a site. There was some thought that it should be located on or near the Square but no suitable site was found available in that congested district. It was decided that further study was in order.

Much as the Square was the civic and commercial center, so Battery Park Hill was the social and cultural center. Committee members came to agree that Battery Park was the appropriate place. And they recommended formation of "an association of citizens." On September 18, 1900, the Asheville Auditorium Company was incorporated with able, affable Duff Merrick as chairman.

Shares of capital stock were offered immediately and enthusiasm was so great that some 400 subscriptions were received by close of business the following day. The social Four Hundred all wanted aboard, it seemed. Aston, Rawls & Company, a leading real estate agency, already had an option for the site, more than an acre of the spacious Penland estate directly across Haywood Street from the north entrance driveway to the hotel grounds.

On October 4th, an organizational meeting of stockholders was held at the hotel, standing room only. Professional theater consultants came down from New York. J.M. Westall & Company was engaged as building contractor. On March 9, 1901, good weather prevailing, the groundbreaking ceremony was held.

The formal, handsome new structure was in the Federal style of architecture, brick with limestone trim. It proved to be as popular as its proud backers had hoped, a symbol of progress and an object of civic pride. The initial performance was given before a full house on April 14-15 in the following spring, with the formal opening on May 7th. The coming season was a full one at both theaters, auditorium and opera house, and the season following started off strong with visitors from Florida and the East in attendance.

Before long, the city had gained wide recognition as a center for the performing arts. On the evening of October 23, 1903, *The Favour of the Queen* was presented. Then during the night, the building caught fire in a howling wind. The first alarm came in at 4:15 o'clock. Every available fireman was summoned to duty. Several were at risk of personal danger but made the utmost effort.

Flames were visible from the fire station on the Square and from the Biltmore House, Kenilworth Inn, and other vantage points around town. Sparks from the fiery inferno slightly damaged a section of roof at the Penland house nearby and for a while, there was fear that the blaze might spread to the hotel or the downtown business district on the southeast, depending on how the windstorm veered. It was finally extinguished but by then the building had nearly burned to the ground. A night to remember.

The business community was stunned. Directors met in special session the very next morning, even before the embers had gone out. The mood was sombre but not one of hopelessness.

The project had been a success and no one had been harmed physically, something for which to be grateful. There was no question but that they were in the right location. There had been complaints about acoustics but there was also a positive side. After newspapers published side elevation drawings showing sight lines, directors had tentatively approved raising the building in stages, first the main floor, then the stage, and finally the roof.

The question was whether to act or postpone a decision. A motion was offered to rebuild. The vote was unanimous in favor. The leadership set to work with determination, again raising funds in a short time without waiting for help from city government, which was unlikely anyway.

Then on December 30 came news that shocked the community and the nation. The Erlanger theater in Chicago, known as the *Iroquois*, had caught fire during the holidays and 600 persons were trapped, unable to open exit doors from the inside. Some were trampled to death in the ensuing panic and all became part of a monstrous human funeral pyre, the worst indoor disaster in American history.

The new building was an entirely different architectural proposition with various measures taken for fire protection, including a huge silo on the south side, with a circular sloping ramp inside, one on which patrons could slide to the bottom in safety during an emergency. Seating capacity was 1,955 persons, later expanded to 2,305. The opening beneath the proscenium arch was fifty feet wide and thirty feet high. In all, a phoenix rising rapidly from the ashes. Workmen were dedicated and some building crews worked triple shifts. Eight to four, six to two, two to ten.

Opening night was September 29, 1904. The attraction was a production of *Human Hearts*. Introductory remarks drew heavy applause, which could be heard at the hotel across the way. And once again it was a gala occasion with a full house to greet those onstage, formal attire worn by those in the orchestra section, balcony, four boxes on each side, and elsewhere.

Over the years, there followed a broad panoply of great stars, including the world famous. A long line of interesting personalities that made the socially inclined want to wine and dine guests and take part in proceedings...Caruso, Galli-Curci, Madame Schumann-Heinke. Sarah Bernhardt, called "the divine Sarah." The great Helen Hayes and the incomparable Maude Adams. William Gillette, Walter Hampden, DeWolfe Hopper. Olga Petrova. Anna Pavlova. (Pavalowa.)

Beginning with the 1907-8 season, both theaters came under control of the Schuberts, in collaboration with the powerful Erlanger syndicate. Starting that year, only productions of the highest quality were booked into the Auditorium while touring attractions and other stock companies went to the Opera House.

The opera house was somewhat sheltered but when a February cold mass roared through, Battery Park Hill was the coldest spot in town and the Auditorium was hard to heat. On occasion, those near the orchestra pit had seen a famous player shivering. In late February of 1909, Sarah Bernhardt played *Camille* there. Interviewed after the performance, she was asked what she thought of the Auditorium, then relatively new.

"Ah, it is so large," she replied. "It is grand. C'est magnifique." Then with a characteristic Gallic shrug, the world's most famous actress relapsed into her native French. "Mais, c'est froid. Mon dieu, c'est le pole du Nord!" Whether or not this motivated transfer of the property to city fathers, they acquired it that same year, before the next season opened. And changed the name from Asheville Auditorium to City Auditorium.

These were the halcyon days. The second decade was even more successful, despite some distraction from the war. There were many big name draws such as the Barrymores, royal family of the legitimate theater. And Englishman Caryl Florio, the noted music director at All Souls, gave concerts there.

It became tradition for A.G. Fields and his jovial minstrels to open the season by putting everyone in a mood of good spirits for the upcoming schedule. No one could name all the players...or all the prominent members of the audience...but they might include Adelina Patti or Rosa Ponselle. John McCormack. Eddie Foy for comic relief. Sir Henry Irving. Richard Mansfield. Ruth Chatterton.

There was Jan Paderewski. Fritz Kreisler. Charles Wakefield Cadman, the composer and pianist whose work was often inspired by romantic interpretation of Indian themes. John Philip Sousa. The Philadelphia Orchestra. The San Carlo Grand Opera Company was a regular seasonal feature. Paul Whiteman & His Orchestra. *Rhapsody in Blue.* The sound of an era nearing its shocking finale.

Helen Keller. James Whitcomb Riley. Clarence Darrow. Billy Sunday. Sir Harry Lauder. Houdini. Jack Dempsey. Will Rogers. Calvin Coolidge speaking on world affairs of the day before a well educated audience.

Somewhere along in here, the first rudimentary motion pictures began to make their appearance, first in a primitive form at the Berkeley where a room off the lobby was set aside for a contraption into which viewers could peer for glimpses of the flickering pictures. They certainly posed no social challenge...in fact, they were rather disreputable...but they piqued curiosity.

Within a few years, advent of the nickelodeon brought a more regularized schedule although wooden benches proved the rule, along with a plain muslin sheet for a screen. They were centered along Patton from Battery Park Place, where the Dreamland lit up the corner in a blaze of light bulbs on the wall, to the Square where several houses were clustered at one time or another, including a few whose names would later become long forgotten.

Some traditional citizens thought these early cinematic houses...the Classic, Airdome, Dreamland, Nickelodeon, Theato, Galax, Gayety, Gayoso, Vance, Palace, Princess, Sapphire and Strand...were like toadstools but they attained a measure of public acceptance. And while they were lumped together in many a mind with saloons, pawn shops, pool halls, and brothels, they had an innate potential for improvement far beyond the imagination of many who saw them as a transitory nuisance.

As for the opera house, late in 1911 fire marshals warned that the building was structurally unsound and there was the possibility of "a terrible catastrophe." Use by an audience was prohibited although the ground floor continued to be used by various commercial enterprises. Talk of a second remodeling came to naught and acting on the report of an investigating committee, City authorities ordered closure.

One evening, following a final presentation of *The Bishop's Carriage*, the doors were closed forever.

***

When the Twenties came to a close, and the Dismal Thirties began, the number of events declined precipitously and then another problem arose. Fire marshals declared the building a hazard. Fire Chief A.L. Duckett said that such a situation also threatened the new George Vanderbilt Hotel next door since the 15' alley in between was insufficient to afford protection from a major fire.

The Auditorium was condemned by City Council and remained vacant during most of the Depression days that lay ahead, a tangible ghost of Fashionable Asheville in a time of lowered spirits. Just as the second world war was starting, it was replaced by an ordinary sort of facility. An all-purpose vehicle, serving no purpose well, it would cause problems from the very night it was opened.

Endnotes

1. The Board of Trade was established on January 12, 1898. On September 9, 1922, the name was changed to Chamber of Commerce.
2. The program that evening was a musical comedy, *Sergeant Kitty.*
3. Asheville was the smallest Southern city on leading circuits, sometimes the only one in the state.
4. The disaster forever changed fire protection laws and had a profound effect on the institutional side of architecture as well.
5. The black silo was later painted with white letters running vertically down the side, reading RADIO-KEITH-ORPHEUM, often known by the acronym, RKO.
6. The ubiquitous R.S. Smith was involved with architectural details, as he would be later with the Catholic church across the street.
7. A wag said the strange exit device enabled the fashionable to flee for the bottom in their glad rags without singeing their own, even if friction burn might cause some "smoking derrieres." Another alluded to petty complaints about acoustics by remarking that the fire could be a case of "acoustical arson."
8. For the year, there were more than a hundred performances at the Auditorium, of which eight could be identified as world class events, and 91 in all at the opera house, the latter representing a wide variety of entertainment.
9. Ethel Barrymore was the last prominent thespian to trod the boards.
10. The hotel was on the site of the Penland house, purchased (1869) from Melvin E. Carter, a prominent attorney who had just been elected mayor that same year, but in 1912, it had become Dr. Briggs house and later office.
11. The building was condemned on June 18, 1931. The new Auditorium (1939) had a peculiar seating capacity. Ostensibly the same as the old, it was actually dependent on the event being staged. A sports event one night, symphony the next, everything jerry rigged in between. No fixed seating, no sloping floor.

TWO

RIDING TO HOUNDS

One Saturday morning, a group of perhaps two dozen colorfully well dressed outdoorsmen gathered at the stables of Battery Park Hotel to go fox hunting at Sulphur Springs. Their aims were not so ambitious at the time but actually this was the origin of country club life in the city.

These energetic socialites mounted their horses, cantered down an equestrian path, and left the grounds through the western gate. After following the car line out Patton to Haywood, they wound down the slope to Smith's Bridge and once having crossed single file to the other side, proceeded on to the springs, some three miles from the river as the crow flies.

It was early 1893 and hunting was good in this section. Nearby stood charred remains of the Belmont, still smoking only six months before. Some guests had enjoyed occasional forays into woods and fields of surrounding areas and there had been talk of forming an English style hunt club, but nothing came of it. Now there was renewed interest.

Since the grand opening in 1886, the fashionable social leadership had made its headquarters at Battery Park but Belmont and Kenilworth were providing benign competition, until each burned to the ground. For some weeks after the fire, however, there was talk about what a shame the Belmont disaster was and how unfortunate those guests had been, unable to go hunting and enjoy other activities that had been part of the scene since earliest days.

Someone pointed out that the area was available and a consensus was reached that opportunities should be explored. The Swannanoa Hunt Club was informally formed for purposes of fox hunting and those objectives relating to hunting in general. Among prominent members was Mr. J. E. Rumbough, socially active mayor of Montford. From this, development of club facilities would extend over the nest 35 years.

The time was ripe. At *Biltmore*, construction at the great house had just reached its halfway mark. The opera house was in full stride. The first permanent post office had opened at the foot of Battery Park Hill and the Carrier line from Sulphur Springs had been extended to connect with it. Mission Hospital had recently moved into a new building of its own. And the first city hall was now open on the Square.

Many prominent citizens would be involved in this social enterprise but one was essential. And Dr. Thomas Patton Cheesborough had special qualifications. His mother was a Patton of Asheville his father a Cheesborough of Charleston. He himself was a cross blend between Charlestonians and native stock, basic components in the equation. Thus he was in a unique position of being the logical catalyst to lead all elements of high society into an organizational structure.

Under the circumstances, no one fit the part more naturally. A friend and social companion of the Vanderbilts, he loved people and was active across a broad spectrum of society. He had been instrumental in earlier beginnings of several smaller private associations and had been a member of

The Asheville Club since its opening. And as a physician, he was engaged in practice with Dr. Battle at Battery Park, a good combination of medical and social interests.

Although not well understood because of its confusing complexity, the saga of Tom Cheesborough's familial connections, this Scottish and Scotch-Irish tribal clan, is virtually that of social development for real society in the mountain kingdom. It incorporated all elements, Charlestonians, pioneer stock, hotel spectrum, business and professional presence, and landholding class. It was fashionable Asheville in microcosm.

When John Cheesborough asked Louisa Patton for her hand in marriage, it all came together in something far more than a single matrimonial couple. The Pattons were prolific. James of Asheville and William of Charleston had already married Kerr sisters there. John Cheesborough of Charleston had married a daughter of one of the Kerrs but she later died.

After the war, he came up to visit her mountain relatives and met Louisa, daughter of James Patton and Henrietta Kerr. Dr. Cheesborough himself married Alice Connally of the Thomas-Connally family. And Haywood Parker married Thomas Patton's daughter. With over a hundred relatives involved, anyone could understand that even family members sometimes got confused.

In the sphere of real property, the situation was similar. These extensive holdings could be found along the river east of Main, south of Beaucatcher, west of Sunset. In town, there were buildings around the square, down Main, west for several blocks, south of Patton, much of which was built on Patton property. They stretched from parts of the road leading out of town toward Sunset and up the slope to the ridgeline further north, out to the north fork of the Swannanoa, and some tracts all the way to Mt. Mitchell in The Blacks, where James had a place called *Mountain Lodge*. A land inventory would be as confusing as a roster of family members.

The Scots Presbyterian Pattons and the Anglican Episcopalian Cheesboroughs were loyal supporters of the church. The Pattons had owned property toward Willow Street, renamed Aston after conveying part of it to the mayor, and had become the "founders of Church Street" by providing land to establish the city's principal churches there, along with Ravenscroft School, an Episcopal training institution. As for land along the river, the Trescotts of Charleston had built a fine house there for a summer home and shortly after it was completed, it was purchased for that same purpose by William Patton.

The newlywed Cheesboroughs went to live there while plans of their own were being completed. It was called *Azalea* by Mr. Patton after the spectacular flame azalea, a native plant found growing there. The river was a source of many an admiring ode...*Swannanoa, nymph of beauty, I would woo thee with my rhyme...wildest, brightest, prettiest river, of our sunny Southern clime*. Fashioned after the Greek Revival style, the house was comfortable, one of several worthy Patton houses. All in all, it was a pleasant place for a honeymoon. Or married life.

The bride this Charlestonian had chosen was equally pleasing. She and her sister Clara were considered to be among the city's most eligible young ladies. Bright, talented, and charming, Louisa had turned down more than one worthy offer of marriage. Now the time had come for a dowry or an inheritance. The two sisters tossed a coin. Clara was by then the mother of the Murphy family and since that portion of these lands toward the mountain already had a fine house on it, she elected to take ownership where she was, and Louisa took the lands lying along the river.

The site of *Azalea* was on the north side of the banks. The couple chose a site a little further upstream on the other side and built their own place. They called it *Springvale*. An infant born there was named Thomas for one of many family members with that name, a middle name for the mother, and last name from his father.

***

Riding to hounds and life related thereto were conducted under auspices of some luminaries in the world of sportsmen and the related circles of high finance and military adventure.

On December 29, 1891, members of the renowned Meadow Brook Hunt Club on Long Island held a special meeting for the sole purpose of deciding whether Thomas Hitchcock, its master of foxhounds, should bring its entire pack to Asheville for the next winter season. The eminent Mr. Hitchcock, a ten-goal ranked international polo star, was allowed to bring with him whatever was deemed fitting and appropriate under circumstances at the time.

Word of the decision was received on New Year's Eve during a party at the Battery Park and the interested sponsoring parties agreed that they would organize a hunt club. The season at hand would be one devoted to learning the rules of the sport, obtaining proper gear, establishing necessary facilities, and engaging in extensive practice.

A member of one of the most aristocratic families in the Anglo-American realm of sporting events, Hitchcock was an Asheville visitor who early saw its possibilities. He had established an 18-square-mile estate at Aiken, South Carolina, and it became the most famous schooling ground in the world for young horses. Fox hunting and yachting were his chief recreation but he had charge of training for the U.S. Polo Association, organized the previous year, and won wider fame in training steeplechase jumpers and hunters. Indeed he became the greatest trainer of such horses in American turf history.

Born at Aiken in 1900, Thomas Junior joined the illustrious *Lafayette Escadrille* with his Asheville friend, Kiffin Rockwell, son of Paul Rockwell, the city's distinguished liaison with the French Army. Shot down behind enemy lines, Hitchcock was taken prisoner but managed to escape to Switzerland. As a result of his exploits, he was awarded the *Croix de Guerre*. A frequent visitor in Asheville, he became the world's greatest polo player, a dashing symbol of the Roaring Twenties and, like Bobby Jones and Bill Tilden, a household name.

The fraternity of sportsmanship in Asheville began life with impeccable credentials on a playing field where new money and political influence did not determine rules of the game.

***

Attracted by accounts of fashionable Asheville in the Eastern press, two Irish Catholics of Boston decided to explore possibilities of moving into the realm of Anglo-American society. Mr. John Francis Fitzgerald and Mr. Patrick Joseph Kennedy set out to "consort with the swells" by making reservations for a drawing room on the *Asheville Special* and a suite at the Battery Park. The winter season.

On June 7, 1895, the first golf links were opened. With valet and secretary, the Boston pair arrived in mid-December, just before completion of *Biltmore*. One time mayor of Boston, Congressman Fitzgerald had become known as *Honey Fitz*. Or *Money* Fitz. Both were reported to have the magic touch with moneyed interests in political circles, various aspects of municipal government, and certain business groups, particularly hospitality and the liquor business.

Here where Appalachian, Southern, and Eastern social strata converged, these ambitious visitors closely observed the social scene. They dressed properly for the popular carriage rides, attended fashionable events at the hotels, and donned "glad rags" for presentations at the Opera House, just around the corner from hotel grounds. Some guests rode while others, weather permitting, strolled down the pedestrian walkways. Congressman Fitzgerald made trips to the capital from time to time, keeping in touch with whatever of interest was going on.

In late afternoon of March 25, 1896, he left Biltmore Station for return to Washington. Mr. Kennedy left for the Bay State about the same time. On October 7, 1914, not long after the guns of August began their colossal barrage, this close association became a family affair, when the Fitzgerald daughter, Rose, was married to the Kennedy son, Joseph.

Under his strong direction, three sons of this union would become major Presidential candidates.

Endnotes

1. In addition to hotel grounds, tennis and badminton courts, bowling alley, croquet yard, the hill included paved streets with electric lamp posts, infirmary, several houses with lawns, nursery and greenhouses, club house, carriage house, gazebo and band shell

2. The five locations were Sulphur Springs, Ramoth, Edgemont, Charlotte Street Extension, and Grove Park Inn.

3. The Belmont burned August 24, 1892.

4. Prior to that, municipal offices were maintained at several small locations on the Square.

5. She was the daughter of his first wife's mother's sister, a result of William & James (second) both having married members of the Kerr family in Charleston.

6. Over the years, John Cheesborough took control of the property and business affairs of much of the family interests on both sides of the inheritance.

7. Louisa Patton was a graduate of old Salem Academy. Zeb Vance and James Evans Brown of *Zealandia* fame were among her many admirers, as described in Vance's published volume, *Love Letters.*

8. Major Breese followed Mr. Cheesborough into the banking business in Charleston and became cashier of the First National there. Through him, he kept apprised of the banking situation in Asheville. When he decided to establish the First National in Asheville, he moved to the city and later on the advice of Mr. Vanderbilt, built a house located centrally between Azalea, Kenilworth, Victoria, Biltmore & Asheville. It later became known as *Cedar Crest.*

9. Starting in 1890, visitors arriving at Biltmore station were met by carriages from Kenilworth Inn that had been erected just above for that purpose.

***

1. Like his father, young "Tommy" was educated at Harvard and Oxford. After helping win the international cup from the British in 1921, he became the toast of Anglo-American sporting society. On December 15, 1928, he married into the Mellon family of Pittsburgh, a relationship that made headlines in the society pages, and at the bottom of the Depression became a partner in the investment banking firm of Lehman Brothers. He worked in Wall Street, Southampton, L.I., and London.

2. He visited friends in Montford, rode horseback and played golf at both Asheville and Biltmore, visited Linville and Highlands. The epitome of romantic derring-do in heady days of *Lucky Lindy,* he enjoyed challenge. In addition to polo, he excelled in six other outdoor sports, was sometimes compared to Douglas Fairbanks or Errol Flynn. While commanding fighter plane group during the second war, he was killed in a plane crash at Salisbury, England. 4-19-44.

3. The senior Hitchcock's father was a noted lawyer, author, and journalist. Called the mother of American polo, his daughter-in-law organized the great Meadowlarks team at Westbury, L.I., N.Y.

THREE

BRINGING SOCIETY TOGETHER

The extended family of Tom Cheesborough reflected the social framework of pioneer settlement as it developed from the Swannanoa northward to the Square. It was one that would touch every facet of city life in some way. And leave its mark.

The original <u>James Patton</u> left Tamlachte parish of Derry, later Londonderry, in Ulster and sailed for America from Larne, north of Belfast, in a wave of emigration to lands of opportunity in the New World. He arrived in Philadelphia after a frightful journey lasting exactly two months through many rough & turbulent seas.

Slowly & laboriously, he worked his way across the traditional Pennsylvania route and down the Great Wagon Road, finally settling in Wilkes County. Along the way, he saved his pennies and provided funds for his mother and ten brothers & sisters to emigrate. Following recovery from illness brought on by his debilitating experiences, he decided on a healthful climate and came to the Swannanoa, settling on a farm. After seven years there, he moved into town early in 1814, 31 years after landing in America, and built the Eagle Hotel.

From Wilkes, a brother's son, <u>William Patton</u>, went to Charleston where he made a fortune dealing in land. He became a prosperous merchant, importer of goods from Britain, and used his capital to acquire numerous tracts. Indeed he owned parcels of land all the way down to Florida. He loved the mountains, however, and came up often to visit his relatives. In Asheville, he acquired the pioneer Pressley house and land tracts as far north as the Black Dome, later named for Prof. Elisha Mitchell. From the Trescotts of Charleston, he learned about their new summer home on the river and purchased it from them. He also built a summer home on the Black Dome.

A plantation owner at Georgetown, <u>John Weaver Cheesborough</u> saw his affluence come to an end when his ship, carrying a full cargo of cotton owned by him and some of his friends, sank on the high seas en route to Liverpool. To meet his rightful obligations, he sold the plantation and removed to Charleston where he went to work in the Customs House on matters of trade with Britain.

As the eldest son, <u>James Weaver Patton</u> of Asheville inherited his father's estate and continued his work ethic and lifetime objectives. He divided family inheritance in such a manner that every sibling was satisfied. He built a street running west from the Square, a thoroughfare later named for him as Patton Avenue. And he built a handsome house at No. 86 South Main in the first curve below the Square.

<u>Andrew Kerr</u> of Kelso, Scotland, just above the English border, was a member of the clan about which Sir Walter Scott wrote. He was an heir to the line of the dukes of Roxborough but did not pursue his claim to a title. After arrival in Charleston, he became successful in the same lines of endeavor. Of him, it was said that he had the finest ship, the most beautiful wife, and the handsom-

est residence in his district. In one year, the ship was captured, his wife was killed by accident, and the house burned down.

The Kerrs had five daughters and two sons. Riding in a carriage to the St. Cecelia Society, he and his wife were accompanying their eldest daughter to her first formal ball. In the social excitement, a pair of frightened horses ran into them from behind, violently upsetting the carriage. Both ladies, mother and daughter, were so seriously injured that they died soon afterwards. He was struck so forcefully that he hurtled through the air. He landed on his head in a cobblestone street, rendering him partially incapacitated.

John Cheesborough was born on his father's plantation. Active as a banker in Charleston, he saw his fortunes consumed by the war. During its closing days, it was believed that Sherman would come through the city seeking revenge. Assigned responsibility for carrying important records to Columbia for safekeeping, he successfully completed the task...only to find that the Union commander would come through there on his famous "march to the sea." Setting the torch to the city, his troops destroyed these official papers in the conflagration.

His first wife died of consumption before the war (1858) but after cessation of hostilities, he came to visit relatives in the Skyland-Arden-Fletcher area and those of his wife in & around Asheville.

To ongoing confusion of Asheville residents, these lines crossed as Pattons & Kerrs traveled back & forth between French Broad & Swannanoa in the high country...and Ashley & Cooper in the low. William married Elizabeth. James (second) married her sister, Henrietta. Unmarried sister Charlotte came to live with the family of James' son, Thomas. And John Cheesborough, in a phrase of the Bard...created confusion worse confounded...

First, he married William's daughter, also named Elizabeth, and then Louisa, daughter of the James Weaver Pattons. In Charleston, he had five children and then after his first wife's death, eight more in Asheville. Thus he had 13 children, the seventh of the girls being named Septima. Judge Parker married Tom Patton's daughter, Josephine, and they had seven children.

From early days, the Patton family was a pillar of the First Presbyterian Church. James Patton's sons, John E. & James W., took over the Warm Springs resort and supplied visitors with a popular round of entertainment which included picnics & excursions, musicales & balls, and deer hunts in surrounding mountains.

The last of the major progenitors, Haywood Parker began law practice with Judge Joseph Adams, father of Judge Junius G. Adams, who ran the affairs of Biltmore Estate after the death of George Vanderbilt. A trusted advisor to Colonel Bingham, he was a faculty member of the famous military academy at Mebane near Chapel Hill when a number of buildings were destroyed by fire. He suggested Asheville as a better location and gave him letters of introduction to Mayor Charles Blanton.

Judge Parker was born on a plantation in Halifax County during the final year of the war. He first came to Asheville to teach at Ravenscroft, where he remained two years as headmaster. As head of the Asheville Library Association, it was he to whom Mr. Pack confided his intention of giving the building vacated by the failed First National Bank, to be used as a library. During the Twenties he was a regular member of the university building committee which planned attractive & appealing structures being erected at Chapel Hill during that era.

To complete the picture, if such a mosaic may be said to be completed, Thomas Cheesborough married Alice Connally. Along the way, many offspring of this interrelated chain of perhaps a dozen families were named James, John, or Thomas....Patton, Parker, Pearson...Cheesborough, Connally, Coxe...Rumbough, Holmes, Erwin...Thomas sisters of Richmond & Kerr sisters of Charleston. Seven was a lucky number...but so were 11 & 13. And in the life of the city, there was ample room for all.

**

The Patton story would be woefully incomplete without mention of <u>Thomas Walton Patton</u>, by all accounts Asheville's best loved citizen. Graduating (1860) from Colonel Lee's celebrated school, he went to Charleston to acquire business training in the office of his uncle, Thomas Kerr, a successful cotton factor. He was preparing to go to Chapel Hill, when war clouds burst over a doomed land...

At the age of 19, he enlisted in the Buncombe Rifles and went out with that unit as it moved across the mountain and over past his school on its way to report for duty at the state capital. He served throughout that great conflict. He was at First Bethel, the opening engagement, and at Bentonville, the last. His two older brothers perished in the service. And he believed that God had spared him for some useful purpose.

Returning home to deprivation of the times, he settled in to work, married one of the Waltons of Burke County, and built a house. As soon as he was in a position to do so, he set out to be a Good Samaritan. And he wasted no time. He found homes for helpless little wards of the county, black or white alike, and afterwards kept in touch with them. He was the first to suggest the need "of a home where erring and fallen girls could go and by gentle and loving care be brought back to the paths of virtuous womanhood" and he helped make that a reality.

When it was determined that the Mission Hospital should have a building of its own, he, with his friend Lawrence Pulliam, bought property at the next corner (Woodfin) with purchase money that he had borrowed from personal friends. Through his generosity, the library association obtained its property on Church Street and he encouraged Mr. Pack in his benevolences. And he was a loyal member at Trinity Church, serving as treasurer and trustee of the district from its inception and as vestryman & senior warden of the parish over a span of more than forty years.

Passages from a statement by one familiar with the facts clearly describes the true man..."He was not content to pray for those in prison, but gave much time to visiting the jails and his wisdom & kindness were manifest in the fact that he was the friend & advisor of jailers no less than prisoners. The condition of Federal prisoners engaged his helpful aid in large measure. Men, arrested on vague suspicion of violating revenue laws (laws they neither knew nor could understand) were brought away from their families whose sole support they were, and herded in overcrowded jails to wait long months for trial.

"It touched him deeply. He not only exerted influence with Federal judges to prevent unsanitary crowding, but by painstaking investigation obtained release upon bond of many of these poor men. Nothing gave him more pleasure than to tell of the numbers of men upon whose bond he had gone, who came back for trial, walking many weary miles over the mountains to give themselves up that 'the Captain' should suffer no loss through them. For many years, a portion of every Sunday was spent at jails & convict camps, distributing newspapers & magazines and taking notes for letters that he would afterwards write to friends of these unfortunates.

"When elected county commissioner in 1878, he made it his first duty to visit county paupers, whom he found 'farmed out' to the lowest bidder and living in huts far from a public road or any possibility of public inspection. This was at once changed. He had them moved into new & sanitary quarters near town where they were visited by him and other kind friends. It was touching to see an eager joy light up the faces of these waifs & strays of humanity when 'the Captain' was seen coming, pockets bulging with gifts of tobacco, knitting yarn & sewing materials...each one remembered and a gift for each to brighten weary days."

Thomas Patton had a surprising versatility. He was secretary-treasurer of the first utility companies in the city. For a time, he was superintendent of the street railway company. At one point he controlled and edited the *Citizen*. His capable services were in demand because when *he* was in charge, everyone knew that moneys would be accounted for down to the *last penny*.

When the city administration became inefficient and many even suspected corruption, he was called on to serve as mayor and elected to clean it up. He did so with a vengeance. His candidacy was that of an independent and the vote was overwhelming so he was beholden to none. He reduced expenses by half, while actually increasing efficiency of public services. Streets were cleaner, police more active, accounts kept more carefully, city property better guarded & protected than ever before.

He had a new city charter prepared which, when approved by the legislature, became a model of its kind. As far as possible, he brought all pending litigation to a prompt conclusion. He had an inventory made of all city property and held the head of each department responsible for its safekeeping. All floating debts were carefully investigated and accurately determined. He so arranged and systematized public finances that *any citizen could readily determine not only expenses but liabilities and income from all sources as well.*

Captain Patton never forgot the men with whom he served during the war. His health had almost failed as a result of those experiences and he was grateful for his recovery. When the *Maine* was sunk in Havana harbor and the country geared for war, he enlisted in the 1st N.C. Volunteers. He was nearly three score years of age and it had been 37 years since he enlisted before. Both times he entered as a private. This time he was commissioned by Governor Russell, the adjutant of one of the regimental battalions.

The thoughts that entered his mind would be difficult to fathom. As a comrade wrote of the experience, "he did not delude himself in a belief that his country needed his services as a mere soldier, with sword or rifle, but he did believe that his experience in camp & battle could be made beneficial to young men of his native city...He went with this object in view and never lost sight of it for an instant." April 1861. April 1898. By a curious coincidence, he left the city on the same day of the same month.

He could not have known what dangers would be faced but as it turned out, his presence was most appropriate. All wars involve mishap & disaster but in Cuba, they were found in disease and absence of sanitary conditions more than gunfire, which was somewhat limited. An experienced hand was invaluable, rather than a bayonet. And satisfaction was realized when Company F from Asheville was the first to enter the capital city at the successful conclusion of hostilities.

The last winters of Tom Patton's life were spent in Florida at a place he had discovered while training with troops at camps of instruction in the Tampa Bay area. He bought a house in Dunedin in 1904 and made it into a hospitable home with numerous guests. In October of 1907, acute illness set in and he was taken to Philadelphia for specialized treatment. He died on November 6. When word of his demise was received in the city, every mark of public respect was shown...

Courts were adjourned, classes suspended. Stores, all places of business closed. Flags lowered to half staff. The city bell tolled. A large delegation met the funeral party at the station. Gray headed veterans of the War Between the States accompanied his bier, followed by vigorous young manhood of war with Spain. Before the services, crowds gathered on Church Street, white & colored, persons from all walks of life. Inside at the service, the congregation sang in full unison.

Dr. Campbell knew the man well and had other family members in his congregation next door. Indeed both James Patton and James W. Patton had been elders. After the services, he went back and sat down at the old desk in his little study just up the street. In meditation, he took pen in hand and wrote these words to the widow of the departed...

"...I could not always agree with him, but I could never withhold my respect for his absolute independence of thought, and my profound admiration for his utter fearlessness of speech...words always courteous but never cringing...Another quality was his great-heartedness, his tender sympathy, which reached out...to the suffering and the sorrowing, especially those who suffer shame and sorrow in obscurity...the despised and neglected classes of society...Take him for all in all, he was the first citizen of Asheville..."

And finally, there were words from the Colored Men's Organization of the state. Tom Patton's compassion had never been influenced by race, and everybody knew it. Confronted with unfair or demeaning treatment of anyone, he grew hot with indignation. From his home in Wadesboro, E. H. Lipscombe sent a message that began as follows: "Please grant space for a colored man's word of humble tribute to the memory of Capt. T. W. Patton. From the goodness of his heart, he stood by and befriended me and my household through many checkered years...so many, in fact, that I saw my children grow from babies to manhood & womanhood.

"During these years, there often came to me days that were dark but no day so dark that it was not relieved in some way by his goodness. And amid his other kindly deeds to me, I count his good advice & counsel as no means least, though there were times, perhaps, when I was not as observant of these last as I might have been...What wonder, then, that I should feel impelled to lay upon his honored grave some sprig or leaf in token of grateful remembrance?"

In 1911, Dr. Campbell organized the Good Samaritan Mission that carried out important work along lines established by Tom Patton. It was supported for many years by the Churchmen of Church Street and clergy of various downtown churches. He remained its guiding light throughout his pastorate. This was the forerunner of a larger ecumenical organization.

Endnotes

1. Over the years, John Cheesborough took control of property and business affairs of much of the family interests on both sides of the inheritance.
2. Louisa Patton was a graduate of old Salem Academy. Zeb Vance and James Evans Brown of *Zealandia* were among her many admirers, as described in Vance's published volume, *Love Letters.*

3. Major Breese followed Mr. Cheesborough into banking with First National in Charleston and they kept each other informed of the situation in Asheville. After establishing First National in Asheville, Breese was advised by Mr. Vanderbilt to build his house on South Main at the entrance to grounds of Kenilworth Inn. It later became known as *Cedar Crest*.

4. Arrivals at Biltmore Station were met by carriages from Kenilworth Inn that had been erected just above, partly for that reason.

5. He was a founder of the Young Women's Christian Association (Y.W.C.A.) and a liberal subscriber. Guardian of many minors and administrator of several estates, he was an advisor and supporter of church related educational programs.

6. Historical research later showed that the Spanish did not blow up the battleship whose sinking precipitated conflict with Spain but instead, war was fomented by Pulitzer and Hearst newspapers as part of an intense circulation war, activities which led to the term *yellow journalism*.

7. They sang No. 636. How Firm a Foundation, Ye Saints of the Lord. And No. 396. Ten Thousand Times Ten Thousand. At the cemetery, which he helped plan and beautify, the *Gloria in Excelsis*. And No. 679. There Is a Blessed Home.

**

1. From oppression to opportunity was the way some saw it. In a lengthy explanatory letter, he described his reasons for wanting to escape "high rents and haughty landlords" of the times.

2. He married a daughter of Francis Reynolds, by whom he had eleven children. In a letter setting forth some of his moral precepts and ethical views, he expounded his conviction that men should deal with women in a benevolent fashion. Mr. Reynolds was one of the first settlers of the Yadkin River.

3. Protestants who settled Londonderry were strong proponents of the Presbyterian faith and under later siege there, grew more and more resolute. Indeed the place became the most strongly fortified town in Ulster. A number of Pattons emigrated to the middle colonies and to Bermuda and British islands of the Caribbean, their faith undiminished.

4. Francis Landey Patton, whose family migrated from Londonderry, was born in Warwick, Bermuda. He came to the United States and after a distinguished career in higher education and the Presbyterian church, became president of the College of New Jersey. During his administration, a graduate school was founded and the college's charter name changed to Princeton University. He later became president of Princeton Seminary.

5. As with many of his forebears, Dr. Patton's attitude toward church order and heresy was epitomized by General Patton's attitude toward military adversaries in a later generation.

6. In partnership with Jeremiah Cleveland and Andrew Erwin, he evolved an informal network of general stores, inns, and itinerant trade from Pennsylvania to Georgia, an early forerunner of the franchise concept.

7. Along with George Swain & Samuel Chunn, he was directed by the General Assembly "to lay out and make a turnpike road" from state line to state line. In 1827, while carrying out this formidable task, he turned over management of his estate to James, his eldest son.

8. In 1831, he purchased Warm Springs where he built a fine two-story hotel on the turnpike. His son, John E. Patton, became its manager.

9. James M. Smith married Polly Patton, James Patton's niece, in 1814, the year Patton built the Eagle. Smith, Patton, Chunn, Swain, Cleveland & Erwin were Presbyterians, mostly serving at one time or another as elders & deacons in the First Church, for which Patton & Chunn gave the land.

10. Church, for which Patton & Chunn gave the land.

11. Partly by default, Mr. Cheesborough came to assume control of much of the family fortunes, including those of William Patton and the Kerr sisters. Three trustees had been appointed in Charleston but after Mr. Kerr met with the bizarre accident, Mr. Roper, the third trustee, succumbed to a circulatory ailment.

12. The driveway at *Springvale* was connected to the north bank by a bridge that became a local landmark. It was washed away in the big flood but later replaced.

13. Jas. W. Patton married Clara, daughter of Thos. Walton of Burke County.

14. After the Beacon plant was built, Sayles Bleacheries built a plant on the old Cheesborough farm.

15. In the fall of 1896, Mr. Parker formed a partnership with his old friend and classmate, Louis Bourne, a principal in M.V. Moore & Co.

**

1. Thos. Patton was the son of Jas. W. Patton, known to later generations as "James the Second."

2. On his way home from the battlefield at Bentonville, he was given shelter at *Struan* by Alexander Robertson. Since renegade Federal soldiers were engaged in wanton killings at this time, moving in the opposite direction, this kindness may have saved his life.

3. The city's foremost military encampment was on this family property. Known as Camp Patton, it extended northeast from the intersection of Charlotte & Chestnut.

4. He married Martha Bell Turner in April, 1871. They had two children, Josie Buel & Frances McLeod.

5.   This small library stood on the corner of the Presbyterian church grounds between the Presbyterian and Episcopal churches. Original library facilities had been located on the second floor of a building across the way on South Main.

6.   So satisfied was the public that he was elected to a second term by near unanimous vote. A supporter said that only three categories voted against him: those who didn't know the candidates, those who hoped for personal gain, and those who did not understand the ballot.

7.   DeSoto Park in Tampa was a scene of encampment for volunteer units.

8.   For his role in leading the contingent to Cuba, the Spanish-American War veterans camp was named for him; the United Daughters of the Confederacy (U.D.C.) chapter was named for his sister, Miss Fanny Patton.

FOUR

ORGANIZING THE LINKS

The father of golf in Asheville grew up on Patton lands along the Swannanoa at a time of transition from the old society...of Scotch-Irish pioneers based on land and trade...to a new society influenced by Charlestonians but increasingly dominated by Eastern capitalists.

After schooling at Ravenscroft, young Cheesborough attended the University of Virginia and was graduated from its School of Medicine. He married an affluent widow, Emily Herrick, and they went to live in Scotland where he enrolled in the School of Medicine at the University of Edinburgh. Receiving a second degree, he returned home to become a pulmonary specialist, then the city's leading medical specialty.

While a medical student at Auld Reekie, he often made the 35-mile trip to St. Andrews, cherished cradle of golf. There he played the historic Old Course of the Royal & Ancient, established before 1754. He became familiar with great traditions of the game. The Royal Burgess Golfing Society had been founded before 1735 and the Honorable Company at Edinburgh Golfers had been in organized existence before 1744.

After his return to Asheville, the new "chest doctor" was ready to play. Fresh out of college, he was the youngest and most enthusiastic of the downtown social group. When the hunt club was formed, he arranged to have it named after the "nymph of beauty" along whose tranquil waters he had come into the world. He became one of the first masters of hounds and he recruited additional members. Meanwhile, he continued to practice with his Scottish club but as to testing his skills on the links, no course was available.

As it turned out, a Scot named Angus McNorton had already introduced the game to Asheville. He practiced strokes on vacant ground near Sulphur Springs and was then joined there by Dr. Cheesborough and an enthusiastic friend named Joseph J. McCloskey. There were discussions about the significance of golfing in general. As the genial doctor was probably aware, informal variations of the game had come much earlier and there were golfing clubs in Charleston & Savannah dating back to the 1780s.

In the venerable history of the game, however, no championships had been recorded until the British Open was held at Prestwick in 1860. Then in 1873, the Royal Montreal Golf Club was formed on this side of the Atlantic. And in 1887, the first permanent golf club in this country was founded at Foxburg, Pennsylvania. Tom Cheesborough had simpler things in mind at the time but he was on his way to inheriting the mantle of his medical partner as the city's unofficial social organizer.

After the Spanish-American War broke out, he followed his relative, the other one named Thomas and Patton, into the service, entering the army medical corps, perhaps the most necessary branch of the army in that basically naval conflict. After U.S. entry into the world war, he again volunteered and at the end was assigned to the new hospital in Azalea, by coincidence coming back to this same small corner of the world, virtually within walking distance of his old home.

The year 1894 was a significant turning point. The British Open was held on English soil for the first time. The first unofficial U.S. Open was held at the pioneer St. Andrew's Club in Yonkers N.Y. On December 22, the U.S. Golf Association was organized. And the national amateur championships, both men's and women's, were held the following spring. Thus the forthcoming opening in Asheville matched the beginnings of tournament play in the United States.

It was the start of a unique chapter in major American club history, one that over the next four decades would see most of the game's recognized masters play the city's three leading courses. Names such as Anderson, Smith, Ross, McDermott, Travis, Travers, Sweetser, Evans, Walker, Mac-Farlane, Farrell, Little, Armour. And eventually that superb trio of all time, the great "moderns" Hogan, Snead, & Nelson. And it all began with riding to hounds from that celebrated downtown hill one Saturday morning on the way to the springs.

The Henry House on Battery Park Hill (hotel grounds) was club headquarters, an attractive building with checker, chess & whist rooms. Mr. McCloskey became the club's secretary & treasurer and large groups of both men and women mounted and rode out on trips to Sulphur Springs. They began noticing a nice area of ground about a mile to the east near Strawberry Hill. The place Mr McNorton had chosen for his practice. Land was acquired and to complement the city club house a country club was erected.

Here Cheesborough & McCloskey arranged some crude golf holes and many members took up the game. McCloskey then laid out a simple but proper course nearby and construction of both links and tennis courts began in late 1893, one of the first such in the South. Then on November 6, 1894, subscribers signed articles of agreement and links were made available for informal use Work was suspended during winter months, however. On January 28, the name was changed and the group incorporated as Swannanoa Country Club. In late April, work was resumed and links given finishing touches.

Fellow members Martin & Winans were recruited in a foursome, which gave an informal demonstration to some confused or bemused onlookers. The following day, Friday, June 7, the "links were opened to a curious public." Persons of all ages were seen in carriages and the electric line ran special cars filled to seating capacity. The throng was impressed. Members of the foursome were back, dressed in correct golf costume of flannel cap, shirt, & knickerbockers, with long grey woolen stockings. Shirtsleeves rolled up, this being considered important "for no one may expect to attain any brilliancy as a player unless his sleeves are rolled to exactly one inch above his elbows."

In late 1896, membership gave up hunting, other clubs were formed for that purpose, and attention was devoted to golf. Once the game had taken hold, other residents wanted to participate but the idea of having to cross the river to do so drew resistance and a new site was sought. By now Dr. Von Ruck's land holdings had become the location for his new sanitarium but he was persuaded to make part of them available. The following year, another nine-hole course was built there, running in a northeasterly direction through Woolsey Dip toward the Kimberly lands.

With availability of additional land limited, however, commitment to further investment was found imprudent. As membership continued to grow, interest in getting a better location grew with it. Consideration was given to possibility of moving in the direction of Sunset Mountain, northeast across adjacent Kimberly farmlands. Plans for the Manor were then underway and the idea of having a new clubhouse nearby was appealing. At this point, Mr. Pack, a fellow member, offered to make a 100-acre tract available, a fortuitous circumstance.

Starting at the creek, the property was several hundred yards upstream from the existing course, right in line with their thinking, and within walking distance of plans to develop Albemarle Park. The land had a house on it and it was immediately converted to a clubhouse. Beginning in Edgemont Park, Manager McCloskey laid out still another nine-hole course without professional assistance. By this time, he had a lot of practice and although incomplete, the new Swannanoa Country Club & Golf Links were opened in February of 1899. The Manor was opened the following January and after links were completed, the club was used by some guests & residents of Albemarle Park, also known as the Manor Grounds.

In 1905, a new clubhouse was erected a little further up the slope and the electric car line extended from The Manor gate house straight out Charlotte to the club. It became known as the Charlotte Street Extension. Two stations were established there, one by the city transit company, the other by the Howland suburban lines, for transfer to Grace & Weaverville as well as Sunset & Overlook and other destinations then in the planning stage. Then in 1909 additional property was acquired, the course extended to 18 holes, and the name changed to Asheville Country Club.

Opening of Grove Park Inn in 1913 provided a linchpin in development of the area between Merrimon and the ridgeline, building on earlier development of Charlotte Street and Ramoth. Grove Park. The Manor, Albemarle Park, Edgemont Park, Proximity Park. Norwood Park. All coming together with a championship golf course. On December 19, 1906, the Asheville Rapid Transit Company proposed to build a new rail line via Lexington from the old Grand Central to the golf club in competition with the first two.

Then in the early Twenties, Mr. Jackson established Kimberly Avenue through to Beaverdam. In 1925, Griffing Boulevard completed the pattern at the crest of the rise known as Kimberly Heights. Throughout this period, the game of golf was the attraction that gave status to residential neighborhoods. The man who had the most lasting impact on Asheville country club life was not known as a player, however, but an architect. His name was Donald J. Ross and he was as Scottish as the *haggis*.

***

Son of a Dornoch stone mason, Mr. Ross was born in Sutherland on the Dornoch Firth, which forms a boundary with Ross & Cromarty in northern Scotland. He learned the golfing business at St. Andrews and elsewhere, before emigrating to America at the turn of the century (late 1899) as professional director & club manager. Thus began his remarkable career in the year in which the Asheville course was opened at its permanent site below the Sunset slope.

Within months of his arrival, the golf master established winter headquarters at Pinehurst. He held positions at a number of Eastern clubs, many of them new on the scene, and in the course of his work began redesigning layouts in his spare time. Eventually he was able to raise American standards to a level approaching that of his native land. During summer vacations, he started visiting the Asheville area and played the links. In 1913, he attended the opening of Grove Park Inn and discussed possibilities of redesigning the course stretching out below the great stone walled terraces there.

Club governors persuaded him to come to the city immediately and undertake the task as highest priority. They were so impressed with his work that he was advised to forget regular duties for the time being and devote full time to architectural design. Upon completion of this commission, he did exactly that and went forward on that basis. Returning to Pinehurst, he began design of several courses there, including redesign of championship course #2, founded in 1901. This superb work was so successful that many believed the 6,879-yard result to be the finest course in the world.

Ross was a staunch Presbyterian who exhibited all the traits associated with that social and work ethic. In Asheville, he returned to design the Biltmore course, followed by Beaver Lake and then the municipal layout along the Swannanoa. He described Beaver Lake as his masterpiece. At 639 yards, the 13th hole there was believed to be the world's longest but it was also esthetically pleasing. To attain perfection, he redesigned the course and continued to design others in state & nation. When his life career was over, he had designed, redesigned or modified an estimated 700 courses.

Along the way to this astonishing accomplishment, America's foremost course designer became honorary president of the Society of Golf Course Architects and a permanent & honored resident of Pinehurst.

***

In Asheville, many newcomers began play after the course was redesigned. Not only that but their imaginations were stirred that summer when 20-year-old Francis Ouimet scored his National Open upset in Brookline's historic playoff against the English lions, Vardon & Ray. First Scots and then British (Scottish & English) had dominated the game. Harry Vardon won six British Open championships between 1896 & 1914.

The greatest impetus to the American game came at Brookline, a residential section of metropolitan Boston and home of one of the three oldest clubs. An unknown former caddie there, amateur Ouimet (pronounced *we met*) tied the professional British team at the end of regulation 72 holes of play and went on to become the national sports hero with 72 vs. 77 for Vardon and 78 for Ray.

From Ouimet's dramatic victory to the end of the era in 1930, the great Walter Hagen was a prime factor in golf, both in Asheville and elsewhere. Jim Barnes won the Asheville Open in 1920. Not until the following year, however, did an American representative, Jock Hutchison, break through in the British Open, and he too learned the game in Scotland. He was another Asheville tournament champion. Other Americans played on a par with the British. But the greatest of them all, Bobby Jones of Atlanta was a frequent visitor to Asheville and it is appropriate & fitting that he serve as a closing epoch. He came to Biltmore on his honeymoon and the city never lost its appeal for him.

After learning how to curb his temper, Robert Tyre Jones dominated the game from 1923 to 1930 as no other. He won the U.S. Open, his first major title. In 1930, he accomplished one of the most celebrated feats in sporting history by making the Grand Slam, winning both British and American open & amateur titles in a single year. He retired at once, having won 13 national titles in the two great golfing countries.

The opening at Biltmore brought demand for a new clubhouse and its opening brought demand for a public facility as well. The Beaver Lake course was already in operation. In 1926, the old frame structure at Grove park was replaced by a charming Norman-style building. Beautifull situated in front of Grove Park Inn, it afforded a view from its spacious terraces rivaling that of Biltmore, including a few rising outlines of taller new buildings.

Spurred to take action in these days of expansion, the city acquired land for public purposes near intersection of Black Mountain & Charlotte highways. On the day that Lindbergh flew solo to Paris…May 21, 1927…the Municipal Golf Course was officially opened. And at Sulphur Springs, the old original course there became part of a new Malvern Hills residential development.

Senior members of the senior club had much to remember. And those who had not forgotten the past in the excitement of new developments could relax in this splendid setting to consider that it had all taken place over an eventful span of 35 years.

Endnotes

1. Azalea railway station was named after the Trescott-Patton house.
2. After the hospital was turned over to the Veterans Administration, Dr. Cheesborough did not fully resume his private practice. As control of tuberculosis was strengthened, he devoted more of his time & energies to organization of social affairs.
3. In later day terms, it could be described as being about 200 yards from the northeast corner of Sand Hill & Shelburne roads.

***

1. Origin of the game has disappeared in antiquity. When James VI of Scotland succeeded Queen Elizabeth on the English throne, his Scottish train played on *Blackheath*. It was an exotic, however, and remained the only organized club south of the Tweed for 250 years. In the 17th century, the game was espoused by Charles I.
2. The Calcutta Golf Club of India was established in 1829 and the Royal Bombay Club in 1842. Another club was in full vigor at Madras at a somewhat later date. Other clubs were established in several parts of the Empire.
3. In its native land, the game was as democratic as Scots themselves. All classes of society participated so generally that any village in East Lothian could be sure of competitors, from village cobbler to laird of the neighborhood.

***

1. At turn of the century, standard kit of clubs consisted of driver, brassie, cleek, mid-iron, mashie & putter. Variations included such as the spoon, driving mashie, Taylor mashie, lofter, cran-cleek, hollow-faced cleek, jigger & niblick, the latter for playing out of sand or long grass.
2. The ball was made of *gutta-percha*, having a diameter of 1.75 inches and weighing from 26 to 28 pennyweight. It was "swept away" rather than struck as in later fashion.
3. The Americanized "caddy" was adapted from the Scottish military *cadet*. Those who served in Edinburgh as high grade errand boys (during off-duty hours) were referred to informally as *caddies*. The term was then carried over to any young man who carried a set of clubs or other paraphernalia for an older player unable to carry his own without undue effort.
4. According to a contemporary report, the match game "afforded many criticisms and much amusement (for) spectators to whom mysteries of golf are unknown."

***

1. Links were laid out on grounds of luxurious Mountain Park Hotel at Hot Springs in February of 1895. The Linville club was actually organized by Scottish MacRaes of Wilmington in 1892. At one point, there were two courses, old & new.
2. Courses at Linville, Blowing Rock, Boone, Sapphire, Highlands, & High Hampton became popular, with temperatures seldom exceeding 80 degrees.
3. Additional land was sub-leased from various butchers. Cattle roamed parts of it and animal rendering operations produced undesirable effects. Slaughter pens can be obnoxious. Since players were considered to be among the cream of society, this prompted a satirical observer to remark that it appeared to be "a case of casting pearls before swine."
4. A small but comfortable club house for the "Winyah course" was built west of No. 412 Merrimon.
5. When the name was changed, a business office was established on the second floor at No. 12 Church Street north of the Presbyterian church, a convenient location for Scots.
6. On Christmas Eve in 1898, a five-year lease was executed. It continued during his lifetime for a modest sum but in February of 1907, the land was sold by the executor of his estate to C. V. Reynolds, D.C. Waddell, & C.C. Millard who offered it to the club.

7.   The second annual Southern amateur championship event was held there in May of 1903.

8.   After the new building was opened, the old house was moved up the south slope by Mr. Millard to No. 81 Edgemont Road for use as his private residence, continuing in use.

9.   The term "links" originated on seaside courses of Caledonia (Scotland) where the shoreline was irregular and full of small indentations, like links in a chain.

***

1.   In 1915, the first annual invitational tournament was held. It drew 128 entries in eight flights. Judge Adams, chairman of the board of governors, acted as chairman for the event as well. Entrants competed for the Vanderbilt Cup, donated by Mrs. Vanderbilt, an active member.

2.   Held in March every year (1917-22) until the Biltmore club opened, the Asheville Open attracted many outstanding golfers.

3.   In the inaugural event, Gil Nichols set a world record for 72 holes with 277. The following year, Jock Hutchison broke the mark when he birdied the last two holes in a pouring rain, sinking a 20-foot putt with final stroke.

4.   Young Gene Sarazen, then starting to challenge established champions, placed second by a stroke in the 1922 event.

5.   In 1923, the joint Asheville-Biltmore event attracted national attention. Continuing in March, the first 36 holes were played at Asheville, followed next day by the final 36 at Biltmore. Walter Hagen won.

6.   The course at Beaver Lake was opened to the public on August 27, 1932.

7.   The new Asheville clubhouse was dedicated on June 29, 1926.

8.   All sites except the last had a street railway station and Sulphur Springs was also a station (flag stop) on the Southern Railway west of the city, a line known locally as the "Murphy Branch." It served many classes at Asheville School for Boys.

9.   Present for the municipal opening was a young new employee of the city's parks & recreation department, J. Weldon Weir, who would guide the city's affairs & fortunes for half a century.

10. The clubhouse was located at the springs. The course was opened to the public on April 1, 1927.

11. Subscribing to articles of incorporation were S. Westray Battle, Theo. F. Davidson, Henry M. Steele, Jos. S. Churchill, Jno. A. White, Baron Eugene d'Allengh, J. Edw. Rumbough, Otis M. Coxe, Duff Merrick, Thos. P. Cheesborough, W.W. West, T. Wilson Sharpless, M.B. Wilkinson, W.B. Roseneau, John Childs, Wm. D. Hilliard, H.E. Heintsh, Geo. E. Kirkhouse, S.C. Courtland, W.R. Penniman, Jas. P. Sawyer, Oliver Rutledge, Robt. W. Bingham, J.W. Sluder, J.G. Merrimon.

12. Subscription date was November 6, 1894; articles amended October 30, 1907.

FIVE

RESIDENTIAL RENAISSANCE

The war slowed development down again but once it was over and things had settled back to the new "normalcy" of Warren G. Harding, plans for capitalizing on the city's social reputation were under way once more. Arrival of one of the South's foremost civic planners and developers was the first in a series of events that would follow in escalating succession.

Early in 1919, George Myers Stephens, a Charlotte banker, moved to Asheville and established residence near the Golf Club. His reputation had preceded him. Mr. Stephens left his mark on the Queen City where some observers saw him as the leading citizen. Instrumental in development of Myers Park, a model for progressive cities across the country, and many other successful enterprises of highest quality. Among these were the Trust Building, the city's first skyscraper; Independence Park, a showpiece; and the celebrated Mint Museum.

One of the state university's leading trustees, he was in the forefront of ideas to improve the social environment. In 1910, he developed Kanuga Lake as a pioneer Southern summer resort club. He had been visiting the Asheville area since 1898 and early in the century had established a summer residence at Flat Rock. With war ended and his career highly successful, he decided to make his home in Asheville for reasons of health, but not to retire.

He resigned as president of the Stephens Company in Charlotte, and with Charles A. Webb, purchased the *Asheville Citizen* in closing days of 1919. Early the following year, he organized Appalachian Realty Company, a holding company. Its first transaction was purchase of Biltmore Village from the Vanderbilt estate, an unprecedented such transfer of an incorporated town.

The period in which this conservative but versatile and forward looking financier was moving was a difficult one. Although the start of the Twenties has often been described as if workmen were lighting a pyrotechnic display, the actual situation was considerably different. After a short period of wild extravagance in weeks following the Armistice, the public staged a dramatic "buyers strike" brought on by deflation of personal income before cost of living declined.

The effect on finance in Asheville was to restrain entrepreneurial spirit and limit business ventures to small scale projects such as neighborhood drug stores and the like. The national economic situation had little effect on the social and residential scene, however. And having a man with stature of George Myers Stephens in its midst gave leadership reason to consider creation of a new community embracing highest standards.

The new newspaper publisher had been discussing purchase of the village with Mrs. Vanderbilt and he immediately saw possibilities. He had been primarily responsible for establishing Mecklenburg Country Club (later Charlotte Country Club) and knew what success entailed. He was also talking with Messrs. Grove & Raoul about the situation where he lived. The two parks or neighborhoods were contiguous properties and the pharmaceutical entrepreneur was ready to wrap up this phase of his grand plan.

On June 1, 1920, Mr. Raoul sold Albemarle Park to his neighbor, Mr. Grove, who shortly thereafter began directing some of his attention to historic Battery Park Hill, visible from the inn in the
downtown distance. The man who had created the Manor two decades before, and brought it to
social success equal to that of Montford at the other end of Chestnut, was now free to embark on
a new enterprise. Conversations ensued with Judge Adams, ruling elder of the estate. Joining them
were Mr. Stephens, Mr. Colburn, Mr. Knight & Dr. Herbert.

Looking out across the plaza from the station in Biltmore, one would find no real choice of
ways to go. To the south was the Reeds' substantial remaining hill. At his back the river & railroad
right-of-way with now developed Swannanoa Hill behind, divided between Victoria & Kenilworth.
To the east, light development. To the west, the Estate and beyond it the Carrier developments.
There was an avenue, however, although closed, one that might be opened.

Off to the southwest at an angle lay the old abandoned right-of-way of the G.W.V.R.R., the
spur track that ran to Biltmore House. Lying between private roads of the Estate and the public
highway leading south along the Southern's right-of-way were several thousand acres planted in
white pine by Dr. Schenck. The spur line ran into these gently rolling uplands marked only by a
scattered number of farmhouses remaining from the previous century. It was like a finger pointing
to an attractive place.

Edith Vanderbilt sat down for lunch with her most trusted business advisors, at Biltmore and
at the country club. There was agreement that if they adhered to the highest standards, this could
be one of the finest such enterprises in the country, one that would maintain traditions of Biltmore
itself, in a more modern setting. They set out to secure services of the best architect they could find
for that purpose.

George Stephens then turned his attention to organization of a city planning commission and
as chairman, brought John Nolen in to design a comprehensive plan for the city. It covered an area
extending from South Biltmore to lands lying north from the end of city car line tracks at Grace.
There it was envisioned that another fine residential community would emerge, complete with a
large lake, to anchor the city at its opposite end.

From Biltmore Station, a new entrance to town would be designed, one worthy of fashionable
Asheville, and the dawn of a new era would be under way. As an active newspaper publisher, George
Myers Stephens would soon have a hand in every worthy idea, as he had in Charlotte, and his name
meant that Asheville had joined the ranks of other progressive cities.

Dr. Nolen of Harvard was an ideal man for the task of laying out the master plan. One of the
country's leading urban experts, he had performed the task of massive planning for Myers Park.
And he approached the budding mountain metropolis with enthusiasm. Only time would tell
whether the fashionable world of Altamont, and its inspiration from the Vanderbilt family, would
prove to be a catalyst for successful passage into the world of Asheville.

***

The concept at Biltmore was creation of a residential area for the age of the motor vehicle. A
small portion of the estate, less than two thousand acres, could be laid out in the form of mostly
large & medium sized lots, restricted in use to protect natural woods & forest environment.

The main entrance would be designed from the road to a central point where town headquarters would be situated, complete with offices, facilities & a few specialized artisan shops. Opposite

them a reserved site for potential inn or hotel. Along the way, half a dozen other roadway entrances could provide access including that from the village into Vanderbilt & Stuyvesant, the principal through roads.

Thus the layout would be connected directly with the Old English model district that had been created for workers & staff of Biltmore House & grounds, church & railway station facing one another across open central plaza. Estate offices adjoining stores & shops & offices, along with other places of business, readily available around village streets. A place where most daily needs could be met without going into the city.

It was anticipated that owners would travel in vehicles driven by others or drive their own personal automobiles and so no sidewalks or paths were provided, unlike the plan at Grove Park. A bridle path connecting with riding stables would be established, however, along with several neighborhood playgrounds & small parks. At the center of it all would be the club, of course, and from the beginning it was seen as the *piece de resistance*, a place of distinctive charm with formal aspects of relaxed residential style.

***

Son of a wealthy shipping executive in Philadelphia, William A. Knight acquired extensive land holdings in the tree farming business along the St. John's River north of St. Augustine. He ran a profitable operation, primarily naval stores shipped from Jacksonville & Savannah, and acquired *Three Oaks*, a great house in the city.

After Henry Flagler organized the Florida East Coast Railway in 1886, he followed his activities with interest, traveling over the Flagler System with its *deluxe* sleeping cars, chain of luxury hotels, and steamship lines. His wife became a friend of Flagler's wife. Increasingly, he devoted time to his interests in botany & photography.

When Dr. Schenck left Biltmore, he helped organize Mount Alda School, which became the School of Forestry at Penn State. And Bill Knight became a trustee. Harvey Loughead was a student there. Met and married Knight's daughter, Priscilla, known as Polly, and went to Florida to manage tree farms for his father-in-law.

Because of the heat, the Knights began spending summers in & around Asheville, traveling with their chauffeur by automobile, sometimes accompanied by Bill Knight's Ford, which he loved to drive himself, or by Pullman car on the *Skyland Special*. They stayed at several hotels, first the Battery Park and then the Grove Park Inn, sometimes taking a house in Grove Park.

He was staying at a cottage in Albemarle Park one summer when he struck up a friendship with Tom Raoul at The Manor. They found that they had interests in common and Mr. Raoul introduced him to Judge Adams, who often dined there. He also became a friend of C.D. Beadle and they went all over the country by motor car, seeking out fine specimens of azalea, photographing them and bringing their selections back to Asheville. This became a foundation of the famous azalea gardens at *Biltmore.*

Before long, the prominent foursome built fine homes there, Adams & Colburn on Stuyvesant, Raoul on Vanderbilt. Knight acquired three prime lots on Forest Road nearby, one at the intersection of Busbee, one not far from the intersection of Cedarcliff, one at the intersection of Vanderbilt near Park. The first he kept undeveloped, the second he used as site for a handsome Mediterranean style house, and the third for *Knightshade,* a magnificent house in French Chateau style.

As an amateur botanist, Mr. Knight continued to work with Mr. Beadle, who entered into designing & planning this "residential park" and then working on a number of individual grounds. Knight brought plants to his professional community from around the world, continuing in the footsteps of Mr. Olmstead as chief deputy landscape architect at Biltmore. Mr. Raoul became first mayor of the town as many persons of professional or social prominence or both decided to become residents, after founders built their houses and others were in a planning stage or actually under construction.

Just looking at the graceful style of drawings & plans for these elegant & authentic private residences was enough to create a sanguine attitude in the minds of those who saw them. Sketches had the charm & finish characteristic of the period. All done with style & finesse by a competent artist. Illustrations included Lodge Gate, Biltmore House itself, features of the club and the scene from the terrace. Residences of Adams, Colburn, Knight, Raoul, along with Dr. Mason, Dr. Minor and Mr. Spencer. The exemplars.

**

Independence Day came on with intermittent light drizzle. Clad in a raincoat, Edith Vanderbilt walked out to the front center circle and hoisted a 20-foot flag to the top of a tall flagpole that had been used when the village was founded. A thousand invitations had been issued for opening ceremonies and inclement weather had little effect on high spirits of assembled guests. Festivities would include a five o'clock reception & tea, a dance in the large clubroom and fireworks at eleven followed by midnight supper.

Drizzle abated. The new golf professional, Victor East, late of the Royal Melbourne Club of Australia, was on hand, as were distinguished guests such as Mr. H.W. Miller, president of the Southern Railway, and Judge Robert Bingham of the Louisville publishing family. Mr. Raoul, the club's first president, & Thomas E. Byrom, the first manager, were much in evidence.

The site chosen afforded a superb view of the beautiful golf course. Grass & trees flowing like a landscape portrait out across the slopes with spectacular background of Pisgah and the eternal hills. Fading into the distance, as seen from a slate covered open terrace. A timeless scene changing only with hue & clime of the season. A vision of *xanadu* perhaps.

Fairways were clipped by horse-drawn mowers, greens watered by hand at night, and epicurean meals cooked on a six-burner, coal-fired range of the best design, food preserved in a large, reach-in icebox. From the first days, exotic nature of the bill of fare was such that the annual budget ended in deficit. Mrs. Vanderbilt was partly responsible for expensive cuisine and when final figures were audited, she cheerfully wrote a check to balance the books and start the new year off with a clean slate.

**

As months passed, many celebrated personalities mingled with other guests at the club and with members such as General Pershing, respectfully known to men who served under him as "Black Jack." Champion Bobby Jones arrived from Atlanta with his happy bride to begin their honeymoon. On the day Asheville's Locke Craig passed away.

John D. Rockefeller Sr. & his son were frequent visitors...the great oil magnate leaving club managers shiny dimes as he did everywhere he went. Henry Ford & Harvey Firestone were among many notable industrialists, along with Charles Schwab, the famous steel baron. Chief Justice of the United States, William Howard Taft, paid a visit. So did the First Lady, Grace Coolidge. Many others remained incognito in the interests of privacy during travel away from home.

After his party nominated Al Smith for President, he & political advisors wanted to sit down & map strategy. Through connections at upper levels of policy making, Mr. Gerry, by now Edith Vanderbilt's husband, proposed that they get out of New York and come to Biltmore for that purpose. In August, the Smith entourage left the heat of Pennsylvania Station by private railway cars and arrived at Biltmore for a week-long conference, the club being taken over for that purpose by special arrangement.

This was something of a mecca for high society, not the flamboyant or relentlessly ambitious but those who had already arrived and could find time to smell the flowers in an enjoyable atmosphere of social affability. As the Roaring Twenties started to soar, more than a hundred fine homes were built, many designed by master architects such as Erle Stillwell and master builders like Lawrence Merchant. The best of workers were craftsmen. Results from this vision of natural elegance, a setting only enhanced with sensitive restraint by affluence, quickly aroused curiosity & admiration of those already impressed by an almost fictional image of the great castle grounds southwest of the city. In the exuberance of this time for accomplishment, a desire for emulation grew.

And with flappers, speakeasies & raccoon coats beginning to tinge the fringes with less than subtle signs of bizarre new energy forms, tangible results were inevitable. Accompanied by sounds ranging from the Charleston & Black Bottom, or *When Yuba Plays the Rhumba on His Tuba Down in Cuba* perhaps, conversation of conservative social intercourse began to acquire occasional phrases from other circles in more liberal places. Those with ambitions of a builder, and sometimes a streak of larceny to go along with it, began to stay up late or lie awake at night with ebullient plans for converting accomplishments & accoutrements of high society into uses of more plebeian society. The automobile was making the Great American Dream a tangible thing.

If not a king, then every man a prince, or at least a spear-carrier.

***

The Great Florida Boom was another source of inspiration & motivation. Everyone with good sense knew there were risks in that sort of thing. Somehow a lot of people felt that if you could just get all those "fantabulous doings" out of sub-tropical flats and up into solid ground...out of sinking sand and onto bed rock...here in these great mountains, where people were basically reliable and had their feet on the ground, perhaps things would be different. We might be here after they were gone under water. And so when the Florida surge began to sink, some developers departed, like rats leaving a sinking ship, for more economically salubrious climes.

Down in the Sunshine State, that bubble burst in 1926 and some of the frenzy of the craze got transferred to the streets of Asheville. Examples of "Spanish style," rarely defined or delineated, began to appear here & there, notably the handsome & graceful Billy Campbell house at the intersection of Marlborough Road & Midland Drive. It sat on the ridge atop newly commenced Lake View Park on the north side of newly commenced Beaver Lake, which followed inspiration of Biltmore along in the middle of this progressive decade. The lake was created out of Baird's Bottoms, site of an old brick kiln and route of the Weaverville car line's right-of-way.

Bankers making possible realization of dreams by others started setting some examples themselves. The president of the city's central banking institution authorized plans to be drawn for a house, to be situated on a commanding knoll in the center of Lake View Park, patterned after stately homes of England. Brick with turrets on the grand scale, *Stratford Towers* was successfully completed & opened on schedule. Others came to fruition around it on three sides, slope of the mountain behind serving as deterrent in that direction. And hillside gradient was about the only thing that would stop building fervor at that stage, provided setting was right.

Those who did not want to live within confines of a social forest or find a place that suited them in one of the comfortable, old established sections now had an alternative. They could build on slopes above the lake where breezes brought in fresh air and the view wasn't so bad either. One could be up at Grace in five minutes, there where old fashioned, creaky Grace Supply folks would comfortably supply all your needs if they weren't too stylish, or uptown in ten more. It was relatively easy to get on the golf course where links provided pleasant spaciousness to general surroundings.

Even confirmed skeptics, including those who remembered panics of '93 & '07, the latter only two decades past, could see that things were indeed happening. It was not a mirage. Plans & drawings for residential sub-divisions started sprouting like bulbs in the springtime. It was rumored that some mysterious being, larger than life, was coming with plans so great that there wouldn't be room to accommodate them all. (Bigger than Grove & Vanderbilt combined, some whispered knowingly.) Soon fire hydrants appeared on mountainsides where no homes had been or ever would be designed

Leading lights had been embarrassed by the fact that the mountain…serene Sunset and popular Overlook and romantic Beaucatcher…still offered nothing more to the traveler than they did in days of Zeb Vance. Paths & trails wound across the top, albeit now paved in deference to wishes of voyagers from the east. But now there was an answer, a modern tunnel could be bored through & opened to vehicular & pedestrian traffic. To anyone sanguine about future possibilities, the hand writing could be perceived on tunnel walls.

All clichés from the cult of boosterism came to the fore. And those with instincts of an aggressive horse trader wanted to capitalize on something.

Endnotes

1. He first made his home at Albemarle Park near the gate house, after which he settled in a bit further out at 12 Evergreen Lane in the heart of Grove Park.
2. Mr. Stephens was a trustee during consolidation of the university with the college for women and the agricultural & engineering college.
3. The club was opened on July 1, 1909. The lake was destroyed by the great flood in 1916. In the fall or 1927, he helped secure it for the Episcopal church as a conference center. John Nolen of Cambridge, Mass., then working in Asheville, devised the plan and R.S. Smith was architect. The original format entailed 40 cottages.
4. Since January 3, 1911, operations of the *Citizen* had been housed at 8 Government Street in quarters especially designed by the Coxe Estate. In 1922, Messrs. Stephens & Webb moved them around the corner to the Y.M.C.A. building.
5. The transaction was executed on February 23, 1920. Between April 1 of that year and October 1, 1923, Mr. Stephens purchased a number of other properties from Central Bank, Mr. Carrier's widow, Mr. Raoul, L.B. Jackson, Tench Coxe, Electric Building Company, & the Wachovia trust department. Several of these provided land adjoining the village proper.
6. Although not generally recognized then or later, acquisition of the village marked an epoch in the course of events. The age of Altamont as a dominant factor in community life was coming to a close and the rise of Asheville as a modern city was about to begin.

7. From a high of 231 in 1920, the commodity price index plummeted to 125 in April of 1921. Farmers never fully recovered. Over the next six years, average value of farmland declined from $108 to $76.

8. One exception to the 1921 scene was the Castanea Building erected on Haywood by the socially active Woodcock family. Located half way between Elks Club & Penland-Briggs property. Later the Woodcocks & Citizens Hotel Company acquired the Penland property from Dr. Briggs and built George Vanderbilt Hotel there.

9. Shortly after acquisition of the village, Azalea Hospital was turned over to the Veterans Bureau and rumor had it that the federal government was going to reorganize the bureau and create a major hospital there. A group of businessmen organized Swannanoa-Oteen Bank on the grounds. The report about government plans for veterans proved to be true. They decided to open a branch across the street from the estate office in Biltmore and the name was changed to Biltmore-Oteen Bank.

10. Mr. Stephens later helped convince Interior Secretary Harold Ickes that plans for the Blue Ridge Parkway should be approved and funds were authorized for that purpose.

***

1. Tar, pitch, turpentine, & other resinous products used for vessels, particularly naval vessels.

2. The Knight House was a landmark. With many rooms and a ballroom on the fourth floor, it was the tallest residential structure in town. The exterior had a coquina finish.

3. Mr. Knight was active in leadership of both St. Augustine Country Club and St. Augustine Golf Club from the time they were organized until his coming to Asheville.

4. Knight married Anna Stevens, daughter of a wealthy grocer in Zanesville, Ohio, Wheeler Stevens, who bought the house for her. Their daughter, Adelaide, married T. Rogero Mickler, the mayor.

5. The Lougheads later built a house at 399 Vanderbilt Road. Loughead is Scottish (Celtic) spelling of Lloyd.

6. After the war, he retired and spent much of his time in Grove Park.

7. A devout Presbyterian, Mr. Knight attended services at Flagler and other Presbyterian churches in Florida. In Asheville, he and his wife, an Episcopalian, went to church on Church Street, at the Presbyterian church during tenure of Dr. Campbell, and at the Episcopal church next door.

8. A convenient location, the first house was used as rental property and had among occupants several prominent persons, including Chas. E. Merrill.

***

1. In late 1920, a land enterprise known as Biltmore Estate Company was organized and about a year later a small square Tudoresque cottage was built for its office. The purpose was to develop this portion of the estate into "a community where persons of moderate means could build homes that would embody on a smaller scale the same ideas which had actuated Mr. Vanderbilt." The building later became the town hall and served as such for many years. The name was later changed to Biltmore Forest Company.

2. According to one account, he & Mrs. Vanderbilt came upon the idea of a handsome forested community, centered around a club, one day during a card game at Biltmore.

3. Another account had it that she was stimulated to get started because of an episode recounted by a veteran Asheville tennis player. Fifty years later, he said that he had been playing a match with her on the number one court at Asheville Country Club. They went to the mixed grill up above. He went to the bar, she went to a table overlooking the courts, ordered lunch, and lit a cigarette. The manager quietly came by her chair and discreetly reminded her that women were not permitted to smoke in mixed company. The player answered a telephone call from the switchboard and while waiting for the caller to come on the line, inadvertently overheard something. According to him, she went to another house telephone, called Mr. Waddell, chief engineer for the Estate, on a different line and inquired about what sort of undertaking he thought would be involved in building a separate club at Biltmore.

4. A prominent engineer, Colburn became president of the Mayflower Society of America and head of the city's most fashionable bank, with Mrs. Vanderbilt a charter subscriber.

5. John Fisher was employed by the club before it was even opened. After serving his apprenticeship, he was chosen to succeed Mr. Byrom as general manager.

6. Her intention had been to see a 40-foot banner waving in the breeze above the new clubhouse but the elements made the idea impractical.

7. Clubhouse construction had been completed on June 8, after which furnishings were installed & finishing touches added.

8. In addition to founding fathers, the 297 original subscribers included many other distinguished persons. They included Charles S. Bryant, treasurer of Champion Paper & Fibre Company, whose house on the golf course faced the club. Furniture manufacturer David B. Morgan & Arthur F. Rees of the tanneries. Widely recognized names in the medical profession. Non-residents included General of the Armies John J. Pershing. The Bingham family was represented by the judge. The

Westfeldts of New Orleans provided George & Thomas to the roster while the Hugers of Charleston & Savannah were made known by D.E. Huger of Charleston.

***

1. Horses were shod with special wooden shoes for heavy lawn use.
2. An inveterate traveler, Mrs. Vanderbilt would find a delicacy that she particularly liked and bring the recipe back.
3. W.J. Bryan was a club visitor prior to his death in Dayton, Tenn., on July 26, 1925, five days after the Scopes trial ended there. He was the nation's most famous unelected presidential candidate.

***

1. The former President became chief justice in June of 1921, serving until February 1, 1930. He died a month later. Judge Alfred Nippert of Cincinnati, chief legal & political advisor to the younger Taft, later built a substantial house in Biltmore Forest not far from the club.
2. As with all private clubs, prohibition had an effect on service of alcoholic beverages. The first prohibition law was passed by Maine in 1846. A war-time prohibition act was passed by the Congress on November 21, 1918, effective the following June, prohibiting domestic sale of intoxicating liquors until termination of demobilization. After passage of numerous laws the Volstead Act was adopted by Congress on October 28, 1919, and remained in effect until February 20, 1933, when it was repealed. North Carolina did not lift the ban on public sales until long afterward.
3. In 1925, the company published a handsome little book with elegant artwork, quietly dignified, including text of a short essay by D. Hiden Ramsey, the city's foremost man of letters & editorial journalism.
4. Elegant, swan necked street lamp posts, custom ordered from a leading manufacturer, added an urban quality to the aesthetic character of the neighborhood.
5. In addition to a profusion of makes, automotive models seen on streets of Asheville & Biltmore during the post-war era were the victoria, brougham, landaulet, berlin, cabriolet, electric brougham, & limousine, as well as the more common sedan, coupe, roadster, speedster, & symbolic touring car.

***

1. The New York governor had been nominated for president by F.D. Roosevelt in 1924 but the convention in New York was deadlocked into an astounding record of 124 vote tallies. After being nominated at the Houston convention in 1928, he wanted to avoid anything of that sort and careful planning was given a priority.
2. The Happy Warrior was refreshed but the trip was not enough to overcome broad Southern antipathy toward his Gotham personality and brand of politics, which were perceived to be somewhere between a speakeasy and Tammany Hall, despite a long & noteworthy career as a political reformer.
3. The importance of Enka both to Asheville and to Holland was later underscored by a visit from H.R.H. Princess Juliana of The Netherlands, accompanied by Prince Bernhard and her ladies-in-waiting. For two weeks, the club became a private residence for the royal party, complete with barefoot picnic naps by the princess under one of the imposing oaks shading the main terrace. In order that she might feel at home, her suite had been decorated with pictures and similar things provided by Dutch families living in the area. She conferred with officials of the Enka company and its success continued unabated for many years. The visitors said afterward "one seldom finds such agreeable accommodations in so beautiful a setting."
4. Some thought Mr. Fisher would reach the half-century mark at the club but after 45 years on the job, he retired to engage in real estate. At the time of the occasion, there were 13 survivors: Frank Coxe, Harvey M. Heywood, Richard Loughran, Reuben B. Robertson, L.B. Jackson, Silas G. Bernard, Alan C. McDonald, Steven R. Adams, Arnold H. Vanderhoof, Vern Rhoades, J. Gerald Cowan, and Drs. Herbert & Ambler.

***

1. The firm of Lakeview Park, Inc., with J.D. Murphy as president & Fred L. Sale as secretary, began buying property at the mouth of Beaverdam Valley in 1922. Plats based on the Nolen Plan were first recorded during the following June.
2. In later years, anything north of Grace might be called "Beaver Lake" regardless of whether it was in Lake View Park or not, including the other side of the lake. Going out Merrimon, the lowest point on the route was still known as Woollsey Dip, a point where the street began its long rise to Hester's Pharmacy at the top of the hill.
3. By 1927, officials of Central Bank were claiming that it was the largest bank of its kind in the state. On July 31 of that year the president issued a long promotional statement in response to an inquiry from newspapers at the end of the fiscal year. A reporter wrote a few lines extolling virtues of his source and citing it as authoritative. The editor carried it in full, using many columns on front & inside pages for that purpose. In it, the bank president cited figures purporting to show that during the post-war period through June 30, national business had increased by 27% while Asheville business increased 213%. The tenor of his lengthy analysis might be summarized in these words. There isn't a cloud to be seen on our beauti

ful mountain horizon. Folks, you ain't seen nothin' yet. The effect of such hyperbole was to provide additional stimulus in some quarters although, as in every community, there was skepticism about newspaper coverage of sensational subjects.

***

1. His father, Judge Joseph Shepherd Adams, was born at Cane Creek on the Toe River in Yancey County where his father, Stephen Delaney Adams, had come from the family home at Strawberry Plains, 14 miles northeast of Knoxville, in a sort of reverse migration. Stephen married Cordelia Shepherd of Bumsville and their son, Joseph, founded Bumsville Academy.

2. At some point, Joseph became a lawyer in Bumsville and gave up teaching in private school. After being appointed a judge, he married Sallie Greene of Greensboro, both descendants of English & Scottish pioneers in the Piedmont. He was in Statesville on February 8, 1884, when our subject was born. Shortly after Mr. Vanderbilt opened his mansion, he moved to Asheville, establishing private practice near the courthouse. The son later said facetiously that he was born in Statesville "by accident" because they were only there while his father happened to be presiding in district court at the time.

***

1. An honors graduate of the University of North Carolina, he was also a distinguished graduate of the School of Law there.
2. Known to close friends as "June," he became widely known as "Judge" because of highly visible service in the local court.
3. The town of Biltmore Forest was incorporated and from 1923 to 1929, he served as its first mayor.
4. In 1929, Biltmore Forest was one of several towns absorbed by the burgeoning City but after the City's financial structure collapsed and political influence reached its nadir, the town's independent status was restored.
5. A member of the Pen & Plate Club and the Asheville Club and an organizer (1921) of the Asheville Civitan Club, he joined the Lawyers Club and the Southern Society in New York, along with the University Club and the North Carolina Society.
6. When he assumed management of the famous Jersey herd in 1932, it consisted of 332 cattle and produced 4,200 pounds of milk annually. Within a few years, it numbered more than a thousand head and production had doubled, making this the largest distributor in the Southeast and the Estate's most profitable enterprise.
7. He was elected president of the American Jersey Cattle Club and then the American Pure Bred Dairy Cattle Association.
8. He was appointed chief counsel to the Sinking Fund of Buncombe County and served as such until his death.
9. Honorary degrees were conferred by North Carolina State University upon him and Dr. Carl A. Schenck of the Biltmore School, Doctor of Agriculture bestowed to the former, Doctor of Forestry to the latter.
10. When the Biltmore Company was founded in 1932, he was named its president, affirming his long established role in the Estate.
11. In the bleak days of 1933, he sold his home property to his neighbor, Mr. Colburn, and went to live at *Farmcoat* on the Estate for the rest of his life.

DAVID COLEMAN BAILEY

SIX

A MEMORABLE WEDDING

In the invigorating early spring days of 1924, an exciting skyscraper was the big story but it was only one of many stories in the field of real estate, and real estate was not the only thing prospering that year. Together these elements made city society a scene of animated conversation at social functions in various places.

Yes, it was a good year for wizards and weddings, for wishes of many kinds, and in the world of high society the wedding of Cornelia Vanderbilt was the *ne plus ultra* that would make many a socially minded person wish for an invitation. The fictional romance of John and Miriam was published in that year, and its purposeful prose somehow blended into the highly charged scene.

Down at All Souls in Biltmore, there was detailed preparation for an event the likes of which had never been seen and would be unlikely ever to be seen again. In an era of such trans-Atlantic nuptial arrangements, this could top them all. Time and date for the ceremony were set for noon of Tuesday, April 29.

The bride and Thomas Wolfe were worlds apart, at that time he was teaching English in the Washington Square College of New York University, but they were born six weeks apart in the same year. 1900. She came into the new century on August 22, he on October 3. His arrival downtown on Woodfin was unheralded outside the family while hers was comparable to an occasion at one of the stately houses of England.

The betrothed's mother was the former Edith Stuyvesant Dresser of Newport, direct descendant of Peter Stuyvesant, the last Dutch governor of New York. Her father was a grandson of Cornelius, whose honorary title as transportation czar was *The Commodore*. Dr. Battle had officiated at proceedings of birth. The international press took note and hundreds of persons connected in some way with the family or the estate extended greetings and good wishes.

The groom was directly descended from a line of the most powerful family in England, and thus the world. During the reign of Queen Elizabeth I...the first of two great female monarchs of empire...this narrow realm was extended to the far-flung corners of the globe by her adventurous sea captains such as Drake and Raleigh. And her principal advisor was Lord Burleigh of the House of Cecil.

When Queen Victoria ascended to the throne in the golden noontide of empire, the Cecils were still a house of influence on all parts of the earth. And in the Edwardian age to follow, that influence had not disappeared. The father of the bride was not here present, of course, but the father of the groom, Lord William Cecil, C.V.O., was notably in evidence. His mother was the late Baroness Amherst of Hackney.

Accompanied by his father and the British ambassador to the United States, the groom approached the English church. His name was John Francis Amherst Cecil. A diplomat with service in Cairo, Madrid, and Prague, he was first secretary of the Embassy in Washington, an appointment that was expected to lead to a rising career. With his clipped appearance, manner and speech, and dressed in full formal attire, he appeared to be a nobleman from British fiction or legitimate theatre of the first rank.

As a substantial number of officers of the law controlled flow of pedestrian and vehicular traffic throughout the village, the impressive governor of the state, Cameron Morrison, alighted to enter the parish grounds and welcome other guests. Protocol was in capable hands, what with high ranking officials of the State Department, diplomats and military attachés of Britain and America as well as France, ambassadors of all three countries, along with diplomats and noblemen of several other European countries.

The church was decorated with immense palms and branches of spring blossoms from the estate. Large masses of dogwood, azalea and other native shrubs and trees mingled their bright flowers with clusters of dark green fronds. Full transepts and their entrances were reserved, right for employees of the estate and left for nurses of the Biltmore Hospital. Prominent members of Vanderbilt families and relatives entered, as did approximately 75 friends of the bride and her mother. All told, some 250 guests were present.

Ushers were Capt. F. L. Tottenham, R.N., Leander McCormick-Goodhart, Harold Sims, Geoffrey Thompson, Somerville Tuck, John Francis Brown, Robert Cecil, and Benjamin Barnard. The mother of the bride wore a slender silhouette model of pale green and gold *crepe du chene* with a small gold tissue turban. Several members of the Cecil family were seated among the guests. Guests from Asheville included Colonel Bingham and his son, Robert Worth, who would one day become United States ambassador to the United Kingdom of Great Britain, Ulster, India and all the rest.

The local delegation was led by Judge Junius G. Adams, who was directing affairs of the estate in the absence of its founder. Participants included several residents of Albemarle Park and founders of the new town of Biltmore Forest, carved from lands of the estate, along with those of the old community of Montford, Victoria, Chestnut Hill, Grove Park, and Flat Rock. Attire of some fifty or so of the most prominent ladies, present as guests, was described in some detail, not only in the local press but also in national and international journals of society.

James Alderson was seated at the console of the organ during most of the service, in which he played *O, Perfect Love* softly throughout. There was silence while he relinquished his seat to Ernest Schelling of New York as the party entered. Then suddenly the mighty strains of Lohengrin pealed forth in the wedding march. Miss Vanderbilt was met at the chancel steps by Mr. Cecil and his best man, Hugh Tennant, and there the traditional marriage ceremony was performed by the parish rector, the Rev. A. G. Branwell-Bennett.

The marriage was solemnized by the bride's uncle, the Rev. George Granville Merrill of Stockbridge, Massachusetts, whose words carried clearly to the entire audience. As she repeated the vows of marriage, the bride's voice rang clear and steady. The blessing was pronounced by the bishop of the diocese, the Rt. Rev. Junius M. Horner. And two houses of ancient Dutch lineage on this side of the Atlantic were united with two houses of ancient Anglo-Saxon lineage on the other.

For her entrance, the bride had worn a veil, "an exquisite bit of rose point lace" over a longer veil of tulle, four yards in length. She carried white orchids and lily-of-the-valley. Tall and straight she created a presence not to be ignored, even in lesser circumstances. Now the satisfied couple was leaving the church by the center aisle. As they made their exit through the porch at the front entrance, they were confronted by a battery of cameramen who stopped the procession for a few minutes.

There was much to see. The bride wore a gown of white satin, very straight, with long sleeves. Her veil was caught with orange blossoms from the Florida plantation of the estate superintendent, C. D. Beadle. Her bridal bouquet was exquisite and each of her satin slippers was ornamented with a single orange blossom. All of the delicate accoutrements enhanced and accentuated the straight lines, elegant sleeves, and round neck of her gown, entirely without trimming.

The maid of honor, Miss Rachel Strong of Cleveland, wore a Lanvin model of white organdie in bouffant style with very full skirt. Her large white Crin hat was trimmed with a yellow arum lily. In striking contrast, the bridesmaids, Miss Margaret Cecil, Miss Muriel Vanderbilt, Miss Louise Ross Todd, Miss Augusta McCagg, Miss Helen Moran, Miss Caroline Story, Miss Rebecca Smith, and Miss Alyne Reynolds, wore very narrow, straight gowns. These were fashioned of soft, green, flowered Japanese silk with white tops, almost sleeveless.

The little flower girls, Helen Raoul and Peggy Morgan, fascinated onlookers with their white straw poke bonnets and fluffy white organdie frocks hanging full from the shoulders. They carried miniature replicas of the bridesmaid's bouquets, which were of spring flowers arranged by the superintendent of gardens from selections made there by him.

There followed immediately a reception and wedding breakfast at the residence of the bride. Guests were received in the Tapestry Room. A handsome, horseshoe-shaped breakfast table had been laid forth on the sunken floor of the conservatory, generally known as the Palm Court. Two orchestras broke forth into music and a number of guests began dancing. When one orchestra suddenly played the national anthem...immediately followed by the other with *God Save the King*...rousing cheers rang into the rafters with an appreciation of the symbolism.

And when the married Cecils were seen ascending from the top of the majestic spiral staircase, more cheers broke loudly forth. Several hundred guests were still present as the couple moved toward the front entrance of the house. There an automobile was covered with streamers and decorations, including a pair of white slippers daubed with tar, emblematic of the bride's status, celebrated since birth, as a native Tar Heel. Heavy showers of rice and rose petals descended upon the pair as they approached the vehicle.

Amid social events surrounding formal nuptials, there was speculation as to destination of the disappearing and departing couple. From several clues left behind, it was surmised that Buck Spring Lodge, the family hunting preserve on Pisgah, was a likely possibility. And in ongoing conversation over refreshment, some of the Englishmen, loyal young blades who were compatriots of the groom, cautioned that you could never be sure about such matters. They noted that some observers of the social scene thought that their now married friend was interested in Miss Ailsa Mellon, Andrew's daughter.

And back in the village and over dinner that evening, there were a few pessimists who wondered about the effect so much authority in the family backgrounds might have on marital rapport and harmony. After all, earls and barons, prime ministers and landed gentry, senators and mayors of leading cities, not to mention an honorary "commodore" with more power than any admiral of the ocean sea, might not be precursor of a democratic spirit of accommodation in personal relationship of a domestic situation.

Maybe so, maybe not. There were many unknown factors. And among the many unknowns was the fact that the bride's mother would, in the coming year, become a member of one of the most prominent families in New England. This new groom would be Peter Goelet Gerry, whose family included governors and senators of Rhode Island and Massachusetts, principal landowners of Manhattan Island, landlords at supremely fashionable Newport, and a signer of the Declaration.

Not to mention a vice president of the United States.

Consuelo

The wedding evoked memories of the most famous Anglo-American nuptials of all, that of Consuelo Vanderbilt at St. Thomas Church, Fifth Avenue, on November 6, 1895, during the month before formal opening of *Biltmore.*

In both, grooms were members of the British aristocracy at its highest levels of family tradition. Only daughters, the brides were granddaughters of William H. Vanderbilt, apotheosis of industrial wealth. Their fathers were among his eight children and the bulk of this vast fortune went to three sons.

To a high degree, Consuelo was educated, intelligent, and charming. Her father, William K. Vanderbilt, was jovial, kindly, and warm hearted. Her mother, Alva Erskine of Mobile, was descended from a line of Southern political leaders. She was not only intensely ambitious socially but hostile to her husband and a tyrannical mentor to her daughter.

Her accomplishments were many, however, and on March 26, 1883, she staged the most brilliant entertainment in a private residence in New York social history, a fancy dress ball given to celebrate opening of her new house at 660 Fifth Avenue. Crowds of curious onlookers formed in the streets.

In marvelously detailed memoirs, Consuelo eloquently describes life growing up in aristocracy's golden age on Vanderbilt Row. At beautiful *Idlehour* near rural Oakwood on Long Island. In magnificent *Marble House* on Bellevue Avenue and Bailey's Beach at Newport, and among the peerage amid palatial splendor at *Blenheim* with its autocratic lord and master, the Duke of Marlborough Home of the Spencer-Churchills and only a step removed from the royal seat at Windsor.

Her father owned S.S. *Valiant,* the greatest private yacht ever built, and everything else was on a comparable scale. They traveled in elegant circles to colonial India, ancient Egypt, sophisticated Paris, and Victorian England at the majestic flowering of Empire. A family so impressive that during its peregrinations, it was met by heads of state or their deputies.

At the tender age of 18, she was swept into a complex international world of social and political intricacies with hundreds of servants and other employees and dependents. All under powerful conventions with ramifications in the business and military arenas, her sense of responsibility challenged by demands on her knowledge and natural diplomatic skills.

Endnotes

1. Alongside newspaper accounts of proceedings was an advertisement for Central Bank & Trust Company with a message of frugality & security. "When money is spent," it read, "its earning power for you is gone forever. Start a savings account today. It gives you security, certainty of interest and availability in an emergency." Type of emergency unspecified.
2. Capsule summary: Cornelius married Sophia Johnson and they had 13 children, fourth of which was William Henry who married Maria Louisa Kissam, and Geo. W. Vanderbilt 3rd was ninth and last of their children.

3. Both of Cornelia's parents had ancient Dutch lineage. Jan Aertsen Van der Bilt, born about 1620, was first of that family to come to *Nieuw Amsterdam*, great-great-great grandfather of Cornelius, and George was his grandson.

4. Dr. Battle had sat on porch rockers with Mr. Vanderbilt and discussed beauty of the scene and prospects for the future here.

5. George Vanderbilt died ten years earlier at his mother's home, 1612 K Street Northwest, Washington, of complications following successful appendectomy. He was recovering satisfactorily, in good spirits.

6. Mr. Cecil was third son of Sir William. His brothers were in His Majesty's Service, one in the army, the other in the Royal Navy.

7. They arrived by private railway cars opposite the church. The village was under surveillance of estate, village, town, city, county, & state officers, activities coordinated by aides to the governor. Biltmore & Biltmore Forest were each separately incorporated.

8. Everyone agreed that floral arrangements were beautiful, provided by the estate, with some assistance elsewhere by local florists.

9. Chas. M. Schwab was present in the city that day. King of Pittsburgh millionaires, he was over in Grove Park, playing golf with other millionaires at Asheville Country Club. Partner of Carnegie, Mellon & Morgan, he left for New York on Thursday in his private car.

10. The church was small and could easily have become congested & confused but these men carried out assignments with skill & finesse.

***

. Metropolitan newspapers described the event as having major implications. The New York press called it "a brilliant event of international prominence." An only child, the bride received a concentration of attention. The international press called her "the world's richest bride."

. They wore very small Cloche hats of white horsehair, untrimmed, with a single enamel pin. White shoes were rimmed with black.

. Half a century or more later, some oldtimers would still remember the Tuesday afternoon when they sat on nearby porches, watching Cornelia Vanderbilt get married a few yards away. "I just loved it," one said. "I felt like we were part of the wedding party," said another.

. "Oh, it was wonderful," reminisced a village observer. "So beautiful...and exciting. I was just 16 and thinking about my own wedding some day. It was like a fairy tale." She laughed. "Some of the men looked so grand. And those children were just, well, just adorable."

. Many guests noticed a sincerity of greeting between family & staff members who participated in reception. It was their impression that everyone took part and feelings were personal on all sides.

. According to a report, "the bride wore a smart tan cloth gown with a V-shaped insert of brown from bodice to hem. The V-shaped collar ended in a long scarf slung over her left shoulder. She wore a small black straw hat."

. Buck Spring Lodge was situated at the high elevation in Haywood & Transylvania counties.

. When she was 16, Cornelia suffered an attack of acute appendicitis during the night. Dr. Battle, the house physician, was called. He brought in Dr. James Madison Lynch, who performed successful emergency surgery & became her doctor. During the Twenties, he delivered both her sons, also at Biltmore.

***

. The Mellons were considered the royal family of American wealth. Among other things, Mr. Mellon was Secretary of the Treasury.

. Elbridge Gerry was vice president under Madison, father of the Constitution. Governor of Massachusetts at the time districts were being divided for political advantage to one party.

. Peter Goelet Gerry was a brother of Robert L. Gerry whose widow was a sister of Averell Harriman, scion of the royal family of railroad politics & diplomacy. The brothers died on the same day, Peter at Providence, Robert near Delhi, N.Y. Edith again became a widow.

***

. He received the most inheritance of Commodore Vanderbilt.

. According to Frank Crowninshield, Mrs. W.K. Vanderbilt was "an amazing woman who brought up her children to become people of the greatest cultivation and taste." *The House of Vanderbilt*, Crowninshield, *Vogue* magazine, November 15, 1941.

. Born Maria Louisa Kissam, daughter of a clergyman in the Dutch Reformed Church. The Kissams were an old & distinguished family, Mrs. Vanderbilt's father having descended from "the Benjamin Kissam, who, in 1786, married Cornelia Roosevelt, daughter of patriarchal Isaac, and the President's great-great-grandfather."

4.   Because *Blenheim* was undergoing renovations until March, the Duke & Duchess of Marlborough went to the Mediterranean on their wedding trip aboard an available but ordinary steamer. After ocean motion caused him to suffer a prolonged bout with *mal de mer*, they disembarked at Gibraltar and toured historic Spain & the glittering Riviera.

SEVEN

A SPECTACULAR SKYSCRAPER

Yes, early spring of 1924 was a good time for a real wedding. And a good time for a young man with ambition and ability to be alive on city streets. For one thing, they were clean and well maintained, fifty miles of them washed down every evening. Some years before, the city had launched the nation's first anti-fly campaign.

The first expectoration ordinance had been adopted. Spitting was prohibited on the street, in street cars, and in public buildings. And public loitering by undesirables of various kinds, a practice that had annoyed or repelled many visitors before the start of this era, was not tolerated by law enforcement officials acting under authority of city fathers. A health resort needed to be clean and free from nasty behavior.

Looking upward in the clear air of a nice day, a briskly moving pedestrian might see the symbol of it all rising. Slowly but steadily, week to week, from its foundation where W.O. Wolfe once carved monuments, in a shop that his son, largely unrecognized in his home town, would make famous among book readers everywhere. The Jackson Building was going up. A modern Gothic adaptation in the center of a heavy, low profile projected by this mountain town. Before the year was out, visitors from across the mountain area would travel to Asheville, perhaps spending the night, to see the sights.

A situation like this calls for a catalyst, a man who can ignite diverse energies. And Lynwood B. Jackson was the man. Where Smith maintained a low profile, he maintained high profile. He had a vision shared by few others and it was more than a figment of the imagination. It was an understanding of various factors that had come together at this particular time. He wanted to accomplish something and although he was only 25 when he started planning, he had courage to get the ball rolling. What he had in mind was something beautiful, valuable, profitable.

A native of Cuthbert, Georgia, he came to Asheville in 1914 at the age of 18 when his father, Edmond A. Jackson, after hearing about wonders of Grove Park Inn, decided to move the family to the Land of the Sky. The elder Jackson established Chero-Cola Bottling Works, one of many such fledgling enterprises of the day, eventually merged into the Nehi company. While he was in the soft drink business, however, he developed a bottle inspection device, equipment that enabled a bottler to detect impurities and foreign objects. This was profitable and he used his capital to enter the real estate business on a modest scale.

Modest was not the scale young Jackson had in mind. Before long, he was playing for heavy stakes. In 1922, L.B., as he was known, joined his father in development. The town would never be the same. Immediately, he began negotiating with others for a number of things, including something unimaginable. A classic skyscraper. Five years before his arrival in Asheville, Frank Woolworth had shown the world what a beautiful Gothic skyscraper could be by building one in New

York. Young Jackson must have dreamed about it because his ideas, as seen in an artist's drawing across the room, looked somewhat like it. Where Woolworth went for 79 stories, he decided on 14.

Under agreement, he and William Farr developed land, owned by the latter, east of Merrimon, just north of Woolsey Dip. As a builder, Jackson was working in Grove territory, physically and mentally. The two men had something in common when it came to appearance of neighborhood layouts. The original Grove Park had acquired a charming ambiance with small landscaping and architectural features that made it a quaint adventure to walk along sidewalks separated from streets and protected by trees or shrubbery. North of Evelyn Place, a second, later stage of development was begun in what was known as the Kimberly Lands.

This was one of the great historic tracts of Asheville, originally comprising some 600 acres of prime property belonging to the Kimberly family. John Kimberly was professor of chemistry and geology at the University of North Carolina. After the Civil War, during which the university was closed for a time, he decided to become a farmer and purchased this entire area on the outskirts of town. Since 1913, Grove had been making acquisitions there.

Here obviously was a golden opportunity for someone with imagination and drive. In June of 1923, a plat was completed for the new extension and W.R. Campbell, better known as Billy, was appointed exclusive sales agent for both Farr and Grove. Jackson's perceptive eye fastened on a road leading north through these lands to Beaverdam and he had it paved with asphalt. This prime street was his focus, facing as it did the serene scene of golf course, great inn, and mountain backdrop.

Kimberly Avenue. Large lots were purchased by "the cream of the business and professional community." He constructed two houses and then proceeded from there to buy and develop numerous other lots. Some of the best designers were involved but there was no record of his having obtained the assistance of a registered architect. Before long, he was being called "a wizard of building and land auctions."

In a matter of months, this popular young man was being described as Asheville's "best known citizen," a fame that spread far and wide. In Atlanta, the *Constitution*, the New South's leading newspaper, published a feature in its Sunday magazine of November 2, 1924. It was headlined, "Peanut Vendor to Real Estate King." In it, William W. Browton wrote that Jackson had a unique marketing ability.

"When he showed a man a house and lot," he reported, "he didn't try to hide the fact that there had to be a profit in it for him. If he didn't nearly double his money, there was nothing doing. But what sold every fellow was his guarantee and his guarantee was what marked him as a genius. 'My iron-clad proposition is that if you take this piece of property and then can't sell it, at any time for way more than you paid me for it, you can get your money back from me,' was what L. B. told them."

Houses sold at a fairly steady pace, with a few of the usual ups and downs, but north of Farrwood, a wooded area remained. In 1925, W.W. Dodge, who had built a Tudor Revival house in the original Grove Park section, designed an English Tudor manor house there on Kimberly Knoll. It was admired as a sort of capstone to this handsome district and widely known avenue, the stately street observed from the inn by visitors coming from all over the world.

In the opposite direction, the largest real estate transaction that had ever been made in the

Asheville area took place in 1926 when Jackson purchased a large tract just south of the city for two million dollars in hard money. This property became known as Royal Pines and Mount Royal. Over his career, he built some 500 houses, including those in outlying subdivisions such as these, as well as Lynwood Park, Oakhurst, Oak Park, and Beverly Hills.

See L. B. Large electric signs proclaimed the message. And few were the spectators who did not understand what it meant. Even those could hardly fail to notice when the big searchlight mounted in the observation tower of the Jackson Building came on. With 18-million candle power, its high beam could illuminate the farther peaks visible from the city.

See L.B.

Endnotes

1. Carefully constructed, the building took more than a year to erect. Work was started in the spring of 1923. By the time it was finished, prospective tenants had executed contracts to rent all the space.
2. Mr. Jackson spoke at opening ceremonies.
3. Originally, this building & the Westall Building next door were contemplated as one building & early sketches showed them as one.
4. The Westall Building was completed later. It was cited in Ripley's "Believe It Or Not" feature & in the Guinness Book of World Records as the tallest building without fire escape, elevator or staircase. The answer to this conundrum was that it was connected to the first at all floors.
5. The combined structure, including a five-story annex off the Square on South Market, contained a total of 102 offices.
6. At Oteen, heavy construction was starting that same year on a wooded tract of 179 acres, an overall project ending in 1930.
7. Fear of lightning was an early factor in public acceptance. It had a steel skeleton framework and many could not understand what would happen when it was struck by a bolt from the blue. The answer, of course, was that it was grounded. In order to dramatize its safety, Jackson posed for a photographer while standing on the observation tower during a thunderstorm.
8. A headline in the *Asheville Times* of July 6, 1924, proclaimed ASHEVILLE'S FIRST SKYSCRAPER COMPLETED.

***

1. "Nobody was afraid of that and nobody has ever sold anything back to him," the article concluded.
2. Jackson had his own real estate company. These sales were made through the E.W. Grove Investment Company.
3. During this same pre-war period, the central portion of lands behind lower Kimberly to the west was acquired & developed into Norwood Park by the Central Development Company.
4. Its central street was Virginia Avenue (later Norwood) running parallel to Kimberly, and Woodward running down to Woolsey, each part of a separate stage of development.
5. These were small, moderately priced lots & homes, about a hundred in each phase. This development extended north from Murdock, a link between Charlotte & Merrimon.
6. Because of the close proximity of Norwood, the Farrwood area did not allow sufficient room for inclusion of service alleys, an element that Grove considered important for his motor car-oriented scheme.
7. These lands extended from the creek at the foot of the long slope, north to the top of the hill where Beaverdam Valley began.
8. Later renamed Edgewood Road.

***

1. A native of Brooklyn, John Kimberly was a graduate of Yale, completed graduate work at Harvard, & took advanced studies at Heidelberg. When the University of North Carolina was closed in 1866, President Swain persuaded him to come to Asheville.
2. The Kimberly lineage was historic. His mother's family line settled in Old Greenwich, Connecticut, in 1616, four years before the Puritans arrived from Plymouth. His father's family arrived at New Haven from England prior to 1637.
3. Professor Kimberly purchased lands from where Coleman Avenue was later established, north to Beaverdam, west to Beaver Dam Road and east to the top of the mountain. Shortly after his arrival, he contributed land & logs for Beaverdam mission, later Grace, founded in 1867. He built a house which was numbered 221 when Kimberly Avenue was put through.

DAVID COLEMAN BAILEY

***

1. Here on Farrwood Avenue, Garden Terrace & Vineyard Place, attractive houses on smaller scale were purchased by sales managers, small businessmen and others.

2. The younger man admired results of work done in planning the original 1908-13 band 1914 platted areas.

3. Sometimes he built on commission from the property owner, such as the Ruffner Campbell house at No. 46, sometimes on speculation, often renting until a purchaser could be found.

4. At the turn of the century, two children built houses overlooking the Sunset slopes. In 1918, they were moved to nearby Stanly Street on lots later included in Grove's plat.

5. On Stanly, his three unmarried children built and shared a house whose design was influenced by the Prairie style, a design created by his daughters and constructed between 1913 and 1915.

6. A handsome house of pink granite was occupied by two unmarried women and long known as the Kimberly Sisters house, a city landmark.

7. Starting in 1911, the country club extended its golf links, as they were known, from 9 to 18, after purchasing land from the Kimberly Estate and other families.

8. In addition, Farr had acquired his land north of Woolsey Dip and Norwood Park east of Merrimon.

9. In 1920, Grove purchased 92 acres, last of the remaining Kimberly lands. Thus the familiar Prairie-influenced house would be left standing on the last parcel of farmland remaining in possession of Professor Kimberly's heirs.

10. One of the first two houses, at No. 92, was built as a model for his own residence. He later sold it and moved into another new dwelling.

11. He established several companies to handle facets of the business. Grove Park Construction Company for building, Guaranty Realty Company for real estate transactions, a bond and investment company for financial matters.

12. A total of 18 houses on this thoroughfare have been identified as his. Several manifest his interest in "Spanish-Mediterranean" style of American architecture, often referred to then as Florida, where he owned a residence for a number of years.

EIGHT

A PERSONABLE PANORAMA

As the year 1924 hit its stride, the fashionable world of Asheville was in good order. From Montford to Grove Park, Biltmore to Beaverdam, Beaucatcher to Bingham Heights. From large to small, romantic scenes combined with comfortable old ways and modern new ones in a fortuitous synergism.

From *Zealandia*, a wide range. From Dr. Campbell's little office building, Mr. Grove's little park, Mr. Smith's little chapel at Grace, and Haywood Street's little Bandana Restaurant. From Oates Building and Legal Building to Jackson Building. To *Biltmore* and Grove Park Inn was a leap in time and space. So was Biltmore Station to Pennsylvania Station.

Travel between this and other social centers was maintained by the comfortable Pullman car. This was not a cattle shoot. Or fuming racetrack. And among other features, the popular *Asheville Special* had a certain distinction. Its passenger cars ran between two of the greatest architectural achievements in American history. And they emerged out of the two mightiest empires in the same industry.

In the great era of master builders, none ever reached the heights of those who created the vast Pennsylvania Station in the heart of New York City or the incomparable *Biltmore* on the outskirts of Asheville. Each represented the pinnacle of excellence for imaginative creativity, the zenith of classical architecture in the vigorous environment of a brave new world.

The station was the greatest commercial structure ever built in this country, the estate its supreme house and gardens, the ultimate private residence. And one could leave the one, have dinner and breakfast in the formal comfort of the dining car, and be transported to the station platform of the other while asleep in a berth of his own private accommodations, compartment, drawing room or whatever.

While Mr. Hunt was chief architect in charge at *Biltmore*, and Mr. Olmstead was chief landscape architect in charge of the great outdoors, the chief architect in charge for construction at Pennsylvania Station was scholarly Charles Follin McKim of McKim, Mead & White, the nation's leading firm. Inspired by the famous 33-acre *Baths of Caracalla* in Ancient Rome, the main waiting room alone would be about the size of the nave of St. Peter's, a far cry from the tiny station in the model village of Biltmore.

Passengers making connections with the competing New York Central System would of necessity transfer eight blocks uptown to Grand Central, the beautiful and sophisticated railroad terminal symbolic of Vanderbilt interests from whence had come the wealth which made the vast Biltmore Estate possible. By these gargantuan standards, all else seemed small but size is relative and even the mountains around Asheville were small by comparison with those not far away. And they say variety is the spice of life.

Size alone would have made the Catholic church in Asheville noteworthy but it acquired distinction in terms of its general beauty and superb craftsmanship as well. It was the passion of a lifetime for Rafael Guastavino, an architect who had come from Spain via New York to work on the great Biltmore project. In the process of attaining the perfection he sought, Guastavino erected a new edifice for the cramped St. Lawrence church congregation at the head of Haywood Street adjoining the northeastern edge of the 25-acre Battery Park Hotel grounds.

Where two decades later, Douglas Ellington would take his inspiration from Florence, Guastavino was inspired by a church in Valencia, Spain. In the classic mold, he devoted himself in mind, body, and spirit to the image of his task, which involved many challenges of difficult form and detail. When completed, it was covered with the largest unsupported elliptical dome in all of Christendom, outside of the great dome of St. Peter's Basilica itself.

Soon through a spyglass from atop any component of the city's dominant eastern ridge, from the left, Sunset, Overlook, Town and Beaucatcher, many examples of building enterprise could be seen. In the days when experienced craftsmanship and the skill of fine artisans was a matter of personal pride and professional dignity, there was much to draw a curious and appreciative eye. And before long, hundreds of individual projects took their place in the ongoing scheme of things...

Perhaps the first structure of note, as our epoch began, was *Wychewood*, the picturesque creation of Col. Charles W. Woolsey and named for his ancestral home in England. It was built in 1880 at the northwest corner of East and Hillside. Active in civic and social matters, he was elected mayor of Ramoth, when this area was incorporated as a town. A long drop in Beaver Dam Street, the main thoroughfare that ran through there, became widely known to all succeeding generations as *Woolsey Dip*. The town hall was located near the center of this depression. Colonel Woolsey served with Mr. Vanderbilt on the original vestry of All Souls Church. His house was later occupied by Mrs. Howland.

During the last decade of the era, a feature of the social framework was a structure that did not fit more rigid categories of deluxe hotel, boarding house, private home, sanitarium, or transient facility. It was known as a residential hotel. Finding a demand for this niche, Anne O'Connell built this widely recognized place to house families of patients and other guests in a convenient spot nearby, one that was formal in the sense of propriety and etiquette but informal in the sense of low key, unostentatious atmosphere.

Finding demand for this niche, she built at the next corner from *Winyah* to house families of various sanitarium patients and other guests in a convenient place, formal in a the sense of propriety and etiquette, informal in a sense of low key, unostentatious atmosphere. A hop, skip, and a jump from the Parker house below. A quiet corner like an almost secluded *cul de sac* just out of earshot from hustle and bustle.

Anne O'Connell was a striking redhead known to some guests and friends as Princess Anne and this neat, straight, old fashioned, slightly crotchety place bore that name. Of simple, modified Queen Anne style, the Princess Anne Hotel was perhaps the best known neighborhood facility in the city. And while it defied pigeonholing, neither fashionable nor unfashionable, it was known affectionately to many fashionable persons of the old school.

Even its origin was somewhat off the beaten path. Being built around 1920, it was not a product of the Boom, then just getting ready to get started in a small way, nor was it a product of tuberculosis in full force, the syndrome then beginning to wane just a bit. It was in a class by itself and oldtimers long remembered the feeling it gave as an oasis for one who just wanted to be quiet for a while, without having to deal with the aggressive and ambitious, or expensive charges.

Robert Sharp Smith did not live to see it all come together but he ran the gamut of extremes, a reflection of the city's range. Battery Hill coming down, the new hotel going up along with its neighbor across the way. Rising on the flattened old site until its roof garden was level in space with the lobby of the old. Its handsome competitor, emerging from demolished foundations of the Milton Pinckney Penland residence, the new structure named in honor of Mr. Vanderbilt, an inspiration *par excellence.*

A few blocks away, plans for the Asheville-Biltmore, named in recognition of an obvious relationship between larger community and small, were being subjected to preliminary sketches. Talk of others in similar fashion. For their part, the old Manor, new Kenilworth Inn, and unique Grove Park Inn, were all flourishing. Just off the central square, the formidable Langren taking on commercial business in stride. And as Wolfe well knew, business at the boarding houses was booming, to the satisfaction of his ambitious mother.

It was an election year. In Washington, Calvin Coolidge was running the country in his laconic and taciturn style of cracker barrel wit and wisdom that would make him the butt of national journalism's lampoon and lance, forevermore. His acerbic critics ignored something, however. His was the only administration without deficit, disorder, depression or any of the other major problems of the century, including war. As in every era and every age, some were poor but spirits were high. This was the true *Camelot.* A fable of long ago in the form of modern day utopia. And nowhere was this more true than here in *Altamont.*

Before long, the entrance to the opera house was boarded up, a farewell to the past. Its successor, the Auditorium was beginning an entire annual opera series with strong social support. The new Bon Marche and Denton's , with its traveling network of cables and carriers to fascinate curious young boys, were busy supplying customer's needs, the equally busy shoppers. And on Patton, M.V. Moore & Co. was getting ready for a move down the street. To position itself nearer Haywood in its heyday.

Around the corner, at the head of Church, its new quarters would be next door to where the S&W Cafeteria, an emerging concept from army chow lines, was taking hold as a growing institution. The carriage trade was alive and well. Pullmans still arriving and departing at all hours down at the Depot. Vehicles available for hire at the hotels. Street cars creating traffic jams where Patton comes into the Square. And Mrs. Coolidge, the First Lady, coming to the stores and shops on Haywood with her chauffeur to find out whether their merchandise was as fashionable as she had been led to believe.

For years, the scene as seen from the mountain had been dominated by conventional structural types, schools and churches, hotels and boarding houses, official public buildings spreading out from the low brick business mass described for us by Richard Thornton, clustered within half a dozen blocks of the central square. Rising supreme above it all, of course, was Queen Anne herself, the dignified lady on the comfortable hill sloping down into town from the northwest, the fashionable residential community of Montford just beyond, across a long, relatively level slope, tapering off abruptly down to the river opposite Richmond Hill.

Seen from the other direction, there was little structural evidence other than this to catch the eye except for a few great houses and the king of the mountain, Grove Park Inn, a massive, majestic, montane monument to man and material from mother nature and patent medicine. Queen of the hill and king of the mountain, each clearly visible from the other with this quaint and curious watering hole, one large and modern downtown hotel in the center, spreading out in between. Was it really a good idea to haul the hill away? Something no other city had, this side of Nob Hill.

The panorama was placid and personable, and then, the advent of big steam shovels inching their way up Battery Park Hill signaled the coming of something else even bigger and L.B. Jackson was a young man who caught the vision in a hurry. Excitement spread like wildfire and when his slender, graceful building went up in the center of town, middle of everything, it was a signal that the modern building era had begun. Within the short span of five years, the city skyline would be radically altered.

Years later, oldtimers still got a glint, or a tear, in their eyes when talking to you about it. A camera set up on the front porch at *Ardmion*, taking one picture a day for five years, and then running them through a motion picture projector in a frame-a-second sequence, as in a botanical film display, would show it all emerging like plant life growing from seed. In sixty months, there were sixty new buildings, large and small, completed or underway. Real buildings.

Endnotes

1. Throughout the era, the most popular travel excursion was an early spring trip by special railway cars to Charleston for a guided tour of Magnolia, Middleton, and Cypress gardens. They sometimes ran as a second section to the *Carolina Special*. Participants were met at the station and many stayed in private residences of the old city.
2. Colonel Woolsey served with Union forces.
3. A large house built in 1883 by Edw. I. Holmes on Baird Street remained a landmark of the Charlotte-Chestnut district.
4. The entrance faced the intersection of Chestnut & Pine, changed to Furman. This was the eastern end of Chestnut, which provided the principal east-west connection north of the Square, particularly after the viaduct was opened west from Five Points near the end of the building boom.
5. Although quite different in some respects, ambiance at the Princess Anne would be easily recognized by aficionados of *Tip Top Inn* at Pawley's Island, off Georgetown, South Carolina. After eleven, all one could hear were surf, snores, and the imaginary sound of pages turning in a good book. Said to be the oldest island beach resort on the southern Atlantic coast.
6. *Tip Top* was built by Captain Dingle in the early Twenties, partly in response to the building era in Asheville, where old families had been "going to Pawley's" by rail for generations. Excellent beach and surf. The proprietor was his widow, Lorraine. Kindly Mrs. Dingle supplied kitchens with produce from her own vegetable gardens on the mainland. Buildings were later completely destroyed by a major hurricane.
7. M.V. Moore was located at No. 45, the S&W at Nos. 41-3.

About the Author

Born in New York City and a lifelong writer, David Coleman Bailey is a long time resident of Asheville. As a boy coming to Asheville with his family, he was fascinated in the startling aftermath of this seemingly brand new city.

Educated at the University of North Carolina & Haverford College, he received degrees in journalism and languages and is retired from a long investment career with Merrill Lynch, Pierce, Fenner & Smith. Social & political history is a hobby.

The father of Derrick, Douglas, Thomas, and Caroline Elizabeth, he is married to the former Cathey Massie, owner of Biltmore Forest Realty in Asheville. Family forebears came to American shores during the 17th & 18th centuries. Named for Col. David Coleman, whose regiment reached the climax at Chickamauga, greatest battle in the history of Anglo-Saxon arms.

Mr. Bailey has long been involved in operations of the Penland Company, an hereditary family land management business. He is a founder of the Asheville Arts Council and former chairman of Southern Appalachian Highlands Conservancy, dedicated to preservation of the Highlands of Roan and other mountain conservation projects.